The Berlin Wall
Ch. Links Verlag

Berlin Wall Memorial
Exhibition Catalog

Elke Mathern escapes with her
parents, August 17, 1961
Horst Siegmann, Landesarchiv Berlin

The Berlin Wall

Ch. Links Verlag

Chief editor
Prof. Dr. Axel Klausmeier
for the Berlin Wall Foundation

Editor
Anna von Arnim-Rosenthal

English translation
Miriamne Fields, Berlin

Designer
Weidner Händle Atelier, Stuttgart

**Text editing of
open-air exhibition**
Dr. Gerhard Sälter
Anna v. Arnim-Rosenthal

**Text editing of
permanent exhibition**
Katja Böhme
Dr. Elke Kimmel
Dr. Kay Kufeke
Dr. Susanne Muhle
Cornelia Thiele

**Biographies and quotes
from contemporary witnesses**
Dr. Kay Kufeke

Publishing editor
Margret Kowalke-Paz, Berlin

English editors
Miriamne Fields
Marie Frohling

1st edition, August 2015
Christoph Links Verlag GmbH
Schönhauser Allee 36, 10435 Berlin
Telephone +49 30 44 02 32-0
www.christoph-links-verlag.de
mail@christoph-links-verlag.de
Printing and binding:
Bosch-Druck GmbH, Landshut
ISBN 978-3-86153-859-2

**With thanks to the following
organizations**
Archiv der Berliner Wasserbetriebe,
Der Bundesbeauftragte für die
Unterlagen des Staatssicherheits-
dienstes der ehemaligen DDR,
Bundesstiftung zur Aufarbeitung der
SED-Diktatur,
Deutsch-Deutsches Museum
Mödlareuth,
Deutsches Zollmuseum,
Archiv der Internationale der
Kriegsdienstgegner/innen,
Polizeihistorische
Sammlung Dresden,
Presseamt Land Berlin,
Archiv der Robert-Havemann-
Gesellschaft e.V.,
Archiv des Schwulen Museums,
Senatsverwaltung für Stadt-
entwicklung Berlin,
Staatsarchiv Hamburg,
Archiv der Versöhnungsgemeinde
Berlin-Wedding,
Zentral- und Landesbibliothek Berlin

A very special thanks to all the
contemporary witnesses who
provided photos and documents.

Despite our efforts, we were not
always able to identify the holders of
publication rights. We ask anyone
wishing to lay claim to the publication
rights of photos shown here to please
contact the Berlin Wall Foundation.

This project was co-funded by
the Federal Commissioner
for Culture and Media, the State
of Berlin, the joint scheme
for the "improvement of regional
economic structure," the German
Lottery Foundation of Berlin,
and the European Union – European
Fund for Regional Development
"Investment in your future."

Contents

	Axel Klausmeier	Foreword: Commemoration Needs A Place 7
	Monika Grütters	Greeting 12
	Michael Müller	Greeting 13
	Gerhard Sälter	The SED, its Wall and GDR Society 17
	Maria Nooke	Bernauer Strasse – A Site of the Berlin Wall with Historical Significance 22

Open-Air Exhibition and Memorial Grounds at Bernauer Strasse

Chapter 1	The Wall and the Border Strip 34
Chapter 2	Human Suffering 46
Chapter 3	Rebuilding the Border Fortifications 72
Gerhard Sälter	Surveillance of the Wall: The Example of Bernauer Strasse 94
Chapter 4	Escapes and Escape Agents 100
Chapter 5	The Victims 120
Maria Nooke	The Victims at the Berlin Wall 130
Chapter 6	The Wall in the Cold War 134
Chapter 7	The Fall of the Berlin Wall at the Bernauer Strasse 150

Günther Schlusche	From the Fall of the Wall to the Berlin Wall Memorial: How an Urban Commemorative Space was Created 164

Permanent Exhibition in the Documentation Center on Bernauer Strasse 111

Chapter 1	Leading Up to the Berlin Wall 186
Kay Kufeke	Berlin before the Wall. The Occupied City from 1945 to 1961 192
Chapter 2	Building the Wall 198
Chapter 3	Division Becomes Permanent 206
Susanne Muhle	Building the Berlin Wall and Life in Divided Berlin 218
Chapter 4	Dictatorship of Borders 224
Elke Kimmel	Dictatorship of Borders 239
Chapter 5	Leading Up to the Fall of the Berlin Wall 242
Cornelia Thiele	The Last Years of the Wall 263
Katja Böhme	"You want to stay, we want to go" – The Emigration Movement and the Political Opposition in the GDR 278
Chapter 6	The Peaceful Revolution and Fall of the Wall 282
Marianne Birthler	The Year 1989 – Citizens' Movement and Revolution 288
Chapter 7	The Path to Unity 292

Hermann Wentker	The Fall of the Wall and German Unity 299
Axel Klausmeier	"In order to grasp something, there must be something to grasp." Or: The Remnants of the Berlin Wall as Objects of Monument Preservation 304
Klaus-Dietmar Henke	The Dimensions of the Berlin Wall 310

Appendix

Marienfelde Refugee Center Museum 314
Exhibition Imprint 316
Contributors 318

Commemoration Needs A Place
Axel Klausmeier,
Director, Berlin Wall Memorial

The history of the Berlin Wall has a central site at Bernauer Strasse. The construction of the Berlin Wall began on Bernauer Strasse. Spectacular escapes also took place on this street in August 1961 and later: men and women crawled through narrow tunnels, others jumped from buildings on the border, Conrad Schumann, the border soldier, famously leaped over the barbed wire fence. Photographs of these events were seen around the world and have become iconic images of the history of the Berlin Wall. Many lives were lost here because people tried to leave the east side of Germany and reach the west side. When the Nordbahnhof S-Bahn station was blocked off, it became a "ghost" station where West Berlin subways passed without stopping. West Berliners had to travel beneath East Berlin in order to reach other sections of West Berlin. When the sector boundary was closed on this street, border obstacles cut through busy residential areas and neighborhoods, arbitrarily separating friends and family. More than 2,000 people were forced to leave their homes on Bernauer Strasse; the buildings were razed and the border fortifications expanded. The Reconciliation Church, which stood isolated in the border strip after the Wall was erected, also fell victim to border expansion: it was dynamited in January 1985. Even the graves of the neighboring Sophien parish cemetery were cleared to make room for the death strip. The international press reported on the Bernauer Strasse border. Visitors from all over the world climbed to the top of viewing platforms on the west side to get a glimpse over the Wall to the East. The number of commemorative crosses erected for people who had died at the Wall continued to rise during the 28 years that the Wall stood. Bernauer Strasse is associated not only with the beginning of the GDR "wall regime," but also with its demise. It was here, on Oderberger Strasse, that the first opening was made in the Wall on the night of November 10, 1989 – as a consequence of the Peaceful Revolution. The official demolition of the Berlin Wall also began here on June 13, 1990.

Given the important role of this site in the events of Berlin Wall history, it is not surprising that the Round Table suggested preserving the border fortifications on Bernauer Strasse in the spring of 1990 and that Manfred Fischer, pastor of the previously divided Reconciliation parish, demanded early on that a memorial be erected here to commemorate the division of Berlin and Germany and remember the victims. Anticipating the future, he repeatedly said: "In order to grasp something, there must be something to grasp!"

He led a group that began working towards the goal of building a chapel at the site of the razed Reconciliation Church and incorporating the rubble from the demolition into the design. He also strove to establish a documentation center on Berlin Wall history in the parish building that stood on the west side of Bernauer Strasse. This citizen's initiative eventually won the support of the Berlin Senate and German federal government and in 1998 a monument designed by the architects Kollhoff and Kollhoff was erected on the corner of Bernauer Strasse and Ackerstrasse. At the same time the Documentation Center was enlarged to meet the needs created by growing numbers of visitors. Berliners and their guests began to ask more loudly: "Where had the Wall stood?" and "How did the border regime function in the middle of a major city?" There was growing political pressure to address more seriously one of the most influential events of Berlin's history. Consequently, in 2004, the Berlin Senate summoned a workgroup under the title "Berlin Wall General Concept." Under the supervision of Berlin memorials consultant Rainer E. Klemke, a concept was developed in cooperation with the group led by Manfred Fischer, the association chairman Dr. Gabriele Camphausen, the long-standing project director Dr. Maria Nooke, and with historians and administrators. Their task was to assess how the prominent Berlin Wall sites could be used to make the history more visible. The General Concept passed by the Senate in the Documentation Center on Bernauer Strasse on June 20, 2006 allotted Bernauer Strasse a central position in accordance with its historic role. The plan called for establishing exhibition grounds along 45,000 square meters of land. The mostly privately owned 1.4-kilometer-long border strip was to be bought back from the more than 100 different owners. More than 27 million euros were allotted to the project to expand the memorial ensemble formed by the Documentation Center, Chapel of Reconciliation and Wall Monument. Given the significance of the Berlin Wall to the city's history, the decision to devote a centrally-located space in the middle of a

European capital to commemoration and to create a memorial site there was both long overdue and quite unique. It was clear from the very beginning that the project's focus would be on the victims and on the people against whom this so-called anti-fascist protective rampart was aimed, namely the East German regime's own population. It is this detail that distinguishes this border from the other walls and borders in the world.

The memorial concept focuses on the following basic questions: Why was the Wall built? Why did it exist for 28 years? What conditions led to its fall? The Berlin Wall Memorial addresses these questions from multiple perspectives. The outdoor presentation, with the preserved relics of the Wall and the conscious decision not to use replicas, speaks for itself. The lost border structure is represented by modern architectural elements, allowing the exhibition to bring the focus of the site back to the personal stories and the history. The presentation conveys how deeply the border fortifications affected people's lives on both sides of the border, but of course more drastically on the east side. It also shows how the SED tried to assert its claim to power without free elections. The permanent exhibition in the Documentation Center provides the historical and political context, on the local, national and international level.

The Berlin Wall Memorial and the Marienfelde Refugee Center Museum (also a product of civic engagement) were merged to create the Berlin Wall Foundation, which began implementing this ambitious project in January 2009. In the following years, under the supervision of Klaus-Dietmar Henke, historian of contemporary history in Dresden, the Foundation built the new Visitor Center, created a permanent exhibition in the Nordbahnhof station on the history of the "ghost" stations, and redesigned approximately 5 hectare of the former border grounds on the basis of the award-wining plan by the offices of sinai (open-space planning), Mola/Winkelmüller (architecture) and Christian Fuchs, ON architektur (exhibition design). Its centerpiece is formed by the "Window of Remembrance," which commemorates the 138 people known to have died as a consequence of the Berlin Wall. The new permanent exhibition in the Documentation Center corresponds closely with and complements the information provided by the outdoor exhibition. The memorial's expansion was implemented in stages with the completion of individual sections coinciding with important anniversaries — "the 20th anniversary of the fall of the Wall," "the 50th anniversary of the Wall's construction," "the 25th anniversary of the fall of the Wall." The Foundation also organized prestigious events to accompany Berlin's celebration of these various "theme years."

Each segment was completed on time and opened to the public. The entire project was finished and officially opened on schedule and within budget on November 9, 2014 in the presence of German Chancellor Angela Merkel.

As the Berlin Wall Memorial expanded, the number of visitors rose from tens of thousands to well over a million visitors per annum from all over the world. This clearly countered the view expressed so often in the planning phase that Bernauer Strasse was too out of the way to be a central memorial site. The memorial is easy to reach by public transportation (subway, S-Bahn and tram) and only 1.5 kilometers away from Berlin's central train station. The memorial has become one of the most popular museum institutions in Germany.

Today, the former Berlin Wall "crime site" has developed into an educational site that teaches the importance of freedom, the principles of a constitutional state and the fundamental values of democracy. It is also a reminder that these important assets should not be taken for granted. The site makes clear that the people who built the Wall as a political remedy, at best only gained time. Thus the Berlin Wall Memorial helps maintain faith in freedom, especially in the many crisis-ridden areas of the world where people are denied this privilege. This site of despotism and death, of suffering and grief, has been transformed into an international site that instills hope in the power to overcome repression and dictatorship peacefully.

The Berlin Wall Memorial and Foundation have been able to carry this message out into the world thanks to the commitment of many individuals. Citizens have worked since 1990 to create this commemorative site and continue to support it through the friends association and advisory board. The women and men who developed and implemented the concept and design ideas, as well as all the people in the various administrations who paved the way and supported us, deserve our thanks. Those who provided the funds for the project deserve special acknowledgement: the Berlin House of Representatives and Senate, the German Bundestag and the Federal Commissioner for Culture and Media, the German Lottery Foundation and the European Union. And finally, we also wish to express our gratitude to our partners in the Berlin building authority, the Grün Berlin GmbH, commissioned companies, and to the staffs of the memorial, foundation and former association that worked for many years to shoulder this project and fill it with life. To see their success, one need only glance out the windows of the Documentation Center or take in the view from its viewing platform.

It is our hope that this catalog, available both in German and English, as the final component of this project, will help to inspire interest in the history of German and European division and the commemoration of its victims. It should reinforce an awareness of the value and fragility of democracy – so often taken for granted today – and to remind us that for democracy to succeed, it needs to be filled again and again with renewed life and constantly defended.

Welcoming remarks from Michael Müller, Governing Mayor of Berlin

Twenty-five years after the fall of the Wall, the opening of the Berlin Wall Memorial's new permanent exhibition is another milestone in the commemoration of the division of Berlin and Germany. Bernauer Strasse, the scene of dramatic events when the Wall was first built, is an authentic place of remembrance. The Wall divided Berlin for almost three decades, and at least 138 people lost their lives as a consequence of the GDR border regime.

We must not forget what the denial of freedom and brutal division did to this city. Above all, we must not forget the people who paid with their lives for their desire to be free.

Today, the cityscape shows little evidence of the decades of unnatural division. The people of East Berlin and the GDR triumphed over SED dictatorship and division, and this historic victory included the dismantling of the infamous wall that had forcibly separated East and West Berliners.

But the Wall is an important chapter in Berlin's history. We need commemorative sites that make this history comprehensible, especially to the younger generations that did not grow up in the shadow of the Iron Curtain. Only then can we convey the suffering caused by dictatorship and oppression and show what people struggling for freedom and democracy are able to accomplish.

We owe the completion of the Berlin Wall Memorial to the active citizenship and commitment of many: civil rights activists, contemporary witnesses, historians, architects, politicians, the Berlin Wall Memorial advisory board, Director Klausmeier and his staff. They all helped to create a multifaceted presentation documenting the history of division. For this they deserve our thanks.

Michael Müller
Governing Mayor of Berlin

Welcoming remarks from Prof. Monika Grütters, The Federal Government Commissioner for Culture and Media

On the night of November 9, 1989, events turned the Berlin Wall, the symbol of the Cold War, into a symbol of freedom. Even so, the Germans wanted the Wall torn down – understandable given the memory of injustice and suffering associated with it. It is for this reason that we should appreciate the far-sighted commitment of a few individuals, who lobbied to have a few segments of the border fortifications preserved. Pastor Manfred Fischer led a group of citizens at Bernauer Strasse, in a fight against the complete demolition of the Berlin Wall. It is much to their credit that we are able to see original remains at an historic site today. Both the historical examination of the SED dictatorship and the commemoration of the people who lost their lives at the border are important to the federal government. That is why it has made many millions of euros available since 2009, not only for institutional funding, but also for the purchase of property on Bernauer Strasse, for the open-air exhibition, and for the memorial's new permanent exhibition in the documentation center. The large numbers of people visiting the site – we welcomed the five millionth visitor in October 2014 – is an expression of appreciation for the efforts and dedicated work of the staff of the memorial, and most specifically of its director, Dr. Axel Klausmeier. Bernauer Strasse has become an important site of historical and civic education, especially demonstrating to young people the importance of life under freedom and democracy.

With this in mind, I hope the memorial will continue to attract many interested visitors and that this catalogue will also contribute to preserving the memory of German division.

Minister of State Prof. Monika Grütters MP
Federal Chancellery

The Reconciliation Church
in the border strip, 1968
Klaus Lehnartz, Photonet

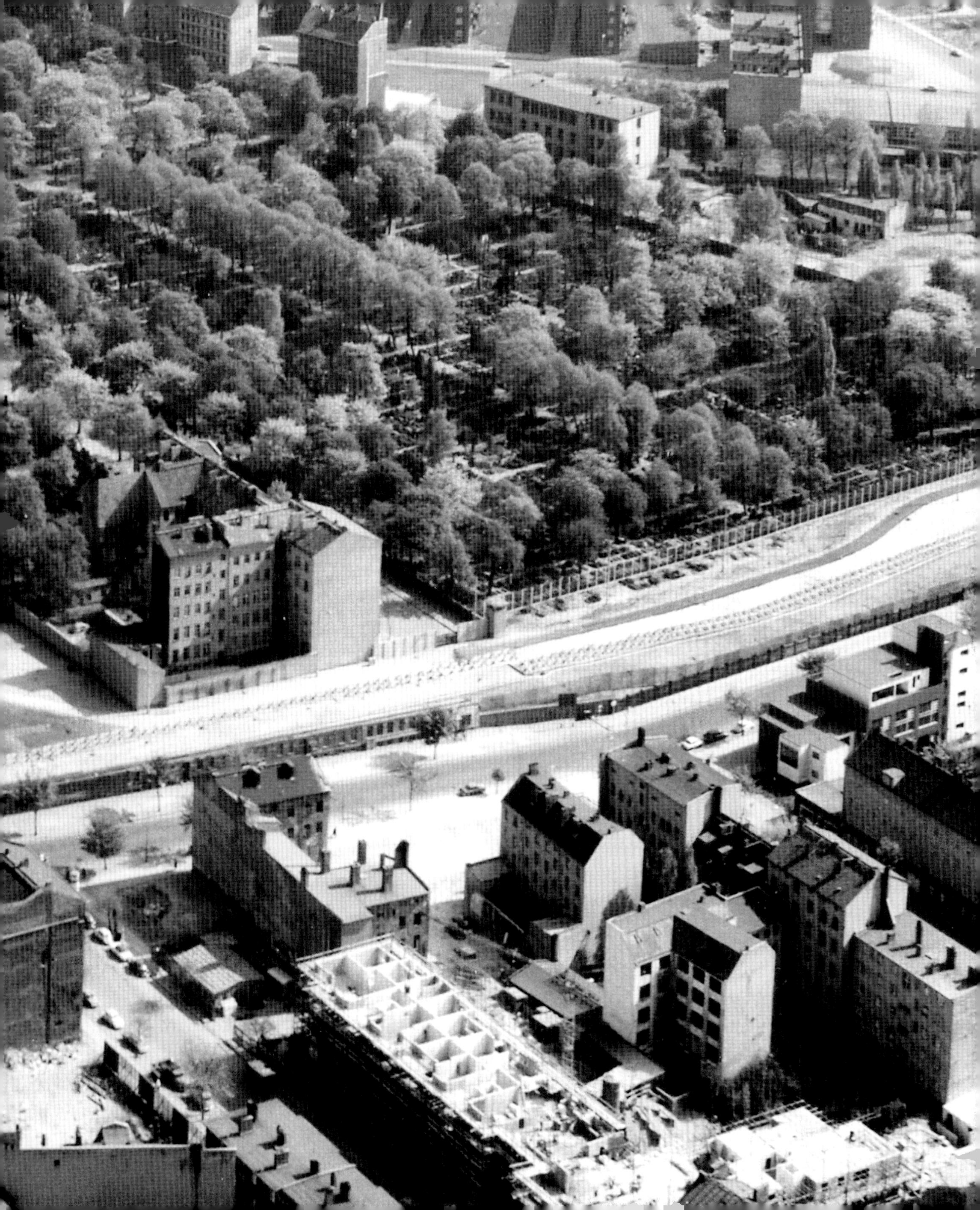

Gerhard Sälter

The SED, its Wall and GDR Society

The GDR would have been unthinkable without its border regime and the Berlin Wall. Along with the Ministry of State Security, Soviet backing and integration, they were essential pillars on which the power of the SED rested in the GDR. The SED's success in securing its power through these methods continues to bear consequences today, especially with regard to those victims who died while trying to escape at the border or under other circumstances at the Wall and inner German border. Additionally, many people were injured by mines, bullets and in accidents that occurred during escape attempts. Tens of thousands were caught trying to flee, arrested by the secret police, the People's Police or the border troops, and sent to prison. The residents who were evicted from their homes near the inner German border also experienced a social upheaval that is still felt today. The border regime pressured its citizens to conform (and participate) to a degree that was even greater than usual in the GDR. Many East German citizens experienced a conflict of loyalty: they were forced to choose between the state and the people in their everyday lives.

After World War II, the SED came to power in East Germany with the support of the Soviet occupying troops. The SED brought with it socialist welfare promises that the course of history had presumably legitimized, but it was also determined to implement necessary social reform without the approval of the people and, if need be, against their will. Following the Soviet model, it established a dictatorship which, believing it could do without the say of its citizens, imposed severe limitations on the rights of individuals and personal freedoms. The population was encouraged to participate and support the political aims of the SED and was rewarded for doing so as long it did not demand explanations or expect to take part in the decision-making process. Anyone who resisted or sought alternatives to these policies faced repression by the secret police, a prison sentence and social degradation.

In the Western part of Germany, a society developed parallel to the GDR that was initially hampered by the fact that many employees who had served under National Socialism had remained in their jobs. West Germany, however, gradually succeeded in moving beyond its authoritarian beginnings, to guarantee its citizens personal freedom and enforceable rights. A thriving economy followed. Both of these aspects – the promises of freedom and the benefits of a growing prosperity – served to lure more and more citizens away from the GDR. The Federal Republic reinforced the incentive by promptly recognizing as national citizens anyone from the GDR who resettled in the West.

By 1961, the GDR had lost almost a sixth of its population through escapes and migration to the West. The SED's reaction to this mass exodus suggests that it regretted not only the loss of desperately needed workers, but also the loss of the country's young people. It saw the exodus movement as a form of resistance, which allowed many to elude the grip of the state and which had the potential to become a mass rebellion against its authority in the GDR. Additionally, the SED recognized that the possibility of escape undermined its political goals in the GDR: every reform measure had to be weighed against the consideration that another thousand people might be driven to flee across the border.

In 1952, SED-head Walter Ulbricht tried to stem the mass exodus to the West by closing the inner German border. Following the popular uprising in 1953, the GDR stopped authorizing most travel because people were using this right to enter the Federal Republic legally and never return. The pressure to escape across the inner German border, or more often to Berlin, increased after 1957, when almost no travel authorizations were granted.

Berlin, the former capital of the Reich, had also been divided, and evolved into a focal point of the Cold War. The SED established the Soviet sector as the capital of the GDR; the three sectors of West Berlin developed into a bastion of the Western world. To GDR citizens, the Western side of the city was like a display window flaunting the Western world; to the SED it was a source of aggravation. The traffic between the two city halves was difficult to monitor, making it easy for East Germans to reach West Berlin at almost no risk. Once there, they were flown to West Germany. As a contact zone between East Germany and Western culture, West Berlin was considered an ideological trouble spot for SED rule. The presence and sovereign rights of the Western Allies put strong limitations on the SED's own sovereignty and made it acutely aware of its dependence on the Soviet protecting power.

By building the Berlin Wall on August 13, 1961, the SED tried to consolidate its power in the GDR and put an end to the mass exodus to the West. The Wall was supposed to be a demonstration of its power to the Western world, but most importantly to the Federal Republic: the SED wanted to show its sovereignty over GDR territory and its people. The Wall blocked the GDR population's access to the West and stabilized the internal political situation. The hope was that eventually, through education and propaganda, those East Germans, whose support was initially lacking, would be won over and the social order imposed within the social realm of the GDR, now enclosed by the Wall, would win acceptance.

By placing a wall around West Berlin, the SED was able to curtail the mass exodus from the GDR, but it was not able to stop it entirely. On the contrary: Many cross-border relationships were cut off by the Wall, particularly in East Berlin and the rural areas outside of the city, which increased the pressure on people to flee. Furthermore, both dissatisfaction with the political and economic situation in the GDR and the allure of the West were great enough to motivate a waning but nevertheless constant exodus. The SED reacted by taking three measures at the border: it intensified the orders for firing weapons, it continually expanded the border fortifications, and it increased surveillance of the border territory. With escapes still possible, and because, in the seventies, East Germans officially began requesting permission to immigrate to the West, long-term surveillance of all GDR citizens was intensified. In the seventies and eighties, the surveillance and repressive activities of the secret police and East German police focused primarily on imposing restrictions on citizens' freedom of movement. The border regime and its Wall were a control and surveillance necessity that penetrated ever deeper into GDR society, playing a decisive role in social life and in the relationship between individuals and the state. It became a fundamental condition of life in the GDR.

In the medium term, the policy of separation and seclusion was successful. There were some people close to the party who had hoped that the situation would ease after the Wall was built, but it instead led to a consolidation of the SED's power within the country. With regard to foreign affairs, it facilitated an increase in the SED's international recognition. Following the construction of the Wall and the Western Allies' restrained, seemingly helpless, response to it, the government of the Federal Republic was compelled to change its foreign policy course. Instead of loudly insisting on the illegitimacy of the GDR government and engaging in a policy of non-communication, it pursued a policy of rapprochement and understanding. The Four-Power Agreement on Berlin, which was signed in 1971, the establishment of the Basic Treaty of 1972 between the GDR and the Federal Republic, and the acceptance of both countries into the UN were also consequences of the Wall.

But the policy of détente between the Eastern and Western blocs, and, in particular, between the two German states, thwarted the SED's internal power gain. German-German treaties created new connections between the two Germanys and served to reinforce already existing bonds. Furthermore, the treaty regarding transit routes between Berlin and West Germany provided new escape routes. The GDR had to increase its legal standards in regard to its own citizens. The SED initially had no intention of honoring them, but diplomacy with the West obliged it to do so and an ever greater number of citizens in the GDR demanded this as well. For this reason, and because of the SED's inflexibility, in the long run, its policies of social isolation that were based on a border regime remained unsuccessful. The SED was unable to convince the majority of the East German population of the superiorityof its social model and its aging leadership chose not to address the needs and ideas of "its" citizens. After Erich Honecker succeeded Walter Ulbricht as head of the party and state in 1971, there was a noticeable effort to at least meet the supply needs of the GDR population, but the state-controlled economy's limited production capacity made this difficult. Given the internal party opposition that emerged in the sixties, the SED leadership became even less inclined to guarantee citizens substantial rights of freedom. The economic problems that manifested themselves more clearly beginning in the seventies proved an additional factor. Despite the GDR media's ongoing claims of production success, the consumer needs of the population, in comparison with the West, were not met, causing even greater discontent. Two new developments emerged in the seventies and more strongly in the eighties: a growing number of young people were turning their backs on the GDR state. The East German youth had adopted other values and wanted to get away from state paternalism. As in the West, an alternative culture developed on society's fringe in the mid-eighties. Finding protection within the Protestant Church in the East, it brought forth an opposition movement.

In 1989 – 1990, pressure within the GDR became so great that a growing protest movement was able to do away with the SED leadership and its established social order with virtually no resistance. The latent dissatisfaction that had been building up since the seventies was organized into a growing protest movement. Following political changes, the Soviet Union ceased to function as the SED's protective power and guarantor of its state power in East Germany. As the Eastern bloc disintegrated, more opportunities opened for refugees to flee in the summer of 1989. Opposition groups that had been forming since the eighties became more active. In the end, the SED capitulated to the growing protest of a broad grassroots movement that had begun on October 9, 1989, the day of the mass demonstration in Leipzig. In addition to the collective resignation of the Politburo, the opening of the Wall on November 9, 1989 was a clear sign of change. The SED leadership had given up one of its main principles: Securing control over the people of the GDR by cutting off their freedom of movement. Three decades later, the Wall and the border regime proved itself to be a flawed strategy for maintaining power.

Official map of Berlin showing Bernauer Strasse, 1963
Stiftung Berliner Mauer

East

Maria Nooke

Bernauer Strasse – A Site of the Berlin Wall with Historical Significance

The intersection of Bernauer Strasse and Brunnenstrasse before the Wall was built
Horst Siegmann, Landesarchiv Berlin

Erecting the Wall between Bernauer Strasse and Ackerstrasse, August 15, 1961
Bernd Thiele, ullstein-bild

Fleeing from Bernauer Strasse 11 to the western side of the street on August 17, 1961
Horst Siegmann, Landesarchiv Berlin

Until 1961, Bernauer Strasse was an inconspicuous and little-known residential street situated between the districts of Berlin-Mitte and Wedding. It did not become famous until the Berlin Wall was erected and the street became the focus of events that were unfolding in August 1961. Until the Wall fell on November 9, 1989, the dramatic impact and personal consequences of Berlin's division were still visible on Bernauer Strasse. As a consequence of this site's historical significance, the central memorial to remember the city's division and commemorate its victims was established on Bernauer Strasse.[1]

The situation before the Wall was built
After World War II, the Western Allies divided Berlin into four sectors that were established along district lines. The boundary between the Soviet and French sectors was drawn along Bernauer Strasse, which created an unusual situation: The buildings on the southern side of the street belonged to the Soviet sector and, thus, to East Berlin. But the sidewalk directly in front of these buildings was part of the western side of the city. The sector boundary was formed by the facades of the buildings that stood along the border. For residents of Bernauer Strasse, crossing between East and West was a normal part of their daily lives.

As was often the case in areas near the border, small businesses were established on Bernauer Strasse that attracted and offered advantages to residents of the 'other' sector. West Berliners patronized the stores and workshops on the eastern side of the street where basic commodities tended to be cheaper than in the West. The East Berlin residents purchased goods on the western side that were not readily available in their part of the city. The many border cinemas situated on and near Bernauer Strasse were also popular among East Berliners. For a small admission fee they could watch films there that had been prohibited on their side of the city because they did not correspond to the ideology in the Soviet-controlled sector.[2]

To prevent certain goods from being imported or smuggled into the East, customs checks were conducted on the side streets of Bernauer Strasse. These inspections were a nuisance, but they rarely had serious consequences since residents had figured out how to get around them.

Consequences of the border closure on Bernauer Strasse
Daily life on Bernauer Strasse changed abruptly when the Wall was erected. On August 13, 1961, East German workers rolled out coils of barbed wire and sealed off the streets that crossed the border. Construction of the Wall began a short time later.

For a few days, residents could still reach the western side of the street and enter West Berlin. During this brief period, they were able to flee East Germany without risk. Three days later, paramilitary workers' militias from GDR businesses began sealing the doors of buildings on the border and creating new exits through the courtyards in back.[3] Residents of ground-floor apartments were forced to vacate their homes and the windows facing the street were bricked up.[4]

East German policeman Conrad Schumann escaping to West Berlin, August 15, 1961
Peter Leibing, Staatsarchiv Hamburg

The 77-year-old Frieda Schulze jumps from a window on Bernauer Strasse, September 25, 1961
Alex Waidmann, ullstein bild

To keep the population under control and prevent spontaneous escape attempts, armed members of the workers' militia were positioned on the staircase landings and back courtyards of the border buildings to keep an eye on all movement into and out of the buildings.[5] Given these dismal circumstances, many residents decided to flee. They jumped out of the windows of their apartments onto the West Berlin sidewalk or they roped themselves down the front of the building. These escapes had to be carefully planned so that the border guards would not notice them and try to stop them. Residents often threw messages onto the street containing the date and time of their planned escape. West Berlin neighbors or passersby informed the firemen and police, who waited in patrol cars on the side streets, ready for action. Dramatic scenes played out during these escape attempts; photographers took pictures and filmed people jumping out of their windows and the images were seen around the world. Conrad Schumann, a 19-year-old East German policeman, attracted attention on August 15: Two days after the border was closed, he threw his weapon behind him and leapt over the barbed-wire fence in an attempt to get away from the cruel situation of guarding the border. According to a statistic from the Ministry of State Security (MfS), he was one of 2,433 border policemen, border soldiers and NVA members who had deserted successfully to the West by 1989.[6]

But most of the people who fled were civilians – even on Bernauer Strasse. Many decided to flee spontaneously during a targeted operation on September 24 and 25, 1961, during which more than 2,000 residents of the border buildings were evacuated from their apartments, mostly against their will.

By October 10, 1961, the border troops had registered 306 successful escapes to the West, 113 of which had taken place on Bernauer Strasse.[7] Not all escape attempts were successful, however. In the first weeks after the Wall was built, two men and two women died while trying to escape out of their windows. In September 1962, border guards shot a man who was trying to reach the western side of the city by fleeing across the grounds of the Sophien parish cemetery.[8]

Measures to prevent escapes

The border fortifications were constantly expanded and improved to make them impassable to fugitives. This was also true at Bernauer Strasse, which had become an eerie site by October 1961: The windows of the border buildings had been bricked up and the residents forced to move elsewhere. Monuments wrapped in barbed wire and commemorative plates set in the pavement reminded West Berliners of the people who had jumped to their deaths or had been shot nearby. The West Berlin police erected wooden platforms at street intersections, providing Westerners a view over the border grounds. Residents and tourists climbed to the top of these platforms to get a glimpse of the border fortifications or to wave to friends and relatives in East Berlin. In 1965, construction units of the border troops began tearing down the deserted buildings along the border on Bernauer Strasse. But the facades of the lower stories, which functioned as a border wall, were left standing and integrated into the multi-layered border fortifications system. A new version of the Wall, called Border Wall 75, was erected on Bernauer Strasse in 1980.

Spectacular escapes

Although the border was under total surveillance and constant efforts were made to improve it, daring escape attempts at Bernauer Strasse repeatedly drew public awareness. Escape tunnels dug along the 1.2-kilometer-long section of the Bernauer Strasse border attracted special attention. Several groups, which had been formed in the West to offer assistance to people in the East who wanted to escape, were active along the Bernauer Strasse border between 1962 und 1971. Of the 13 documented tunnel projects in this section of the border, only three were actually used for escapes.[9] One of them was "Tunnel 29," which was filmed by an NBC television crew. Twenty-nine people escaped through this tunnel on September 14 and 15, 1962. Another 57 people fled to the West on October 3 and 4, 1964 through "Tunnel 57," which acquired notoriety when Egon Schultz, a sergeant in the border troops, was killed during the operation.[10] The third successful escape tunnel ended in a coal yard in the East, but was detected by the MfS the day after completion. Only three young women were able to

Demolition of the church nave, 1985
unknown photographer,
Versöhnungsgemeinde Berlin Wedding

flee through this tunnel before the MfS filled it with tear gas, rendering it unusable.[11] The other tunnel projects were discontinued: They had been betrayed to, or detected by, the MfS during construction or before they could be used. A number of fugitives and escape helpers were apprehended and sentenced to long prison terms in the East. To prevent the construction of more tunnels, the MfS developed a sensor system that enabled technical surveillance of areas where tunnel construction was suspected. The sensors were positioned in the ground within the death strip to measure seismographic and acoustic data. It was believed that by detecting noises and tremors, the construction of tunnels could be prevented.[12]

The Reconciliation Church also fell victim to the expansion of the border fortifications and intricately planned system of obstacles.[13]

The church, which had been dedicated in 1894, became inaccessible within the border strip in 1961. Not only did it hinder border surveillance, it also demonstrated the inhumanity of the Berlin Wall. This may be why it was dynamited by border troops in January 1985. The images of its demolition were seen throughout the world, leading to public protest and outrage. In November 1989, Bernauer Strasse once again became a focal point of historic events. On the night of November 10, just one day after the Berlin population had stormed the Wall, causing it to fall, the first official opening was made through the Wall between Bernauer Strasse and Eberswalder Strasse. Before the eyes of cheering spectators from the East and the West, construction units of the border troops removed the first segments of the Wall and created a new crossing.[14] Bernauer Strasse was also the site where the first official dismantling of border fortifications began. On June 13, 1990, an opening was made in the Wall at Ackerstrasse/Bernauer Strasse, in the presence of the West Berlin construction minister and his colleague from the East Berlin magistrate. A 210-meter-long stretch of the Wall was spared destruction, but the rest of the Wall was dismantled. This piece of the Berlin Wall, the only one to be preserved with its many-layered system of border fortifications, is now integrated into the memorial at Bernauer Strasse.

1 The Berlin Senate's general concept to commemorate the Berlin Wall, pp. 17–21, www.stiftung-berliner-mauer.de/de/stiftung-8.htm, 22.5.2014.

2 Evidence of this and other related activities provided in various interviews, Berlin Wall Memorial Contemporary Witness Archive.

3 See articles in *Der Tagesspiegel* and *Der Tag* on August 17, 1961, Telegraf on August 18, 1961.

4 Interview with Regine Hildebrandt, April 22, 1999, Berlin Wall Memorial Contemporary Witness Archive.

5 *Bernauer Straße 1–50 oder: Als uns die Haustür zugenagelt wurde*, documentary film by Hans-Dieter Grabe, 1971.

6 Maria Nooke, "Geglückte und gescheiterte Fluchten nach dem Mauerbau," in Klaus-Dietmar Henke (ed.), *Die Mauer. Errichtung, Überwindung, Erinnerung*, Munich 2011, pp. 163–180, here p. 171–172.

7 Günter Glaser et al., *Die Nationale Volksarmee in der Aktion vom 13. August 1961*, unpublished transcript 1964, BA-MA, VA-01, 14835, p. 269; Gerhard Sälter, "Zu den Zwangsräumungen in Berlin nach dem Mauerbau 1961," in: *Deutschland Archiv* 44 (2011) 4, pp. 546–551, here p. 548.

8 Hans-Hermann Hertle/Maria Nooke et al., *Die Todesopfer an der Berliner Mauer 1961–1989. Ein biographisches Handbuch*, published by Zentrum für Zeitgeschichtliche Forschung and Gedenkstätte Berliner Mauer, 2nd revised edition, Berlin 2009.

9 Dietmar Arnold/Sven-Felix Kellerhoff, *Die Fluchttunnel von Berlin*, Berlin 2008, pp. 117–150; Klaus-M. von Keussler, Peter Schulenburg, *Fluchthelfer. Die Gruppe um Wolfgang Fuchs*, 2nd revised edition, Berlin 2011; Maria Nooke, *Der verratene Tunnel. Geschichte einer verhinderten Flucht im geteilten Berlin*, Bremen 2002; Maria Nooke/Lydia Dollmann (eds.), *Fluchtziel Freiheit. Berichte von DDR-Flüchtlingen nach dem Mauerbau – Aktionen der Girrmanngruppe*, Berlin 2011, pp. 28–37.

10 Maria Nooke, Egon Schultz, in: Hertle/Nooke et al., *Todesopfer*, pp. 456–462.

11 Interviews mit Wolfgang Fuchs, 12.8.1999 and Dr. Hartmut Horst, 2.3.2001, Berlin Wall Memorial Contemporary Witness Archive; Keussler/Schulenburg, *Fluchthelfer*, pp. 130–146, 154–175.

12 BStU, MfS, BV Berlin, Abt. VII Nr. 1548, p. 75–95; BStU, MfS, BV Berlin, Abt. VII Nr. 1550, pp. 1–166.

13 Christian Halbrock, "Weggesprengt – Die Versöhnungskirche im Todesstreifen der Berliner Mauer 1961–1985," *Horch und Guck*, special issue, Berlin 2008.

14 Articles in *Der Tagesspiegel* and *Berliner Morgenpost* on November 12, 1989; interview with Klaus G., May 22, 2009 and interview with Peter Zeissler, October 22, 2008, Berlin Wall Memorial Contemporary Witness Archive.

Permanent Exhibition and Memorial Grounds at Bernauer Strasse

Section B
The Destruction of the City

Section C
The Building of the W[all]

Section A
The Berlin Wall and the Death Strip

Bernauer Straße

Documentation Center

M10 Gedenkstätte

Visitor Center

B
Chapel of Reconciliation

Monument

Julie-Wolfthorn-Straße — Bus 245, 247

A
Window of Remembrance

Exhibition "Border Stations and Ghost Stations" in the Nordbahnhof Station

M10

Nordbahnhof
S1
S2
S25

Invalidenstraße

Bus 245, 247
Tram M 8, M 12

Park am Nordbahnhof

Gartenstraße

Ackerstraße

Bergstraße

Strelitzer Straße

Anklamer Straße

Invalidenstraße

Stralsunder Straße

Usedomer Straße

C

Map of the Berlin Wall Memorial
Berthold Weidner

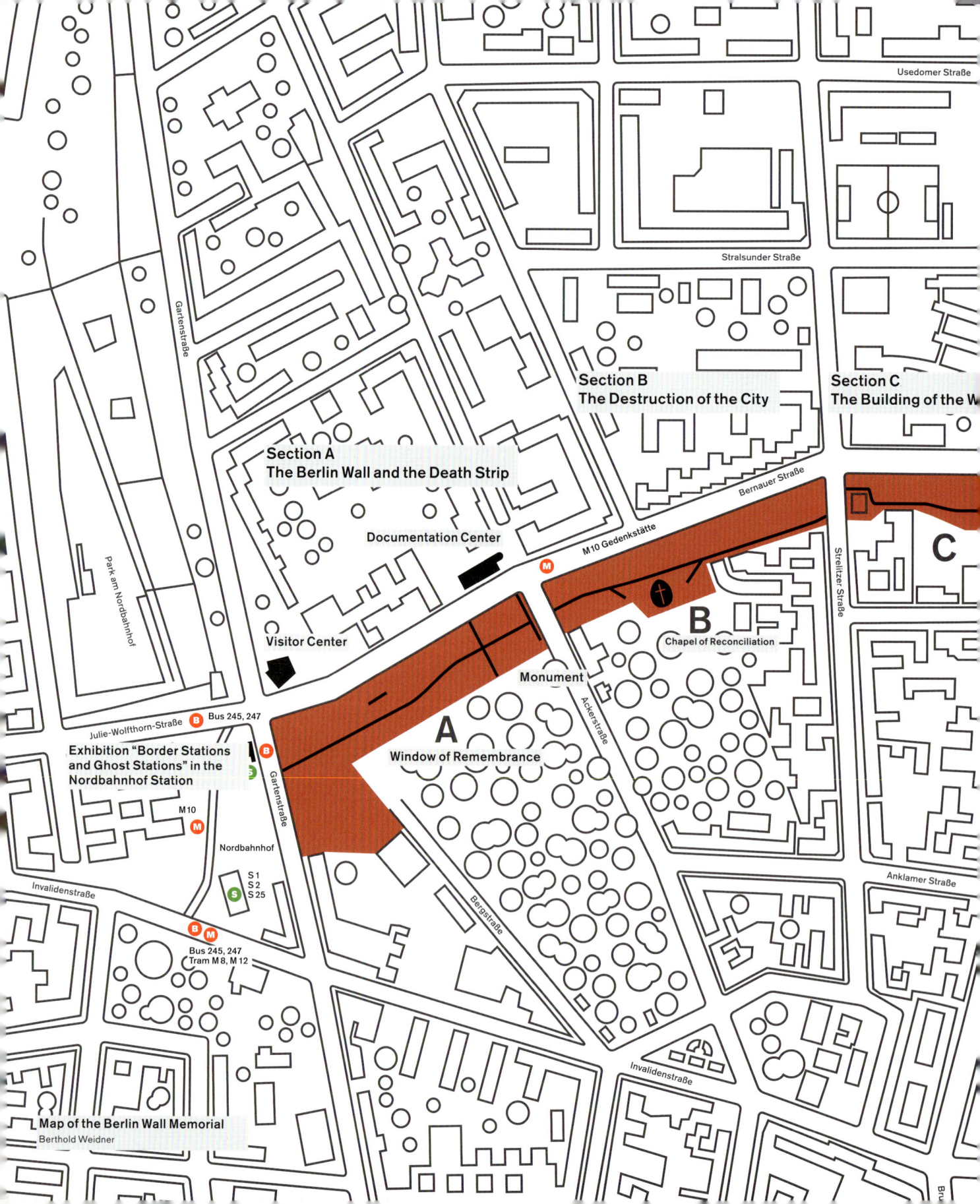

Section D
Everyday Life at the Wall

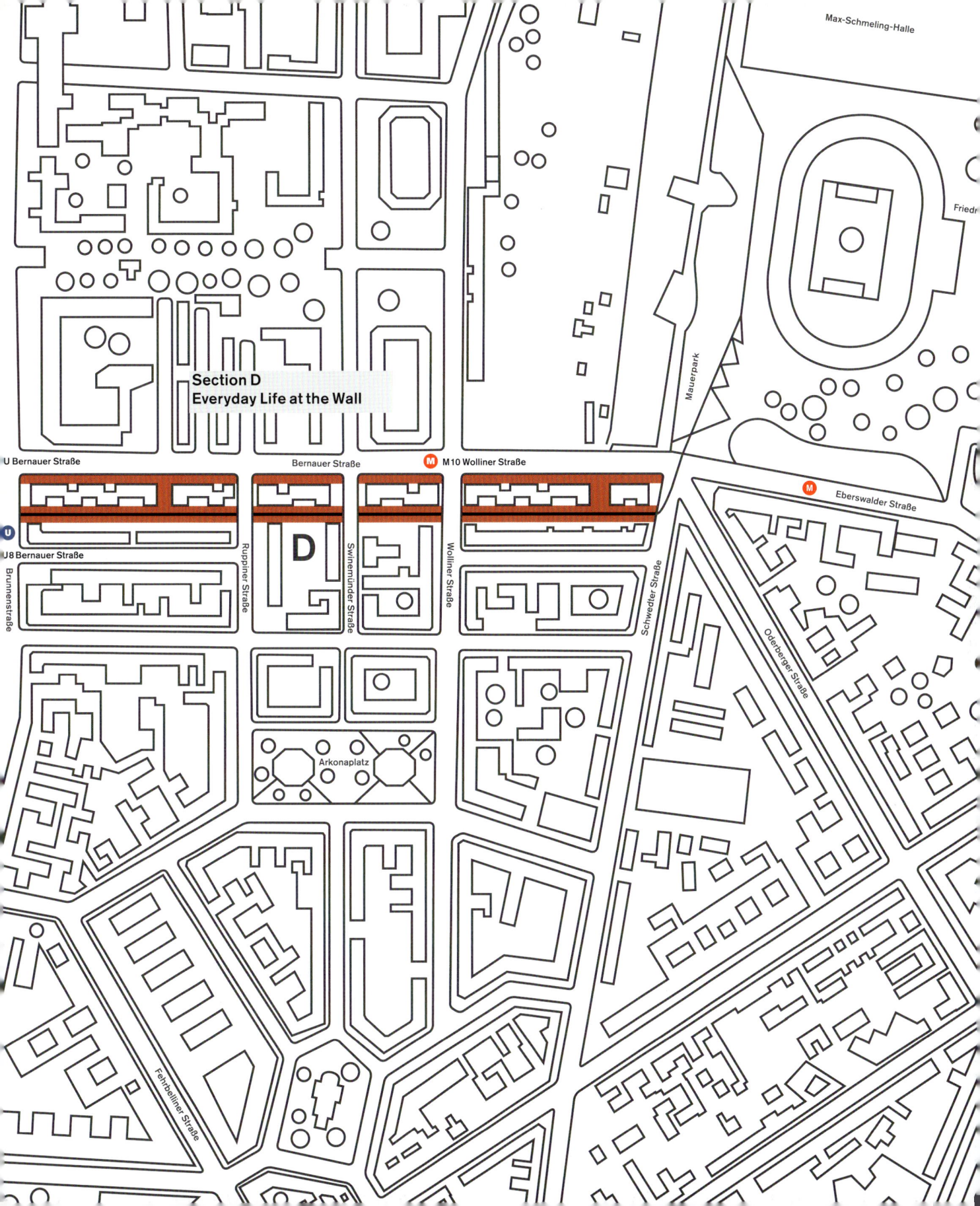

Max-Schmeling-Halle

Friedr

Mauerpark

U Bernauer Straße
Bernauer Straße
M10 Wolliner Straße
Eberswalder Straße
U8 Bernauer Straße
Ruppiner Straße
D
Swinemünder Straße
Wolliner Straße
Schwedter Straße
Oderberger Straße
Brunnenstraße
Arkonaplatz
Fehrbelliner Straße

Open-air exhibition and Visitor Center on Gartenstrasse, 2010
Jürgen Hohmuth, Stiftung Berliner Mauer

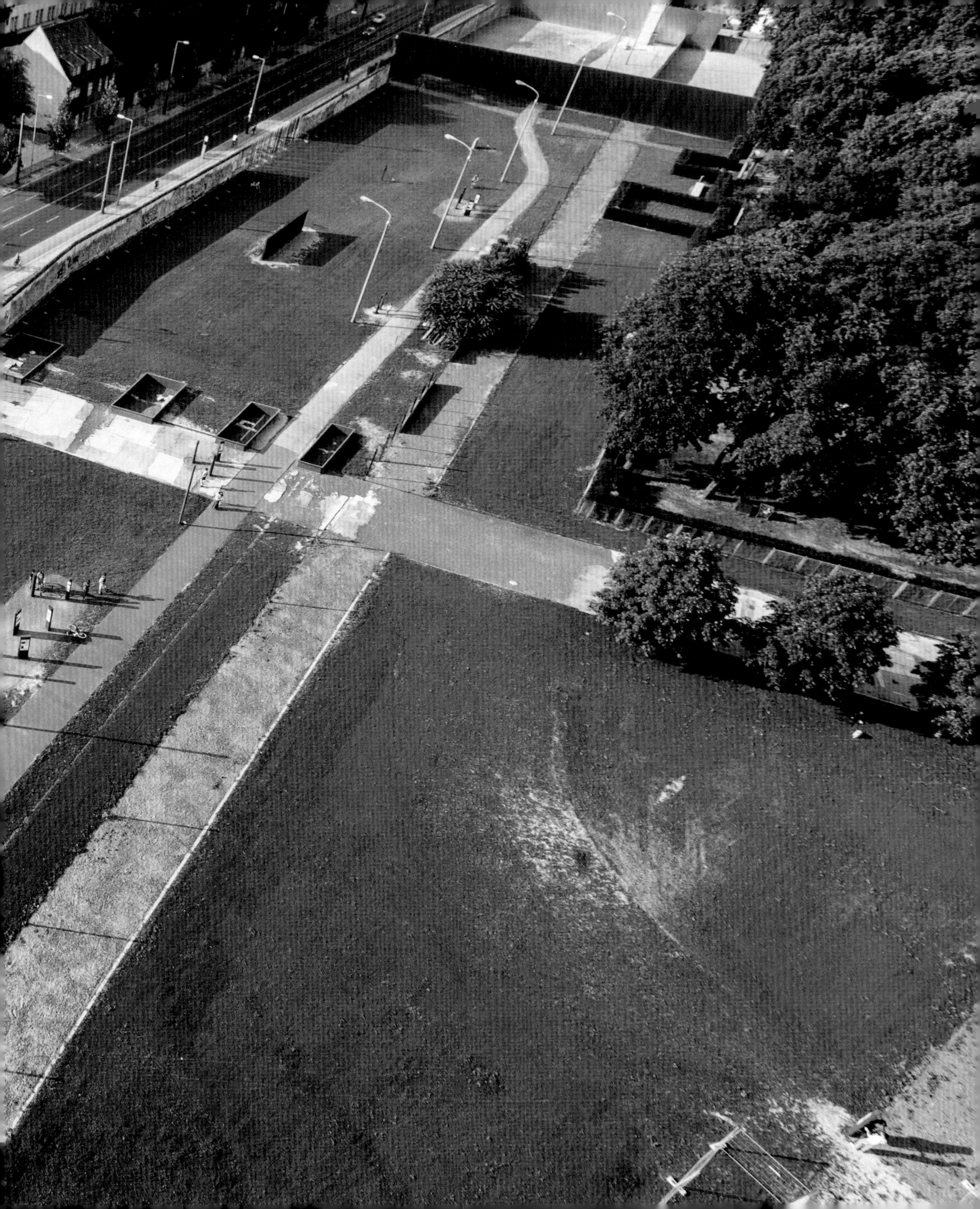

Exhibition theme: "The Wall and the Border Strip" on Gartenstrasse, 2014
Berthold Weidner

Gartenstraße

1989/90

1

The Wall and the Border Strip

With the help of the Soviet occupying forces, the SED state party established a dictatorship in East Germany (GDR) after the war. A large percentage of the East German population did not support the new political and economic system. In contrast, West Germany (Federal Republic), with its offer of freedom, prosperity and modernity, was very appealing. A mass exodus to the West began in the late 1940s that reached dramatic proportions by the 1950s.

On August 13, 1961, the SED tried to stop people from fleeing by closing the border to West Berlin. It also hoped that this act would stabilize its control over the East German people and demonstrate its sovereignty to the world. But the barbed wire and walls did not stop the exodus and the border fortifications in Berlin had to be further expanded and reinforced. The armed guards posted at the border made the many rows of border obstacles dangerous. Soldiers had the order to shoot at fugitives if they were otherwise unable to hinder their escape.

"Sometimes, we'd hear grenades blasting over there in the early morning hours. Why? Because two people had crawled into the open field in the dead of the night, (...) they'd gotten stuck in the wires and set off detonations. Everyone on duty over there came running. The people lying on the ground were expected to stand up, were beaten and taken away – with their shoulders hanging. That was a hard day for us. You can't erase something like that from your memory."

A Lazarus nurse reports on an escape attempt on Bernauer Strasse, 1960s
Interview, Stiftung Berliner Mauer, 2002

Cover of a brochure on the building
of the Wall, 1961
Presseamt des Landes Berlin

Rebuilding the Border Fortifications

The SED leadership did not succeed in putting a complete stop to westward migration. On the contrary, because the Wall separated friends and relatives in Berlin, the pressure on East Berliners to flee became even greater. The SED reacted by developing the Wall into an expansive system of border fortifications.

Initially, when an escape was successful, provisional obstacles were added behind the border wall. Over the years a fence was put up at a number of sites to block off large areas of the border. In the mid-1960s, buildings were torn down and a uniform border strip was created to provide border soldiers with an "unobstructed view and clear field of fire." More and more barriers were installed in what became known as the "death strip." In the 1970s, a "hinterland" or inner wall was added, blocking off the border strip to East Berlin and the GDR. Towards the end, the border wall was replaced by a new wall that was better designed to prevent escapes.

By the 1980s, the border contained a multi-layered system of obstacles.

Blocking off Bergstrasse with barbed wire on August 13, 1961
Beck, Stiftung Berliner Mauer

First measures to seal off Berlin on August 13, 1961
Peter Georgi, ullstein bild

**The first wall is erected
in August 1961**
Bicker, Versöhnungsgemeinde Berlin-Wedding

**Bricked up buildings and wall,
Bernauer Strasse, 1962**
Gerd Schütz, Landesarchiv Berlin

**A border wall is erected on
Bergstrasse, August 15, 1961**
unknown photographer

Border barriers between Gartenstrasse and Bergstrasse, 1962
Günter Malchow, Stiftung Berliner Mauer

View inside the border fortifications on Gartenstrasse, 1962
Karsten Sroka,
Versöhnungsgemeinde Berlin-Wedding

Wall on Brunnenstrasse, viewed from the East, ca. 1965
unknown photographer, Bundesarchiv

Reinforced border wall on Gartenstrasse, 1973
Klaus Lehnartz, Photonet

Border fortifications at Bernauer Strasse between Bergstrasse and Gartenstrasse, 1974
Geoportal Berlin/Luftbild, Senatsverwaltung für Stadtentwicklung

Border strip between Gartenstrasse and Ackerstrasse, 1967
Klaus Lehnartz, Photonet

Inner wall on Brunnenstrasse, 1983
Border troops photo, Bundesarchiv-Militärarchiv

Inner wall on Gartenstrasse, 1989
Klaus Lehnartz, Photonet

The Wall and the Border Strip
Elke Rosin

"My parents were getting increasingly nervous and after a while my father said, 'So, where is this heading?!' – He didn't know the answer, but one thing was certain […], we couldn't continue living there."

Interview, Stiftung Berliner Mauer, 2012

Elke Rosin was born in East Berlin in 1945. She had lived with her parents directly on the sector border on Bernauer Strasse since the 1950s. After observing the situation for a few days following the border's closing, her family decided to flee. On August 17, 1961, Elke Rosin and her parents left their apartment and went to West Berlin. Elke Rosin moved to Darmstadt and completed a commercial apprenticeship. She returned to West Berlin in 1968, where she witnessed the fall of the Wall twenty-one years later.

View into the Monument between Ackerstrasse and Gartenstrasse, 2010

Jürgen Hohmuth, Stiftung Berliner Mauer

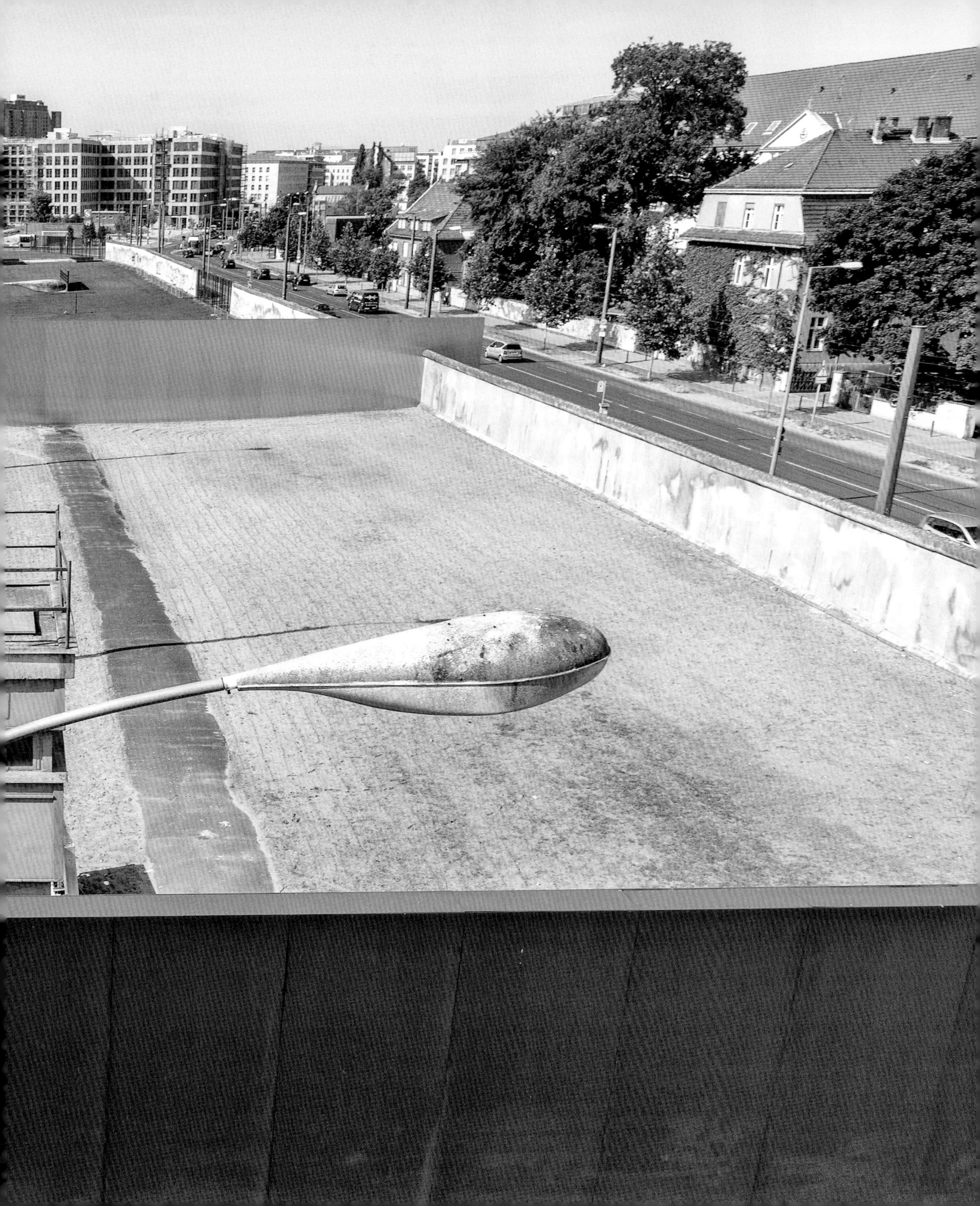

Exhibition theme: "Ackerstrasse in Divided Berlin," 2014
Berthold Weidner

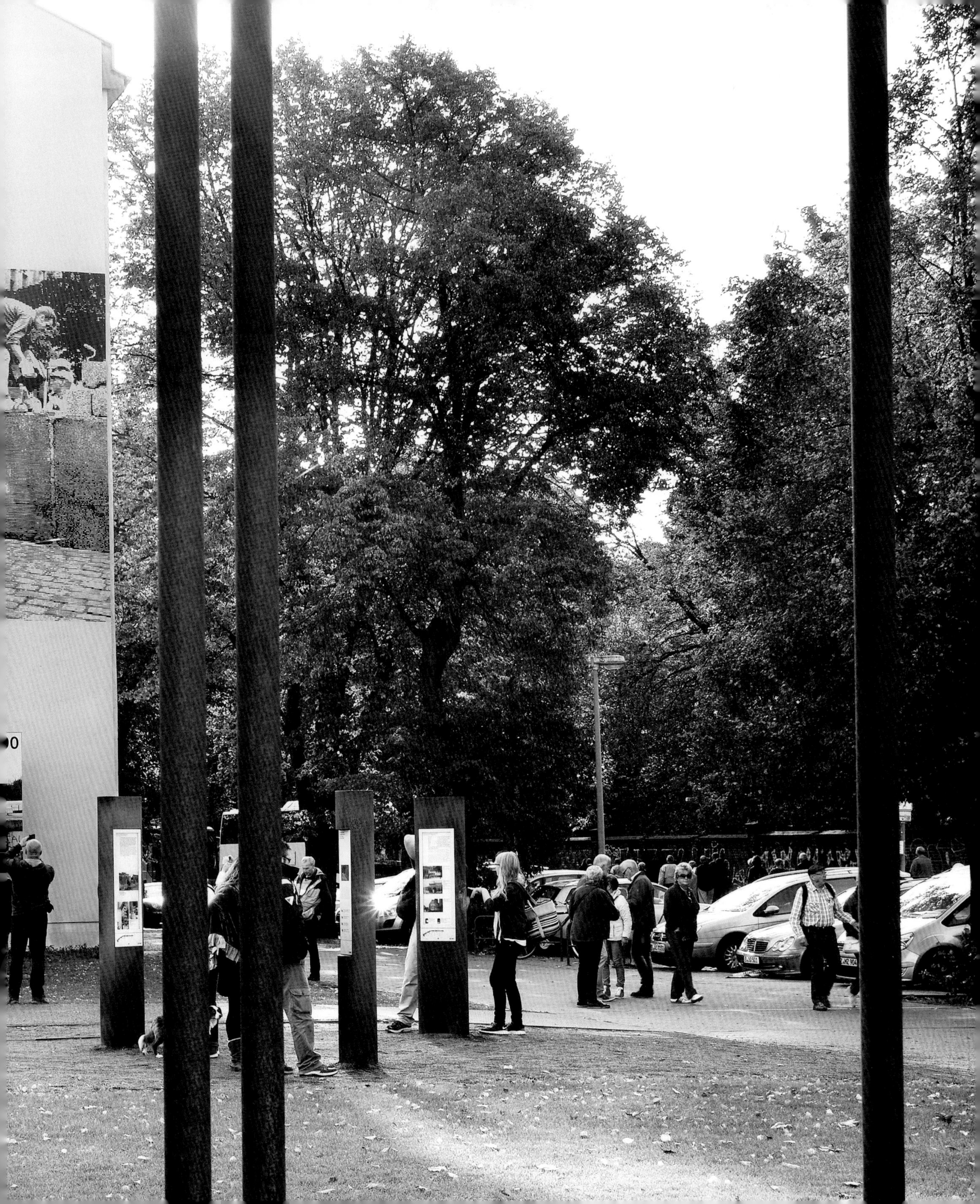

2

Human Suffering

The lives of people living on Bernauer Strasse were altered radically on August 13, 1961. Overnight, families, friends and neighbors were torn apart. Bernauer Strasse became a street where people made dates to see each other across the expanse of the border.

Many people who lived in buildings on the border hastily decided to flee to West Berlin. Those who stayed behind were forced to move out of their apartments. The border houses were bricked up and later torn down. The Wall separated a large part of the Reconciliation parish in the West from its church and pastor in the East. They could no longer hold church services together and the church building was taken over by border soldiers.

For a time, the entrance to the Sophien parish cemetery on Bernauer Strasse was blocked off to West Berliners. East Berlin visitors had to present a special permit before entering.

"On September 24, a Sunday, we heard banging on our door at 6 in the morning: 'Open up right away!' My mother went to the door in her nightgown. The door was forced open and members of the workers' militia rushed to the window to make sure that no one else got away and jumped out. We got up and dressed under their watchful eyes. The trucks of the workers' militia were parked down below. IDs were collected and books carried downstairs. When everything had been loaded onto the truck, they set off. We didn't know where we were moving to."

Regine Hildebrandt, resident of Bernauer Strasse 2 und 10
Interview, Stiftung Berliner Mauer, 1999

**The residents who stayed behind,
September 1961**
Gert Hilde, ullstein bild

The Border Houses

Before the Wall was built, residents of the buildings situated directly behind the border enjoyed the privilege of immediate and uncontrolled access to the West. When the border was closed on August 13, 1961, they lost this freedom. After the Wall was built, residents on the east side were faced with the decision of whether to go or to stay. Many decided to flee.

To prevent this, the doors that opened to the West and the windows on the lower levels were bricked up. The residents were forced to move into apartments on the upper levels.

The SED did not inform the Bernauer Strasse residents of the impending evacuation operation. But rumors spread quickly. The evictions were carried out in three phases: People suspected of planning an escape were vacated in late August. More than 2,000 people were forced to leave their apartments in September. In October, 341 people had to leave their homes. East German police officers and members of the workers' militia forced their way into apartments and ordered the residents to pack their personal belongings. The residents were driven away with their possessions and without knowledge of the destination.

After the buildings were evacuated, the windows facing the street were bricked up. In 1963 the border troops tore down several rear buildings to establish an open strip behind the front buildings. The remaining border buildings were taken down in 1965 and 1966; only the remains of the building fronts were left standing. The buildings had to make way for the "modern border." The actual border wall now ran behind the facades. These ruins were removed in 1980 to make room for a new Berlin Wall.

**Evictions on Bernauer Strasse,
September 24, 1961**
unkown photographer, picture alliance
Jung, ullstein bild

**Bricking up the window,
October 1961**
Klaus Lehnartz, Photonet

The Border House Bernauer Strasse 10a

The front doors to the building were nailed shut about a week after the border was closed. The windows of apartments and the basement level were bricked up after the residents fled to the West. By mid-November, all the remaining residents were evicted. The building remained empty after that. In 1963, a side wing of the building was torn down. In March of 1965, the front building was demolished. After that, only the basement level with no access to the border strip and the ground level façade were left standing.

Fronts of buildings at Bernauer Strasse 10, 10a und 11, December 1962
unkown photographer, Stiftung Berliner Mauer

Demolition of the building at Bernauer Strasse 10a, March 1965
unkown photographer, Stiftung Berliner Mauer

Escapes from border houses, 1965
Landesarchiv Berlin/Stiftung Berliner Mauer

Nr. 13	Nr. 13a	Nr. 11	Nr. 10a	Nr. 10	Nr. 9	Nr. 8
Sept. 22, 1961 one person Sept. 30, 1961 two people		Aug. 17, 1961 a family Sept. 4, 1961 one person Jan. 29, 1962 one person		Aug. 24, 1961 a family Sept. 19, 1961 three people Sept. 20, 1961 two people		Sept. 19, 1961 a family Sept. 24, 1961 one person Sept. 17, 1961 one person

Facade ruins, photographed from the border strip, 1965/66
Border troops photo, Bundesarchiv

Facade ruins after demolition, Bernauer Strasse 10 to 13a, 1965
unknown photographer, Landesarchiv Berlin

Facade ruins after demolition, Bernauer Strasse 5 to 10a, 1979
Karina Raeck and Gary Rieveschl

22, 1961 one person . 22, 1961 a family . 27, 1961 one person					Aug. 13, 1961 one person Aug. 19, 1961 two people Sept. 5, 1961 a family Sept. 14, 1961 one person Sept. 19, 1961 one person Sept. 23, 1961 one person Oct. 15, 1961 one person Oct. 27, 1961 one person May 2, 1962 one person
	Sept. 25, 1961 a family	Aug. 26, 1961 one person Aug. 30, 1961 three people Aug. 30, 1961 five people Oct. 23, 1961 one person Dec. 5, 1961 one person			
June 18, 1961 four people Sept. 24, 1961 one person			Aug. 19, 1961 two people Oct. 23, 1961 one person		
Nr. 6	**Nr. 5**	**Nr. 2**	**Nr. 1**		**Ackerstrasse Nr. 43**

51

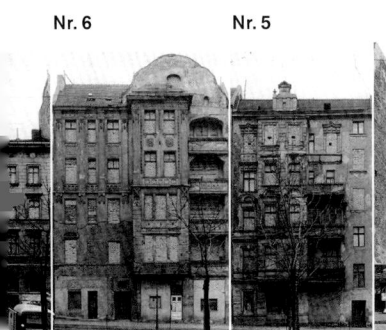

The Reconciliation Church

The parish of the Reconciliation Church that was dedicated in 1894 had been divided since the end of the war. About 90 percent of its members lived in the West. The church stood in East Berlin, where the pastor also lived. Despite the difficulties caused by the city's division and the SED's hostile policies towards the Church, the church community remained largely intact until 1961.

After the Wall was built, the Reconciliation Church found itself situated behind the Wall. After August 22, when the church portal on Bernauer Strasse was bricked up, it was no longer accessible from the west side. Only the few parishioners left on the east side were able to attend church services there after that; the last service was conducted by Pastor Hildebrandt on October 22. He was forced to leave the parish hall the following day. Only border guards, who began using the tower as an observation point, were allowed to enter the church. The parish on the west side made do with various temporary arrangements until a new parish hall was erected at Bernauer Strasse 111 in 1965.

Since the mid-1960s, the church stood in the border strip surrounded on all sides by border fortifications. Because of its name, and the fact that the spire behind the Wall seemed to reach into the heavens almost accusingly, the church became a symbol of Berlin's division. Well into the 1980s, it was commemorated in the media on memorial days as an icon of the divided city.

As preparations began for the city's anniversary celebration in 1987, the border strip was also cleaned up; some of the menacing barriers were removed and with them the church. The SED functionaries had become increasingly annoyed by the symbolic value of the walled-in Reconciliation Church. The church nave was destroyed on January 21, 1985; the spire followed on January 28.

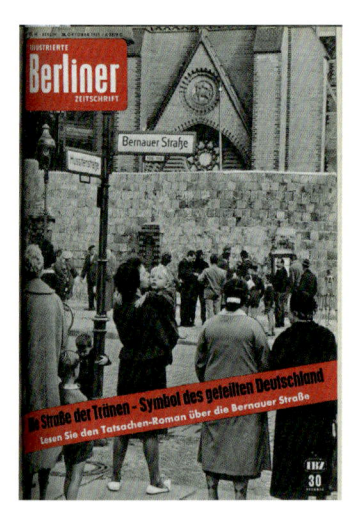

Berlin magazine cover, October 1961

The Reconciliation Church behind the Wall, circa 1964
unknown photographer, Stiftung Berliner Mauer

Prayer services behind the Wall, October, 8, 1961
Bundesarchiv

**Temporary barriers
at the church, 1966**
Klaus Lehnartz, Photonet

Church behind the new Wall, 1980
Blicker, Versöhnungsgemeinde Berlin-Wedding

Demolition of the church nave, 1985
unknown photographer,
Versöhnungsgemeinde Berlin-Wedding

"When the spire fell, the cross flew through the air and onto the other side. I had tears in my eyes. (…) I had lost a piece of home."

Gerda Neumann speaking about
the demolition of the Reconciliation
Church
Interview, Versöhnungsgemeinde
Berlin-Wedding, 2000

"As a child I passed by the church often. I remember that there was a large figure of Jesus giving a blessing over the church door. We weren't religious, but that made an impression on me. As a child I always thought, the Lord Jesus is blessing you. When they blew up the church I was really sad. I thought Jesus has been blown up with it."

Elke Rosin's childhood memories
of the Reconciliation Church on
Bernauer Strasse
Interview, Stiftung Berliner Mauer, 2001

**Demolition of the church spire,
January, 28, 1985**
Rainer Just,
Versöhnungsgemeinde Berlin-Wedding

Separation

After the Wall was built, few visits to the West were authorized by the SED. As of August 23, West Berliners were not allowed to enter East Berlin. People could only stay in touch through letters that the secret police could also read, or by waving across the border grounds. East German police and border troops tried to hinder this kind of cross-border contact. But people continued to come to Bernauer Strasse to wave to their relatives on the other side of the city.

Wedding at the Wall: The bride's parents lived in one of the border houses and were not able to attend the marriage ceremony in the West. Because of the Wall, the bridal couple could only visit the parents briefly (September 1961).
Heinrich von der Becke, ullstein bild

The Monument, exhibition and
Chapel of Reconciliation, 2015
Berthold Weidner

kerstraße

1961

Chapel of Reconciliation
with archeological window, 2015
Berthold Weidner

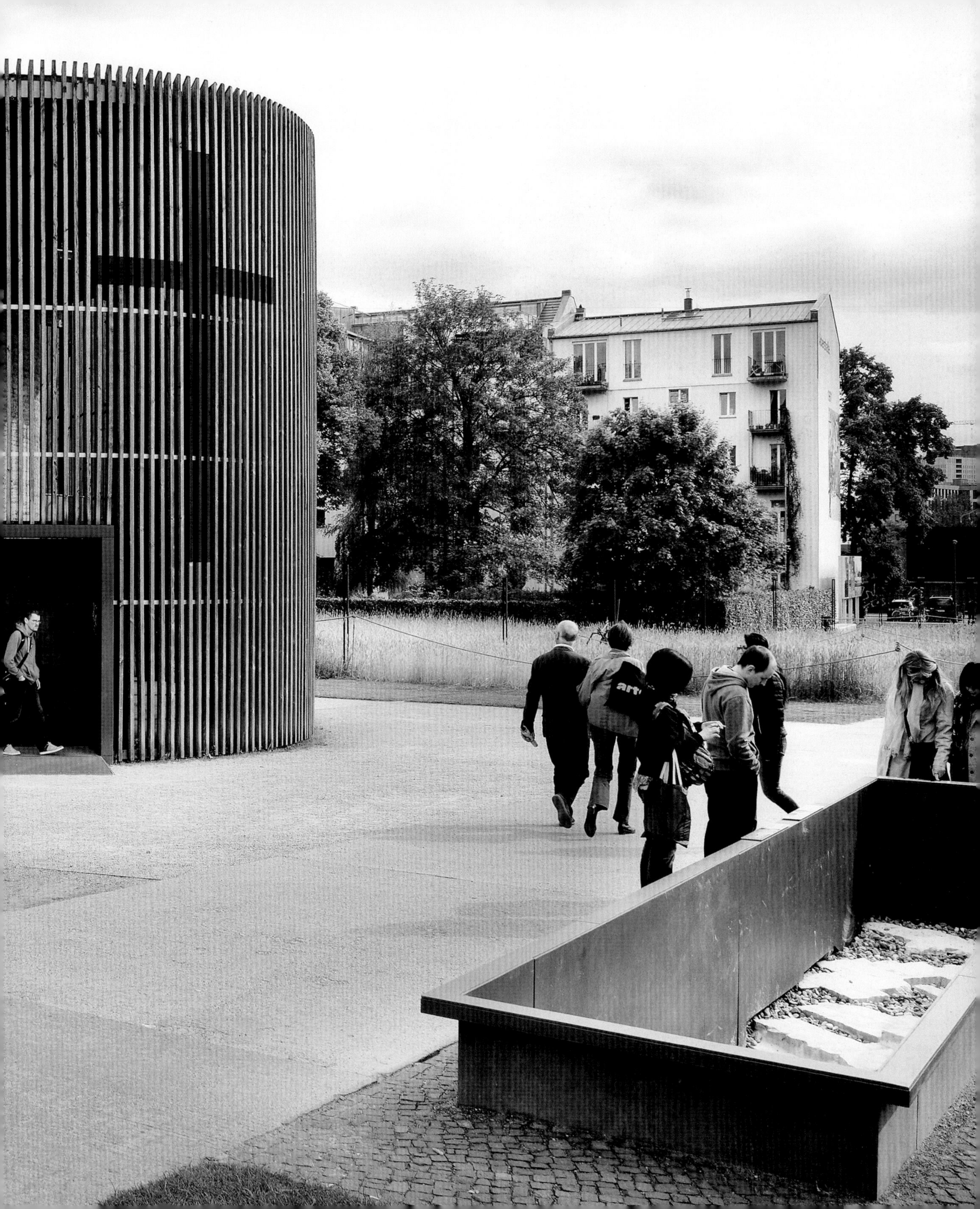

Woman waving, corner of Ruppiner and Bernauer Strasse, 1961
Will McBride, Bildarchiv Preußischer Kulturbesitz

People waving on Bernauer Strasse, September 16, 1961
unknown photographer, ullstein bild/Berlin Bild

unknown photographer, Getty Images

West Berliners waving to their relatives on the other side of the border

unknown photographer, ullstein bild

Will McBride, Bildarchiv Preußischer Kulturbesitz

The Wall through Families

The Radischewski Family

The Radischewski family had lived in building no. 2 on the East Berlin side of Bernauer Strasse since 1945. But they spent most of their time in West Berlin. The daughter, Regine, later Regine Hildebrandt, attended primary school in the West. After August 13, the family thought that the border would not remain closed for long. In late August they were moved to a different apartment on the first floor of Bernauer Strasse 10. The windows of their old ground-floor apartment were bricked up. Regine's brother Jürgen and his wife decided to flee. Regine and her future husband Jörg Hildebrandt chose to stay in East Berlin. For a while they were able to stay in touch with friends in the West from their window. But in September 1961, the Radischewski family was forced to move away from the border to the city center.

Jörg Hildebrandt and his brother having a conversation across the border, 1961
Regine Hildebrandt, Jörg Hildebrandt

"I thought that if I stayed there and things went badly then I would forever blame myself. There wasn't a specific reason, there was no immediate danger. (...) We wrote a farewell letter that made it clear that my parents didn't know anything. We didn't want them imprisoned for this (...). We lowered a suitcase from left to right on a cord from a window. It was possible to hold onto it. I roped my wife down, then some of our things, and then I went down too."

**Jürgen Radischewski,
resident of Bernauer Strasse 2**
Interview, Stiftung Berliner Mauer, 2001

The Lepko Family

Karl Lepko ran a carpenter's workshop at Bernauer Strasse 33. His daughter, Ursula Gesche, lived with her husband and family in West Berlin, but she visited her parents often. One of her sisters was married to an East German police officer, who was not allowed to have any contact with people living in the West. Thus, before 1961, Ursula Gesche only met her sister secretly in their parents' apartment. When the Wall was built, the family was divided. At first visits to East Berlin were not allowed. Later, they remained rare. Karl Lepko fell seriously ill and Ursula Gesche was only able to see her father one more time before he died.

Erika Lepko in front of her father's workshop, 1960
unknown photographer, Ursula Gesche

"We heard on the radio that the Wall had been built and were very shocked that we couldn't visit them anymore (...). We drove to Bernauer Strasse every Saturday to see them. Their apartment didn't face the border, but they were able to wave to us from the window of an apartment of acquaintances. We stood on the border. We could wave, but they weren't allowed to. The police were watching everything. Instead they ran their hands through their hair. We always left there rather dazed."

Ursula Gesche, daughter of the carpenter Karl Lepko, Bernauer Strasse 33
Interview, Stiftung Berliner Mauer, 2010

Karl Lepko with employees in his carpentry workshop, 1959
unknown photographer, Ursula Gesche

Excavated foundations of a building at Bernauer Strasse 10a; exhibition theme: "Human Suffering," 2014
Berthold Weidner

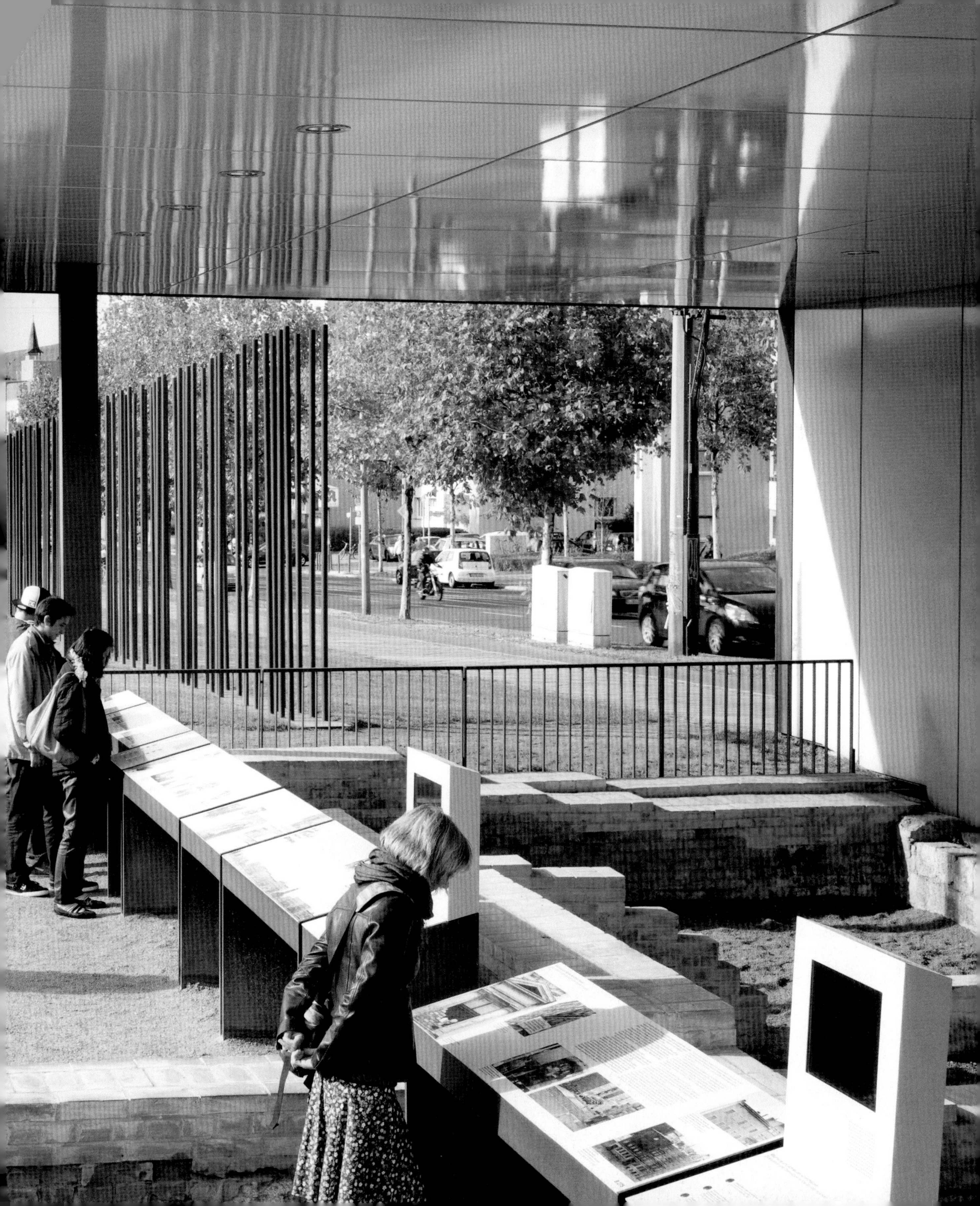

The Wall at the Sophien Parish Cemetery

Beginning on August 13, 1961, the northern wall of the Sophien parish cemetery that ran along Bernauer Strasse was used as a border barrier to the West until a new border wall was erected. A forty-meter-wide strip of cemetery grounds was cut off from the rest of the property. Burials could no longer take place there and the first obstacles were installed.

On the remaining cemetery grounds, which had been part of the border area since 1962/63, gravesites could only be visited at specific times. Visitors had to present a special pass, called a grave card, before entering the cemetery. For a long time West Berliners were not allowed to enter the grounds at all. Even later, when the largest section of the cemetery no longer belonged to border territory, the East German police continued to monitor the grounds.

The GDR border regime gradually displaced the Sophien parish cemetery and its graves. Beginning in 1962, border troops and the East Berlin district of Mitte had numerous graves exhumed and reburied elsewhere, after which the grounds were leveled to make room for the border fortifications. These measures affected two collective graves and a field of single graves containing bomb victims from late 1943. By the 1970s, use of the cemetery grounds outside the border strip had normalized somewhat. West Berliners were allowed to enter again and grave passes were no longer required.

After 1989, this strip of land was returned to the Sophien parish, which planned to reintegrate it into the cemetery. But this conflicted with the plans to establish a memorial at this site. To draw attention to its own point of view, parish members knocked down two sections of the Wall and rebuilt a part of the cemetery wall with an entrance gate. Two crosses identify sites where collective graves from World War II were believed to exist. The parish had the inscription it had preferred for the memorial engraved into a memorial stone.

Border strip and guard post on Ackerstrasse, 1963
unknown photographer, Lazarus-Stift Archives

"On Friday afternoon a funeral (...) took place at the cemetery on Bernauer Strasse. The wife of the deceased, who lived in East Berlin, had chosen a gravesite right behind the East German police patrol road. This made it possible for the West Berlin relatives and acquaintances to attend the funeral, albeit separated by barbed wire. The brother and his family, who lived in West Berlin, (...) stood on a ladder at the Wall and watched the funeral service from there."

Funeral on the Sophien cemetery
Newspaper report, June 1, 1963,
Die Welt

Commemoration of the dead at the Sophien parish cemetry, 1962
West Berliners lay wreaths at the cemetry wall, taking part in the ceremony despite the dividing wall.
Günter Malchow, Gedenkstätte Berliner Mauer

Border soldiers on the cemetery grounds, 1966.
East German border guards patrolled between the graves on the Sophien parish cemetery and checked visitors' papers.
Klaus Lehnartz, ullstein bild

Border strip on the Sophien parish cemetery, view towards Nordbahnhof station, 1969
Dieter Lohse, ullstein bild

The border strip after a border wall was erected behind the cemetery wall, 1971
Horst Siegmann, Landesarchiv Berlin

Border strip after a new border wall was erected, 1985
Klaus Lehnartz, Photonet

Human Suffering
Klaus Abraham

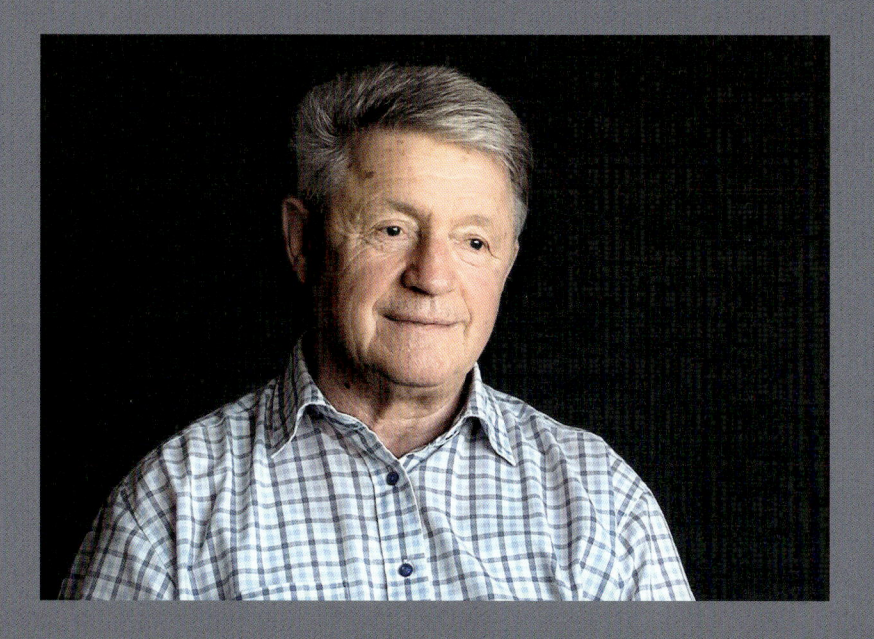

"And then this dreadful thing: […] the waving and crying and people, […] families that had lived so close together for decades were suddenly torn apart."

Interview, Stiftung Berliner Mauer, 2012

Klaus Abraham was born in Berlin in 1937. He trained to become a bricklayer and then applied successfully for a job with the West Berlin fire department in 1960. After the Wall was built, he had frequent assignments along the border. East Germans were fleeing to the West by jumping out of their apartment windows. The buildings were located directly on the border and the people fell into the rescue nets of the West Berlin firemen. In 1972, when Klaus Abraham was working as a fire department diver, he was involved in the search for a child who had drowned in the Spree. The West Berlin firemen were prevented from conducting the search because the river was part of the GDR. Klaus Abraham's rescue unit had to wait for the GDR border soldiers to arrive with their divers before the body could be retrieved.

Exhibition theme: "Rebuilding the Border Fortifications"
near Strelitzer Strasse, 2014
Berthold Weidner

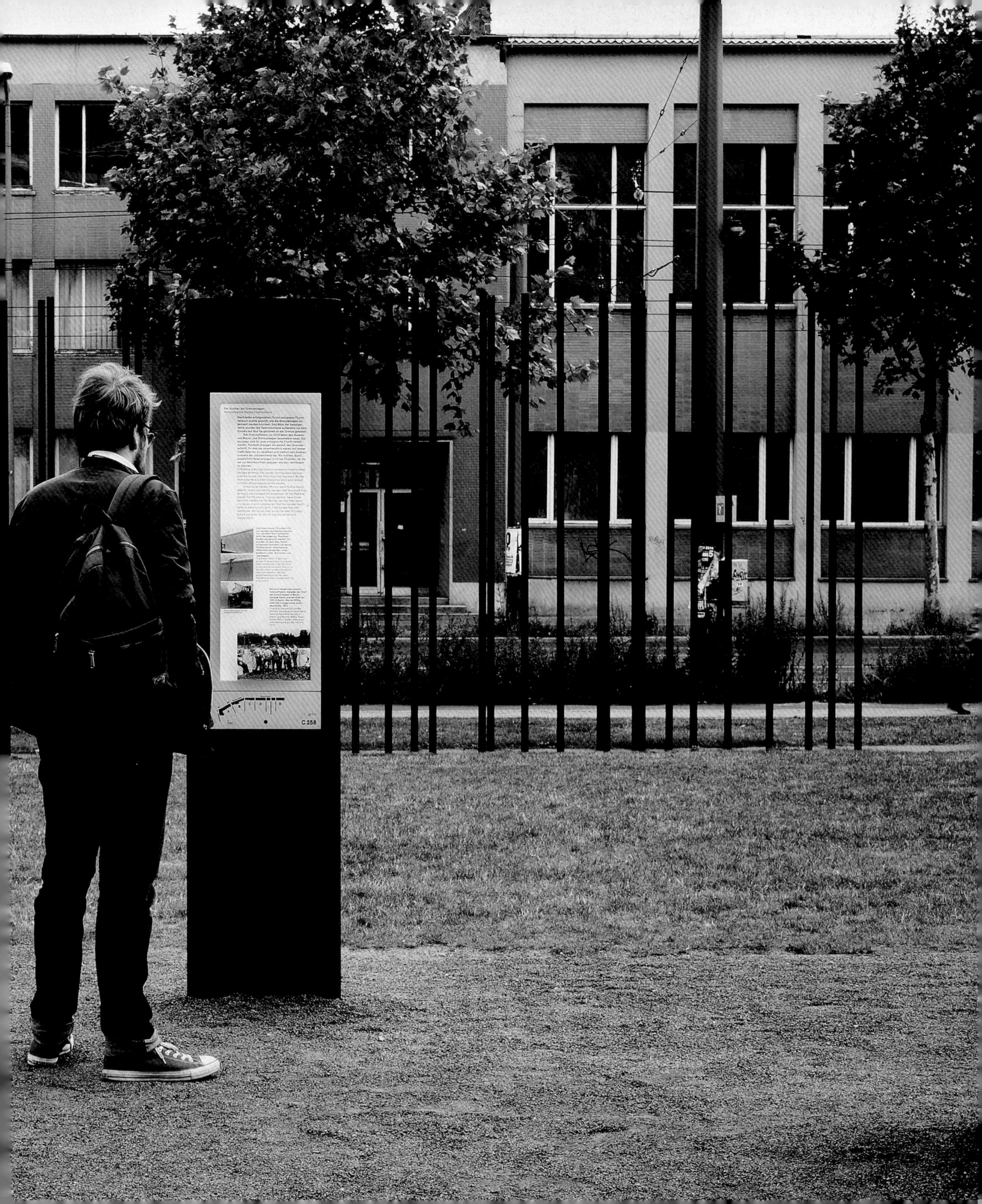
Der Ausbau der Grenzanlagen
C 258

3

Rebuilding the Border Fortifications

After August 13, 1961, it became clear that some people would not be deterred from fleeing to the West, neither by border soldiers, nor by barbed wire. Consequently, beginning in the mid-1960s, the first rather temporary walls and barriers were replaced by a centrally-planned uniform border strip: East Berlin's "modern border." But the pressure to conform and the many divided east-west relationships meant that despite the danger it posed, the Wall actually became the very reason that people decided to leave. The SED responded to this situation by persistently expanding the border fortifications. The expansion and development of the border continued until the Wall fell in November 1989.

"Bernauer Strasse at the corner of Brunnenstrasse: The Wall has gotten tall now. It can be measured, centimeter for centimeter, one layer of hollow concrete blocks after another, there is no getting over it anymore."

A Lazarus nurse reports on an escape attempt on Bernauer Strasse, 1960s
Interview, Stiftung Berliner Mauer, 2002

During an inspection, border officers, including General Geier, head of the border troops in Berlin, and Werner Wittig, head of the SED in the Potsdam district, discuss expanding a section of the border on the outer ring of West Berlin, 1972
Border troop photo,
Militärhistorisches Museum Dresden

The Role of Officers
Since local border officers were held accountable for every successful escape that occurred, they strongly encouraged the expansion of the Wall and border fortifications. They pushed to have more barriers installed at the border section they were in charge of and complained that the current fortifications were insufficient. They hoped that with additional obstacles they would be able to hinder future escapes for which they would be held responsible.

The Expansion of the Border Fortifications

The border fortifications installed between 1961 and 1989 can be broken down into three building phases. During the first phase, a wall secured by barbed wire stood directly on the line of the border.

Anti-tank obstacles, screens and additional fences were erected behind it. Border troops began creating the "modern border" in the mid-1960s. It was a uniform border strip sealed off by a wall facing West Berlin. Usually a fence, later another wall, faced the East. Buildings were torn down to make it easier for the border soldiers to monitor the border strip.

The SED had towers and a patrol road built. The third phase began in the mid-1970s when the border wall was replaced with a new wall that remained standing until 1989.

The SED leadership became increasingly concerned about the appearance of the border strip, which is why, bunkers, surface obstacles (mats with steel spikes), and most of the dog runs, were removed in the 1980s.

In the 1980s, the Hinterlandmauer (inner wall) was the only barrier visible from the east side. A signal fence stood a few meters away that triggered an alarm in the nearest watchtower when someone climbed or touched it. At night lights illuminated the border strip, making it as light as day. A raked security strip next to the patrol road showed the tracks of an escape. The 3.6-meter-high border wall stood at the edge of a broad open strip of land.

Diagram of the provisional border barriers, late 1961
Reconstruction, Yvonne Kavermann, 2009

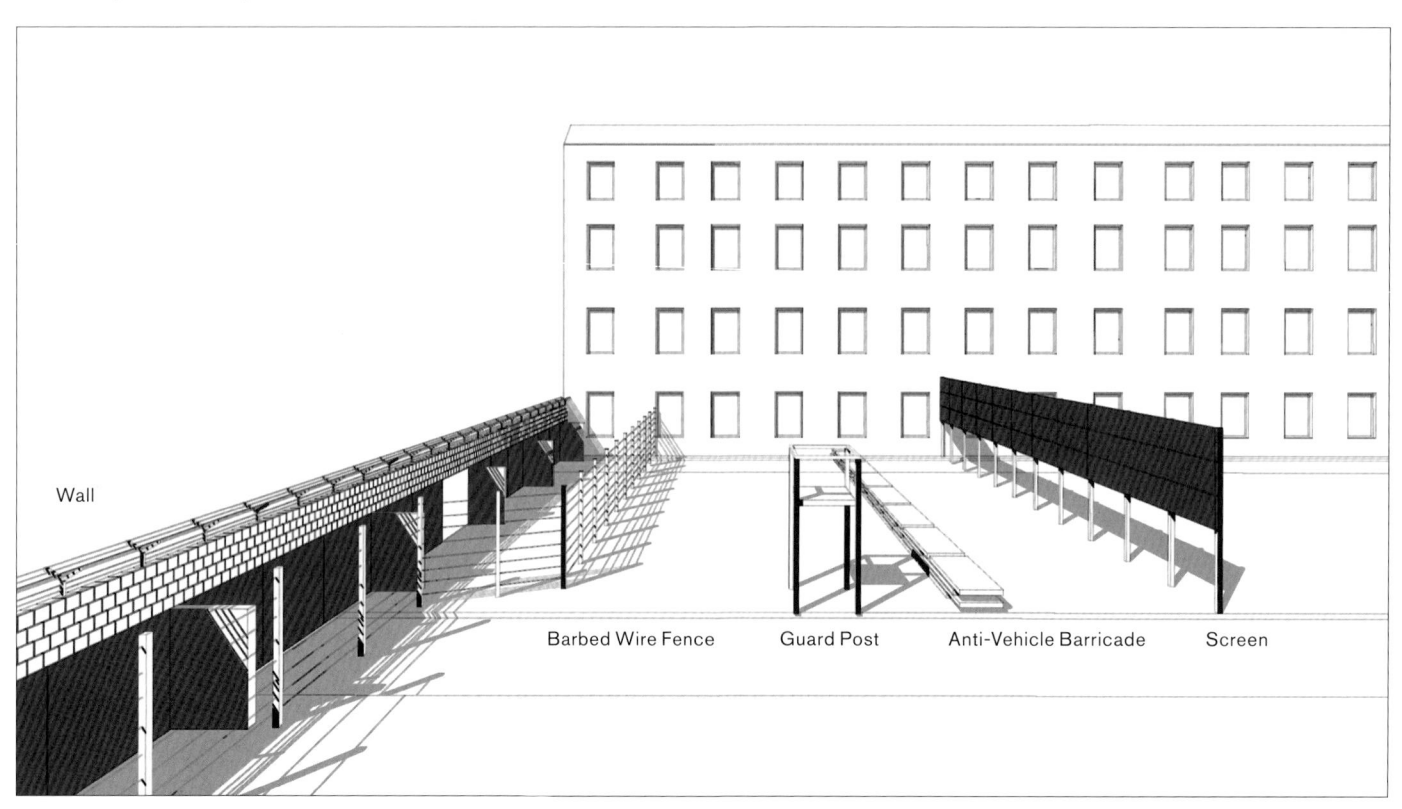

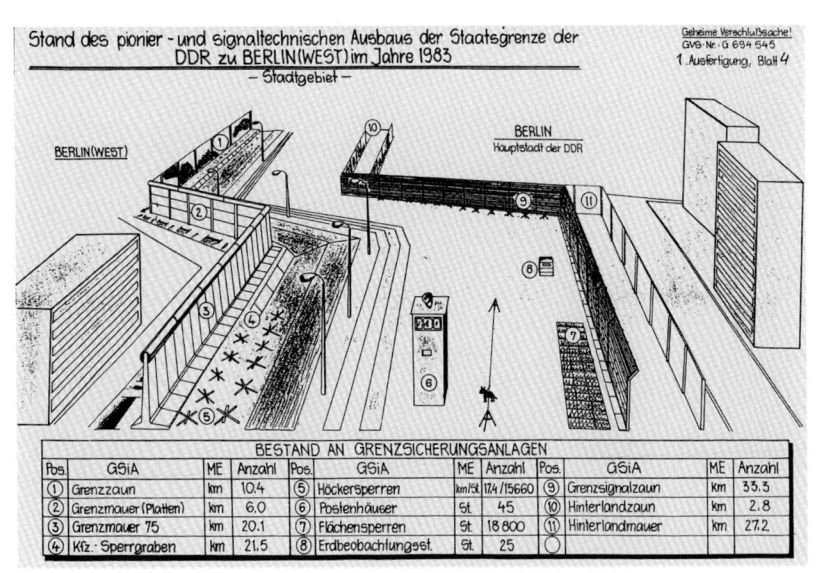

Diagram of the fully developed border strip, 1983
GDR border troops, Hagen Koch Collection

Testing the new border wall: border guards and athletes simulate escape attempts, May 1974

The Border Wall 75 was supposed to appear less menacing, while continuing to be effective in preventing escapes. Before its construction, escape scenarios were simulated to test the effectiveness of certain aids, including ladders, kedge anchors and trucks.

Border troop photo, Bundesarchiv-Militärarchiv

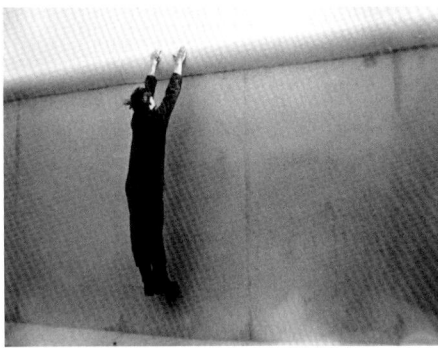

Blocking off Bergstrasse

Segments of the new border wall along Bernauer Strasse
It was welded together in summer 1980. A pipe element was added to make it more difficult to climb.
unknown photographer,
Versöhnungsgemeinde Berlin-Wedding

The new border wall on Bergstrasse, September 1980
Klaus Lehnartz, Photonet

Blocking off Ackerstrasse

The Wall on Ackerstrasse, August 1961
Berthold Noeske

The fully-developed border strip on Ackerstrasse, 1985
Günter Schneider, Landesarchiv Berlin

The evolving border strip, April 1966
Klaus Lehnartz, Photonet

The inner wall and "front-end security," April 1990
Klaus Lehnartz, Photonet

Blocking off Brunnenstrasse

Building the Wall in front
of the underground station,
August 23, 1961
Horst Siegmann, Landesarchiv Berlin

The sealed off underground station
entrance, August 13, 1961
Beck, Stiftung Berliner Mauer

Removing the subway sign,
August 19, 1965
Gert Hilde, ullstein bild

Blocking off Schwedter Strasse

The Wall at Schwedter Strasse, 1960s
Klaus Hartmann

Blocking screens and anti-vehicle obstacles behind the Wall on Schwedter Strasse, 1968
Klaus Lehnartz, Photonet

Blocking screens and additional obstacles on the east side of the Wall, 1964
Border troop photo,
Bundesarchiv-Militärarchiv

79

Border strip between
Gartenstrasse and Ackerstrasse,
late 1989
Matthias Kupfernagel

Final state of the border strip on
Strelitzer Strasse with most of the
additional barriers removed,
ca. 1988
Border troop photo, Hagen Koch Collection

The Individual Border Obstacles

Border soldiers repairing the signal device, September 1969
In 1964, a signal fence was erected a few meters away from the inner wall. When fugitives touched it, an alarm horn and flashing light were triggered. By 1984 the alarm simply set off a light in the watchtower, so that fugitives would not know that they had been detected.
Klaus Lehnartz, Photonet

Dog run in Treptow, September 1983
Dogs frightened off fugitives, barked to alert border soldiers, and apprehended fugitives. In the beginning, the dogs were kept on steel chains, but later they ran freely between the fences.
unknown photographer,
Bundesarchiv-Militärarchiv

Watchtower and Border Wall 75, Strelitzer Strasse, June 1986
From the watchtowers, known officially as observation towers, border soldiers had a good view of the border fortifications and the rear border area of East Berlin.
unknown photographer,
Bundesarchiv-Militärarchiv

Inner wall and screens, Strelitzer Strasse, 1966
Screens were installed at cross streets and on empty grounds in September 1961 to prevent people from waving or communicating across the border. They were dismantled in 1965 when the inner wall was erected.
Klaus Lehnartz, Photonet

81

**Border soldiers
on the watchtower, 1981**
unknown photographer, picture alliance

**Anti-vehicle obstacles in the
border strip, near Strelitzer Strasse,
July 1971**
Tank traps, in place until 1983, were
designed to stop people from
escaping in vehicles. At broad areas
of the border strip, anti-vehicle
ditches also served this function.
Horst Siegmann, Landesarchiv Berlin

**Obstacles with spikes at the inner
wall, Brunnenstrasse, 1981**
Surface obstacles, also known in the
West as "Stalin's lawn," consisted of
upward-pointing spikes. Placed at
the inner wall or signal fence, they
were designed to hinder fugitives
from jumping down from the wall into
the border strip. The iron spikes
caused severe injury.
Hans-Peter Stiebing

**East Berlin view of the inner wall on
Strelitzer Strasse, September 1983**
The Hinterlandmauer (inner wall)
blocked access to the border strip
from the East Berlin side. These walls
were supposed to hinder fugitives
from entering the border strip and
getting close to the Berlin Wall. They
also blocked the view into the border
strip and hindered contact to West
Berlin.
unknown photographer,
Bundesarchiv-Militärarchiv

The Berlin Wall stood a few meters
behind the actual border, alongside
the fence, 1980
Bicker, Versöhnungsgemeinde Berlin-Wedding

Door in the border wall
on Brunnenstrasse, 1990
unknown photographer,
Versöhnungsgemeinde Berlin-Wedding

Exhibition theme: "Escaping to the West" on Strelitzer Strasse, 2015
Berthold Weidner

1961

Bernauer Straße

Surveillance of the Border Area

Since the mid-1960s, SED leadership directives demanded that fugitives be arrested as far away from the Wall as possible – ideally as soon as they left their apartment. In the summer of 1963, part of the residential area near the Wall in East Berlin was established as a restricted area which could only be entered with a special permit. Border troops, the civilian administration and East German police, who were assisted by voluntary helpers, worked closely with the secret police to keep this area under surveillance. It was one of the most intensely monitored territories in East Germany.

The East German police helped the border troops and were in turn examined by the secret police. About half of the police force of a single precinct near the border was on duty exclusively at the Wall. They investigated suspects, intimidated with their strong presence, and searched for fugitives during a border alarm.

Functionaries in the civilian administration were involved in evictions and nationalizing property in the border strip. They also took part in inspections and made sure that the East Berlin rear border area near the Wall offered few opportunities to escape.

Propaganda constantly promoted the border regime so that residents near the border would come to accept it and participate in the surveillance. The propaganda was not very successful, but some East Berlin residents did support the security agencies as informants and by providing emergency services. The secret police hired border informers ("Grenz-IM"), who patrolled within the border area, passed on information and helped apprehend fugitives.

Map for planning surveillance in the border area, 1984
Map from the People's Police headquarters, Landesarchiv Berlin

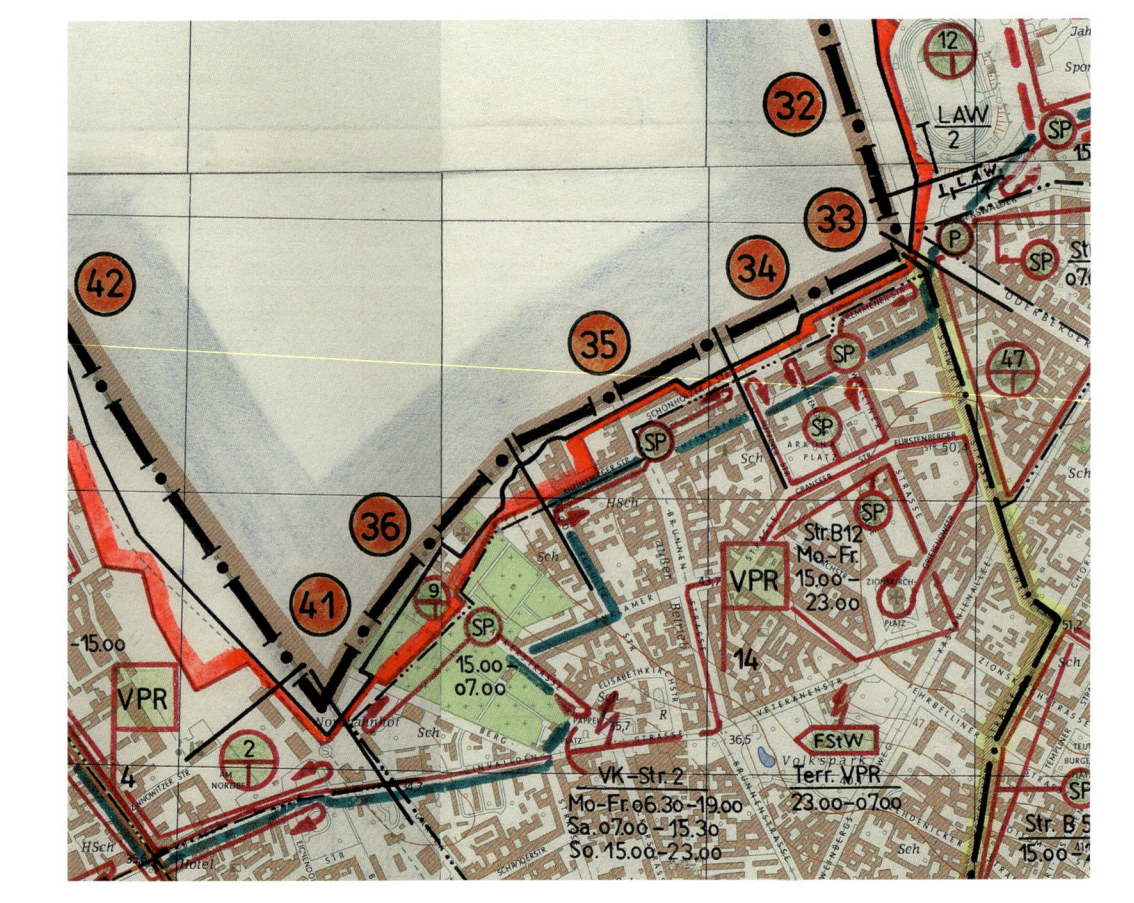

Inner wall

Border area

Border troop patrol area

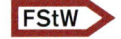

Territory where East German police patrolled
Time of work shift is indicated, if not: 24-hour duty

Border officers and border soldiers were strategically sent to local elected committees to demonstrate their closeness to the people and to represent the concerns of the border surveillance.
Call to vote in the Alex-Spiegel, 10.10.1965

Border soldier and border assistant patrolling together in a garden community, September 1965
Border troop propaganda photo, Spremberg, Militärhistorisches Museum Dresden

"I would like to think that one reason the border of our county is impassable and reliably secure is because there are thousands of class-conscious workers, cooperative farmers and employees of all classes everywhere making a valuable contribution to the border area's security and order. The border troops' voluntary assistants are a positive example of close cooperation and close collaboration. All of our units work with these kinds of voluntary assistant collectives. Our border soldiers draw strength from the daily experience of having our people of the German Democratic Republic involved in the security of our country's borders."

General Gerhard Lorenz, leading political officer of the border troops, Pulsschlag der Zeit, Rundfunk der DDR, Nov. 26, 1977
Deutsches Rundfunkarchiv Babelsberg

Border soldier checking an ID in the border area, June 1966
unknown photographer,
Militärhistorisches Museum Dresden

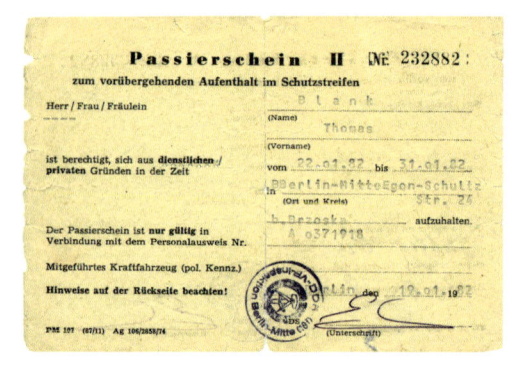

Entry permit for a limited stay in the border area, issued for Strelitzer Strasse (at that time Egon-Schultz-Strasse), 1982
Stiftung Berliner Mauer

Advertisement for the East German police and its "voluntary assistants," ca. 1980
People's Police poster,
Polizeihistorische Sammlung Dresden

88

Border security committee meeting, 1981
"Border Guard," NVA Army Film Studio, Progress Filmverleih

Instructions for residents in the border area, ca. 1973
Landesarchiv Berlin

MERKBLATT

Liebe Bürger!

Zur Erleichterung Ihrer Bemühungen um die weitere Festigung der Ordnung und Sicherheit im Grenzgebiet geben wir Ihnen eine überarbeitete Aufstellung von Ärzten sowie von Reparaturwerkstätten, die für notwendige Hausbesuche im Besitz eines Dauer-Passierscheines sind:

ÄRZTE:

Sanitätsrat Dr. Rudolf Hartmann	Facharzt Praktischer Arzt	1058, Wörther Straße 42 Telefon 44 56 44
Sanitätsrat Dr. Fränze Kindler	Facharzt Praktischer Arzt	1058, Kastanienallee 83 Telefon 44 20 20
Dr. Elisabeth Grosser	Facharzt Praktischer Arzt	1071, Wichertstraße 22 Telefon 44 35 31
Dr. Margarete Wegner	Praktischer Arzt	1058, Schönhauser Allee 49 Telefon 44 24 49
Dr. Arthur Giebel	Facharzt für innere Krankheiten	1071, Willi-Bredel-Straße 39 Telefon 44 34 60 (privat 44 33 55)
Dr. Werner Kressin	Facharzt für Chirurgie	1058, Gleimstraße 10 Telefon 44 47 46
Dr. Bernd Ohmstede	Facharzt für Chirurgie	1058, Kastanienallee 2 Telefon 44 22 54
Medizinalrat Dr. Sigrid Schmidtke	Facharzt für innere Krankheiten	
Dr. Maria Küchler	Facharzt für innere Krankheiten	
Dr. Gisela Behne	Facharzt für innere Krankheiten	
Ursula Müller	Facharzt für innere Krankheiten	
Annelies Lunze	Praktischer Arzt	
Gisela Löser	Praktischer Arzt	Poliklinik Wisbyer Straße Telefon 44 01 56
Dr. Heidi Sachweh	Praktischer Arzt	
Dr. Karl-Anton Pfeiffer	Facharzt Kinderkrankheiten	
Dr. Eva Seltmann	Facharzt Kinderkrankheiten	
Dr. Edith Hübner	Facharzt für Chirurgie	
Gertraude Kirchner	Facharzt für Allgemeinmedizin	
Barbara Strobel	Facharzt für Allgemeinmedizin	
Dr. Hans Pagel	Facharzt für Allgemeinmedizin	1058, Schönhauser Allee 43 Telefon 44 15 41

Wenn ein Rettungswagen oder Bereitschaftsarzt benötigt wird (Rettungsamt-Notruf: 115) bitte angeben, daß Sie im Grenzgebiet wohnen.

bitte wenden!

The Border Soldiers: Aspects of Border Duty
Policemen, and the border soldiers who joined them as of September 1962, were assigned to the border to implement the GDR border security at the Wall. They were expected to fire at mostly unarmed fugitives if they were otherwise unable to prevent the escape. They were also required to keep residents living within the border area under daily surveillance.

Routine border guard duty was generally dull. The only diversion was provided by false alarms that were frequently set off by wild animals at the border signal fence or bad weather. In the border segment at Bernauer Strasse, border soldiers were usually assigned to watchtowers, or to patrolling the border strip and rear border area. Between twelve and twenty border soldiers were usually on duty at one time along the 1.3 kilometer stretch of border on Bernauer Strasse.

Border guard on Ruppiner Strasse, 1961
Gerhard Ringwelski, Stiftung Berliner Mauer

Border soldiers being briefed on routine duty, Nov. 30, 1976
Hartmut Reiche, Bundesarchiv

Border troops on motorcycle and foot patrol, July 1985
Klaus Lehnartz, Photonet

Desertion: The Only Way Out

Many border guards recognized that the border system was cruel and unjustified. Most of the border soldiers knew that shooting at unarmed people was immoral and many tacitly rejected the border regime. They were pressured to fire their weapons at fugitives. A number of guards got out of this situation by fleeing to the West, thus permanently denouncing their allegiance to the SED. Their supervisors and the secret police used coercion and surveillance to prevent these kinds of escapes. It also prohibited any discussions about the border regime. There were several cases of border soldiers who had fled to the West and were later threatened with abduction or even murder. Officially, the GDR blamed these escapes on private problems. Border soldiers continued to desert to the West until the Wall fell.

"After thinking about it for a long time, I decided not to aim my gun at peaceful people. I had seen how brutally our company had dealt with people. In mid-January a sergeant so brutally beat a civilian with his machine gun that he had to be taken to the hospital. The next day the sergeant was presented to us as a role model. That was the clincher that made me decide to go through with the escape."

Rudi Thurow, sergeant in the border police
SFB interview, May 10, 1962, RBB

After fleeing in February 1962, Sergeant Rudi Thurow describes the border regime at a public event in West Berlin, May 1962
unknown photographer, Rudi Thurow

Border troop re-enactment of an escape by a border guard, whose friend beat up his squad leader during the escape, August 1962
Border troops photo,
Bundesarchiv-Militärarchiv

"Of course my thought was: These are my comrades behind us, but I knew they would shoot at me because in that moment it's a desertion. But I just couldn't participate in what they were doing over there anymore. We had the order to call out to the people, to apprehend them, and if they didn't obey, to fire. That was just too much."

Report from a border guard who deserted
SFB interview, Jan. 23, 1962, RBB

Show trial conducted against a border soldier who had fled and was later sentenced to 15 years imprisonment, May 1962
NVA military photo service,
Militärhistorisches Museum Dresden

Conrad Schumann

Conrad Schumann was not the first soldier to desert to the West, but his escape became famous because so many photos of it were seen worldwide. On August 15, 1961, he jumped over the barbed wire fence on the border at Ruppiner Strasse and fled to the West.

Trained as a sheepherder, the young man from Zschochau in Saxony had enlisted with the East German riot police in March 1960. He was transferred to East Berlin in July 1961. When the border was sealed off on August 13, 1961, his unit was posted on the sector boundary at the corner of Bernauer Strasse and Ruppiner Strasse. The newly established border regime is what made the 19-year-old decide to flee two days later. When photographers on the west side realized that he was about to flee, they distracted the other border guards. Schumann jumped over the border and ran to safety in a West Berlin police car. The photograph of his famous jump – as well as his fear of the East German secret police – continued to haunt him up to his very last days. But he never regretted taking that leap. He committed suicide in the summer of 1998 for reasons that are not known.

Conrad Schumann's escape, August 15, 1961
unknown photographer,
Polizeihistorische Sammlung Berlin

Schumann runs to safety, August 15, 1961
unknown photographer,
Polizeihistorische Sammlung Berlin

Gerhard Sälter

Surveillance of the Wall: The Example of Bernauer Strasse

Guards at Potsdamer Platz, August 13, 1961
Dieter Schwertle,
Versöhnungsgemeinde Berlin-Wedding

Border expansion and guard positions on Bernauer Strasse, May 1963
Border troops sketch,
Bundesarchiv-Militärarchiv

The Wall and border fortifications were continuously expanded between 1961 and 1989 to improve the effectiveness of intercepting fugitives.[1] This entailed a two-fold process: regularly evaluating all escape attempts and fundamentally revising the entire border grounds. Although the Wall was constantly being improved, it would have been essentially useless without guards. A ladder was all one would have needed to get through the border fortifications and leave the GDR.

These surveillance measures, which normally would have fallen to the police, were assigned to the border troops, a military force established in the GDR after the Wall was built. The border troops were created out of the border police, which had existed since 1946, and a few units of the People's Police that were involved in guarding the border in Berlin. After the Wall was built, these forces were merged into two border brigades, from which the Berlin border troops units were formed in the fall of 1962. Most of the soldiers assigned to guard the Wall were conscripts who had not volunteered for the post.[2]

The first phase of the border regime in Berlin was characterized by the use of barbed wire and the construction of the first wall in August 1961. During this phase, guards – who at the time still belonged to the People's Police – were posted on the side streets that ran into Bernauer Strasse. Members of the workers' militia, who were also deployed in the first weeks of the border closure, were only posted directly on the border at the Brandenburg Gate. The SED did not fully trust them and did not want to risk their fleeing.

Initially, the residents were permitted to remain in their buildings along Bernauer Strasse. Some took advantage of the situation and roped or jumped down to the West Berlin sidewalk below. To prevent this, police were posted in the buildings. After the residents were forced to vacate these buildings in October 1961, the windows facing Bernauer Strasse were bricked up.[3] Only a few lookouts were posted in the buildings thereafter.

By the end of 1961, the SED leadership understood that the West was not going to accept the Soviet conditions set in Khrushchev's ultimatum. The SED thus remained dependent on the Wall as an instrument to secure its power and it continued to expand the border fortifications. By the mid-1960s, coils of barbed wire, vehicle obstacles made out of railway tracks, screens to block views, vehicle ditches and dog runs had been added to the first wall. These additional barriers added considerable depth to the border fortifications.

A restricted area was established along the Berlin Wall in late 1961 for which an entry permit was required.[4] It was secured with fences and a boom gate, where people had to stop to show identification before entering. For this reason two guards were posted at each side street along Bernauer Strasse: one behind the Wall and one at the boom gate. Between 1962 and 1964, border surveillance between Brunnenstrasse and Bergstrasse was supervised by an officer stationed at Bernauer Strasse 10. The border soldiers on the east side of the Bernauer Strasse most likely received their orders from a commander on Gleimstrasse.[5]

In 1961, border soldiers built the first makeshift shelters and guard stands, which enabled them to view the grounds from an elevated position. In 1962 and 1963, these structures were replaced by provisional guard houses, forerunners to the watchtowers that later stood along the entire stretch of the border. The first ground bunkers were also built at this time, providing border soldiers with a covered position from which to observe the border strip.[6]

Guard house, Bergstrasse, 1962
Border troops photo, Bundesarchiv

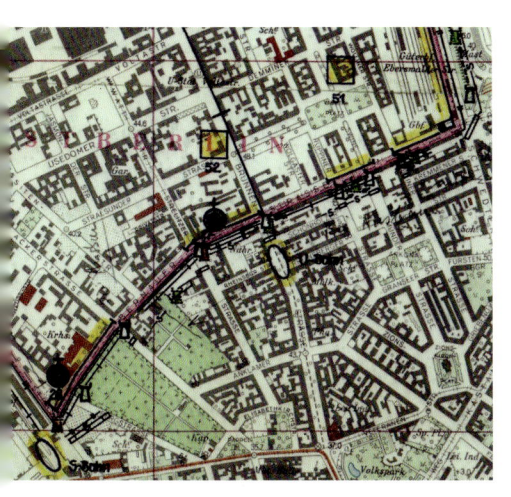

Border fortifications and observation towers on Bernauer Strasse, 1966
Border troops sketch, Bundesarchiv-Militärarchiv

The border fortifications were significantly expanded in the mid-sixties. All the buildings located directly on the border along Bernauer Strasse were demolished. The SED constructed a complex system of border obstacles along the entire Berlin Wall, which was based on a centrally planned and uniform border strip. Specifications for materials, spatial intervals and the "blocking effect," were the same at all areas. The individual border obstacles had been tested in advance.

This border strip was closed off to West Berlin by a wall and to East Berlin – its own "hinterland" – usually by a fence. It formed an enclosed space, which was only accessible to border soldiers. This border strip now included two kinds of observation towers: a simple guard tower, where two or three soldiers were posted, and a "command station" tower, from where an officer oversaw his section of the border.

The border guards were dispersed along Bernauer Strasse in five towers, most of which stood on side streets. This provided the guards with a view of their own "hinterland" so that they could detect fugitives as they approached the border. They also had a broad view of the border strip and a "clear line of fire" both to the right and to the left. Guards were also expected to keep an eye on West Berlin.

In the summer of 1963, the border strip around West Berlin was divided into eleven sections, each one controlled by a single border regiment. The companies securing a section of the border rotated in eight-hour shifts. Each section was divided into three sub-sections that were guarded by a single unit. In 1966, one of these sub-sections extended from Gleimstrasse to Brunnenstrasse and was monitored by a squad leader at a command center on Wolliner Strasse. Unable to view the entire border segment under his supervision, the squad leader remained dependent on the electronic warning system, as well as on reports from his subordinate border soldiers.[7]

In the mid-seventies, the SED once again began to modify the border fortifications along the Berlin Wall. The watchtowers, which had only just recently been built, were replaced by newer models because the earlier ones had proven vulnerable to collapse during strong winds, which rendered them unusable. In the early 1980s, the SED had a new border wall erected that remained in place until its demolition in 1989/90. Additionally, as surveillance of the border's "hinterland" lost importance, the most menacing border obstacles – the dog runs, metal gratings and steel spikes designed to prevent vehicle escapes – were removed. Instead, more signal devices were installed along the border grounds to detect approaching fugitives. The border fortifications were still expected to function, but no longer needed to look so horrifying. Surveillance of the hinterland was intensified; border obstacles were made more efficient; and new observation towers were erected. These changes made fewer border soldiers necessary. In the 1960s, approximately 30 soldiers were on duty at a time along Bernauer Strasse. In the 1980s only twelve were assigned per shift. In 1986, one officer, two sergeants and 20 soldiers were dispersed along the border segment that included Bernauer Strasse and the Nordbahnhof Station. An additional 45 soldiers were on call to join them if necessary. On Bernauer Strasse, the five observation towers were occupied at all times by ten border soldiers. An additional guard was posted in the subway station. Intermittently another eight designated guard positions were occupied by 16 soldiers, who were supported by patrols in the hinterland.[8]

According to plans from 1987, between twelve and 20 border soldiers were scheduled for duty as permanent observation posts and patrols. The number varied according to the various situations: normal "border security," "core times" during which a high number of escape attempts were registered, and "intensified border security," when fugitives were reported to be on the loose or when "interference efforts" from the West were expected.[9]

Border soldiers in the border strip and on the tower, mid 1980s
Hans-Peter Stiebing

The border soldiers were supported by so-called voluntary assistants who were assigned to additional patrol duty outside the border strip. They also worked closely with the People's Police, which closely monitored the area behind the Wall and conducted ID checks. Ideally, fugitives were to be stopped long before they reached the Wall or were arrested as soon as they left their apartment.[10]

In the end, the border troops remained incapable of saving the GDR, just as they would have been unable to prevent an invasion by NATO, which was their second task.[11] When the Wall fell in 1989, not a single shot was fired. The border regime continued to function initially. The last fugitive was arrested on the evening of November 9, when the first East Berliners had already entered West Berlin, and nearby, the MfS officer in charge was about to open the entire Bornholmer Strasse border crossing. At 10:59 p.m. border soldiers arrested the 34-year-old Reinhardt S. at Helmut-Just Bridge (today Behmstrasse) for attempting to "break through the state border to West Berlin."[12] Over the next two days, other people were also arrested at the already-opened border.[13] But these were the last desperate efforts by a system that had already lost its political purpose.

1
On the expansion of and changes to the border fortifications, see Gerhard Sälter, "Die Sperranlagen, oder: Der unendliche Mauerbau," in: Klaus-Dietmar Henke (ed.), *Die Mauer. Errichtung, Überwindung, Erinnerung*, Munich 2011, pp. 122-137; Johannes Cramer et al., *Die Baugeschichte der Berliner Mauer*, Petersberg 2011.
2
Gerhard Sälter, "Zur Restrukturierung von Polizeieinheiten der DDR im Kontext des Mauerbaus," *Archiv für Polizeigeschichte 13* (2002), pp. 66 – 73; Gerhard Sälter, *Grenzpolizisten. Konformität, Verweigerung und Repression in der Grenzpolizei und den Grenztruppen der DDR (1952-1965)*, Berlin 2009, pp. 61 – 90.
3
Gerhard Sälter, "Zu den Zwangsräumungen in Berlin nach dem Mauerbau 1961," *Deutschland Archiv 44* (2011) 4, pp. 546 – 551.
4
Sälter, *Zwangsräumungen*, p. 551.
5
Information report on Bernauer Strasse, 15.5.1963, BA-MA, VA-07, 19868, pp. 14 – 18, 25 – 27; Bericht, BA-MA, VA-07, 16929, p. 432.
6
Protocol of 11th meeting of the NVR on 30.5.1962, BA-MA, DVW 1, 39468, pp. 1 – 3, pp. 9 – 17.
7
Major Treckan, 1st border brigade, final report on desertion, 15.4.1966, BA-MA, VA-07, 17156, pp. 146 – 163.
8
Commander of border regiment 36, Order 20/85 on border security in training year 1985/86, 20.11.1985, BA-MA, GTÜ AZN 14884, pp. 57 – 58.
9
Guard post schedule, notes on Order 22/87 of K GR 36 on border security during the 750th anniversary, 13.4.1987, BA-MA, GTÜ AZN 14886, pp. 102 –106.
10
Gerhard Sälter, "Fluchtverhinderung als gesamtgesellschaftliche Aufgabe," in: Henke, Die Mauer, *Die Mauer*, Munich 2011, pp. 152 – 162.
11
Jochen Maurer/Gerhard Sälter: The Double Task of the East German Border Guards: Policing the Border and Military Functions, *German politics and society* 29 (2011) 2, pp. 23 – 39.
12
BA-MA, DVH 32, 121301, p. 724.
13
BA-MA, DVH 32, 121301, p. 1733.

Rebuilding the Border Fortifications
Volker Wetzk

"[…] but most of them didn't give much advance thought to what they would do if the situation arose. For them it was clear that if someone ran in front of their musket, they would quickly take care of it. That kind existed, too, and was not uncommon. They were not the exception."

Interview, Stiftung Berliner Mauer, 2013

Volker Wetzk was born in 1968. In 1984 he earned his Abitur degree with vocational training as a skilled construction worker in Cottbus. Three years later he was enlisted into the GDR border troops as a conscript. Volker Wetzk was assigned to guard duty at the Berlin Wall, but he made it clear in conversations that he would not shoot at comrades who fled. He was subsequently transferred away from the border and assigned to guard an ammunitions depot. After 1989, Wetzk worked as a heating technician and later completed a civil engineering degree at the Technical University in Cottbus. Volker Wetzk has worked as a research associate at the BTU Cottbus-Senftenberg since 2002.

Exhibition theme: "The Wall on Brunnenstrasse," 2014
Berthold Weidner

1966 1986 1990

WER
DIE STAATSGRENZE
MIT GEWALT
EINRENNEN WILL/
WER AN DER MAUER
PROVOZIERT/
MACHT ALLES
NUR SCHLIMMER!

4

Escapes and Escape Agents

After the border was closed in 1961, people who were determined to flee to the West searched for loopholes in the system of barricades being built. They found one in the buildings on Bernauer Strasse, whose front doors opened directly to the West. Although the buildings were guarded by the police, several people managed to enter them through back doors on the east side.

When the border fortifications were expanded and made permanent, some people tried to go underneath them. Even the sewage system was used as an escape route until the secret police and East German police installed barriers there too. A few used the tunnels of the underground transportation system to flee East Germany. And, finally, both East Germans and escape helpers from the West spent many months building escape tunnels that ran beneath the Wall.

Although the border fortifications became increasingly hermetic and efficient over the years, people who were desperate still tried to get through. These fugitives, referred to in the GDR as "barrier breakers," often did so without using any tools. An estimated 300 escape attempts took place on Bernauer Strasse alone. Altogether about 5,000 people in Berlin managed to escape. But most people were caught, arrested and sentenced to long prison terms. Ninety-nine people died in Berlin while trying to escape.

"I hurried to the window, threw my umbrella and bag down, climbed onto the window sill, closed my eyes and jumped. I made it down and of course I hurt all over but this was rivaled by my spirit. In any case I was quite beat when I heard a woman call out from her building: 'Now now what have we here? I'm calling the police.' And I thought, it's time to get out of here. The people on the other side of the street were screaming and I crossed the street. I couldn't believe it, it was like a dream. I sat down on the curb and cried like a baby."

Rosemarie Platz escaped through a border house on Bernauer Strasse, 1961
Interview, Stiftung Berliner Mauer, 2010

The escapes on Bernauer Strasse became famous – by October 1961 they had already been popularized as a serialized novel in the IBZ.
Illustrierte Berliner Zeitschrift, October 1961 – February 1962

Escape from the Border Houses

The buildings on the border at Bernauer Strasse provided many residents as well as other East Berliners with a good way to escape. They used the doors until they were nailed shut. Then they climbed out of windows on the ground level until these were bricked up. They slid down ropes and jumped from the upper storeys into rescue nets. During the first weeks after the Wall was built, West German firemen stood on alert on Bernauer Strasse, ready to catch people at any time. When the buildings were all bricked up, a few people even jumped from the rooftops down to West Berlin. By mid-October, 113 people had fled on Bernauer Strasse; four lost their lives.

After the escape, Bernauer Strasse 10, probably September 1961
unknown photographer, Bild-Zeitung

The Finder family jumping from Bernauer Strasse 7 on September 22, 1961
unknown photographer,
center: Wolfgang Braubach, ullstein bild

A young woman slides down a rope from a border house on Bernauer Strasse, August 24, 1961
unknown photographer

The Mathern Family

The Mathern family lived on the ground floor of Bernauer Strasse 11 and was able to go to the West without difficulty. When the border was closed, the parents did not immediately see any reason to flee. After the first building entrances were locked on August 16, the family realized that the barriers were going to be permanent. The family decided to flee through their front door that was still open on August 17. Later, their daughter, Elke, later Elke Rosin, drove to the Wall with her father regularly. Her connection to Bernauer Strasse remained strong.

Elke Mathern and her grandmother at the window of Bernauer Strasse 11, 1960
unknown photographer, Elke Rosin

"My mother packed our most important things. She said we were fleeing. I thought that was sort of exciting, but nothing more. We just barely managed to get through the downstairs door. My father stayed in the apartment and handed things down to us. Then people called out to him: 'Hurry up and get out. The police are on their way to your apartment.' If he had gone through the door they would have caught and arrested him. But we lived on the elevated ground level so my father was able to jump out the window."

Elke Rosin,
resident of Bernauer Strasse 11
Interview, Stiftung Berliner Mauer, 2001

Elke Mathern escapes with her parents, August 17, 1961
Horst Siegmann, Landesarchiv Berlin

Gerhard Mathern at the Wall on Bernauer Strasse, undated
unknown photographer, Elke Rosin

The Knittel Family

Rudolf and Helga Knittel, today Helga Kuhn, lived with their young daughter at Bernauer Strasse 8. The family decided to flee when the Wall was built. Although Helga Kuhn was nine months pregnant at the time, she jumped out of the second-storey window with her husband on September 19. They both landed safely in the rescue net of the West Berlin fire department that had been notified of their escape beforehand. Their daughter was born three days later. They were not the only people in the family to flee. Rudolf Knittel's uncle, Rudolf Urban, also escaped from Bernauer Strasse 1, but he was badly injured and died in the hospital.

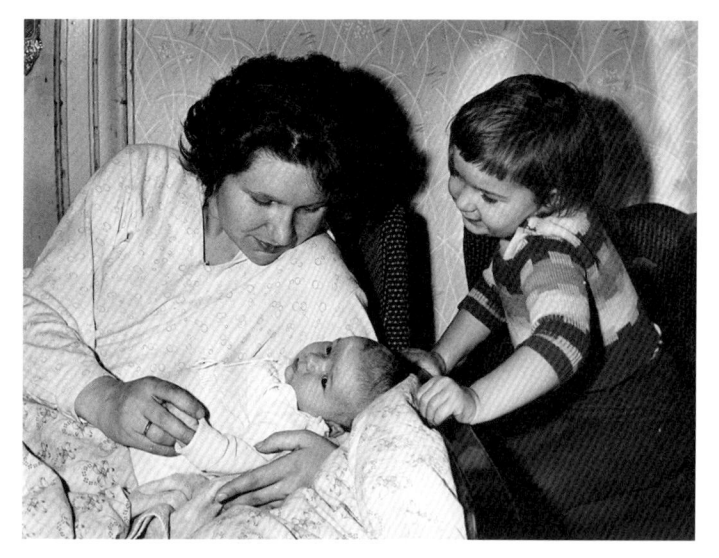

Helga Knittel with her children after the escape, September 1961
unknown photographer, Helga Kuhn

Even the tabloids reported
BZ, 16/10/1961

"Even though I was nine months pregnant I just wanted to be free. We kept everything dark and locked the door so the police couldn't get in. The firemen arrived with a rescue net. I started to feel nervous then: two-and-half storeys! I was the first to jump, or better said, fall into it. Eyes closed and down. My daughter was next and then my husband. Christiane was born three days later."

Helga Kuhn,
resident of Bernauer Strasse 8
Interview, Stiftung Berliner Mauer, 2010

The K. Family

The K. family lived at Bernauer Strasse 10a. After August 13, 1961, Horst K. had to give up his job in the West. After he was conscripted into the East German police force, he got into an argument with the party secretary on September 22 and became violent. The secret police started looking for him. He went to a neighbor, Heinz R., who lived in building 13a and jumped from the second floor into the rescue net of the West Berlin fire department. After his escape, his wife was forced to move out of their apartment. On September 30 she also paid a visit to Heinz R. Guards standing on Strelitzer Strasse let her pass because her identity card still showed her address at Bernauer Strasse. Like her husband, she too jumped out of the window, taking her child with her.

Horst K. after his escape
unknown photographer, Illustrierte Berliner Zeitschrift, 5/1/1963

Horst K. jumping into the firemen's rescue net
unknown photographer, Illustrierte Berliner Zeitschrift, 5/1/1963

Escape Tunnels

Soon after the Wall was built, groups began forming in West Berlin to help East Germans flee. Escapes were becoming more and more difficult. West Berlin students became especially active in assisting escapes. Many of them had escaped from the GDR themselves or had friends and relatives they wanted to help.

Several escape tunnels were built between 1962 and 1971. A few were built from the East to the West, but most of them ran in the other direction. Bernauer Strasse was well suited for building tunnels because the ground was unusually firm. It took three to six months to complete a tunnel, but only three tunnels were actually used to bring people to the West. Difficult conditions, betrayal and counter measures taken by the secret police caused many of the tunnel projects to fail. In spite of these countermeasures, nearly 90 people managed to flee through tunnels on Bernauer Strasse and reach West Berlin safely.

Tunnel 29

One of the last tunnels was discovered in May 1970. People had built it five or six meters below the surface at Bernauer Strasse 80 in the direction of Schönholzer Strasse in East Berlin. After receiving a tip, the secret police increased its surveillance of the east and west sides of the Wall here. It occupied cellars on Schönholzer Strasse and used listening devices beneath the border strip to locate the position of the tunnel. Later it dug a trench in the border strip, exposing the 85-meter-long tunnel. It had the east side of the tunnel filled with mud and debris. Then water was filled into it that flowed towards West Berlin and forced the tunnel to collapse.

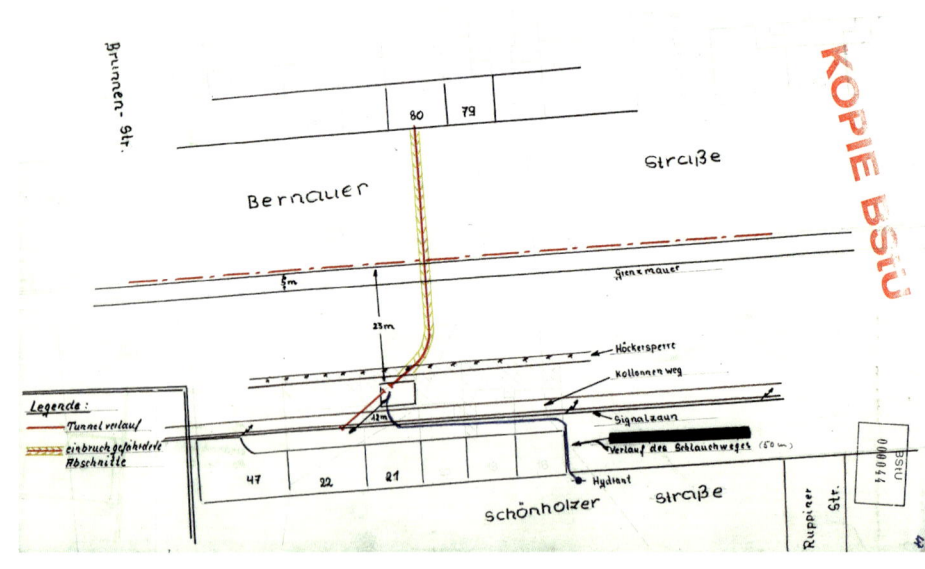

Sketch of tunnel and flooding plan, May 1970
MfS sketch, BStU

Location of tunnel under the border strip, 1972
undated, MfS photo, BStU

Tunnel 29

In the summer of 1962, West Berlin students spent many months digging a 126-meter-long tunnel from the cellar of a factory at Bernauer Strasse 78. Water leaks made digging very difficult and almost caused the operation to fail. The tunnel builders had to shorten the tunnel and move the entrance to Schönholzer Strasse 7, a building closer to the border. They opened the tunnel on September 14, 1962. On two nights, 29 people managed to crawl through mud and leaking water to West Berlin. A film team from NBC, the American television station, filmed their arrival, turning "Tunnel 29" into a media event. Pictures of the escape were seen all over the world. The East German secret police learned about the tunnel from the western press. It located the tunnel eleven days later when the ground collapsed in a back courtyard within the border area.

Entrance to Tunnel 29 in East Berlin, September 1962
MfS photo, BStU

Tunnel 29 with air pipe and border sign, 1962
unknown photographer, ullstein bild

Escape agents' sign marking the border, 1962
unknown photographer, ullstein bild

Tunnel 57

Tunnel 57, named for the number of people who succeeded in escaping through it to the West, is one of the most famous escape tunnels. It began from a cellar at Bernauer Strasse 97 and continued beneath the border strip to a courtyard at Strelitzer Strasse 55. On two nights in October 1964, fugitives crawled through the tunnel to the West.

Fugitives in the tunnel, ascending and arriving in the West, 1964
unknown photographer,
Stiftung Berliner Mauer

Entrance and exit of Tunnel 57 on both sides of the Wall
unknown photographer

Entrance to Tunnel 57 in the courtyard at Strelitzer Strasse 55, September 1964
The dashed line marks the route that fugitives took to the tunnel entrance that was located in a disused outhouse.
MfS photo, BStU

Line of tunnel marked
between Ackerstrasse and
Strelitzer Strasse, 2015
Berthold Weidner

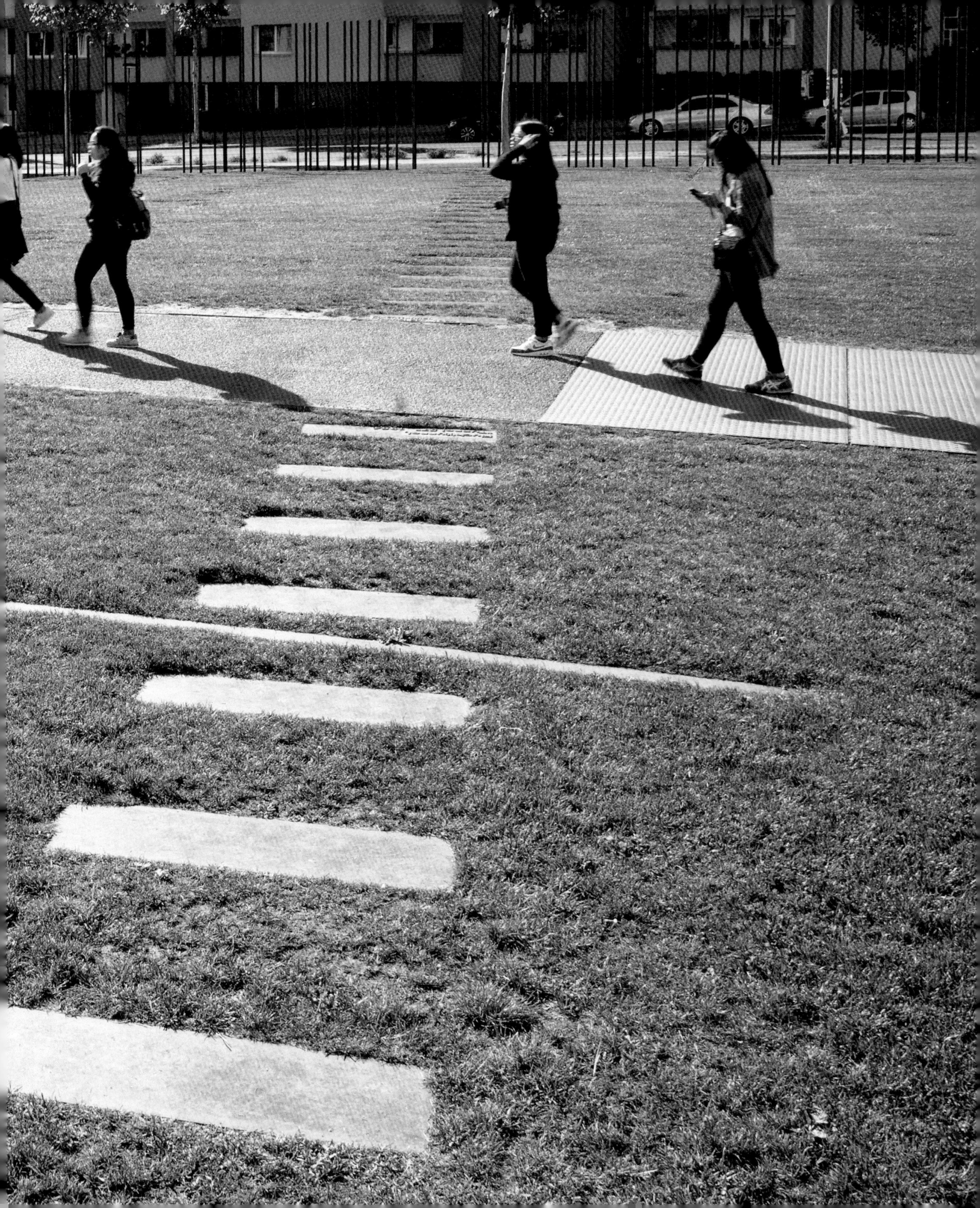

"The escape helpers gave me a little push and I slid through a hole. Someone down below caught me and said that I should duck quickly and start crawling to make room for the others. The tunnel seemed to go on forever. Hats and bags lay along the way, all the things the people had discarded while crawling. But my husband and son weren't behind me. I thought the two of them had been arrested. Then I was pulled up. I was surrounded by friendly people and in that moment my son was also pulled up. Then my husband arrived. When we were brought to the operations room I began to realize: You are in the West. That was the most beautiful moment."

Eva Klein
Interview, Stiftung Berliner Mauer, 1999

Death of Egon Schultz
During the second night, members of the secret police were alerted. Border soldiers were told to stop the operation and arrest the fugitives and their helpers. An exchange of fire broke out between the police and armed escape helpers in the courtyard. Sergeant Egon Schultz was accidentally killed by a bullet fired from the gun of a border soldier. The secret police and the SED leadership made it seem as though the deadly shot had been fired intentionally by one of the escape helpers. The truth did not become known until after 1989.

Memorial plaque for Egon Schultz
dedicated on January 4, 1965
unknown photographer, Bundesarchiv

Rebuilding the Border Fortifications
Karl-Heinz Nagel

"I was a young man, [...] that was the whole reason why I took off. Because I knew both the West and the East [...]. I was young, and wanted to experience something. I didn't want to waste my youth."

Interview, Stiftung Berliner Mauer, 2012

Karl-Heinz Nagel was born in 1942 and grew up in Müggelheim, a suburb of East Berlin. He completed a bricklayer apprenticeship and then – like thousands of East Berliners – became a "border commuter," working on construction sites in West Berlin. In 1961, the GDR government banned its citizens from working in West Berlin and built the Wall soon after. It was then that Karl-Heinz Nagel decided to flee. Running across the rooftops of buildings on the East Berlin side of Ackerstrasse, he reached the last building before the border. Using a clothes line, he roped himself down to Bernauer Strasse on the West Berlin side. When he hit the ground he injured his leg and hip. Passersby brought him to a hospital and he was later flown to West Germany.

Escape through the Sewage System

The underground sewers offered another way of getting to the West. West Berlin escape helpers provided maps of the sewage system. They sent people to East Berlin to escort fugitives to West Berlin and close the manhole cover so that the police would not discover the escape route. Not all escape attempts were successful. Wolfgang H. had already climbed down into the gully on Gartenstrasse on October 6, 1962 when he was discovered by border soldiers and arrested. The secret police tried to stop these kinds of escapes by blocking the passageways with grating and checking them regularly.

Barrier grid in the sewage system
Rene Quabbe, Berliner Wasserbetriebe

Border soldiers climbing down into the gully at Bernauer and Schwedter Strasse to inspect the sewage system, 1965.
unknown photographer, ullstein bild

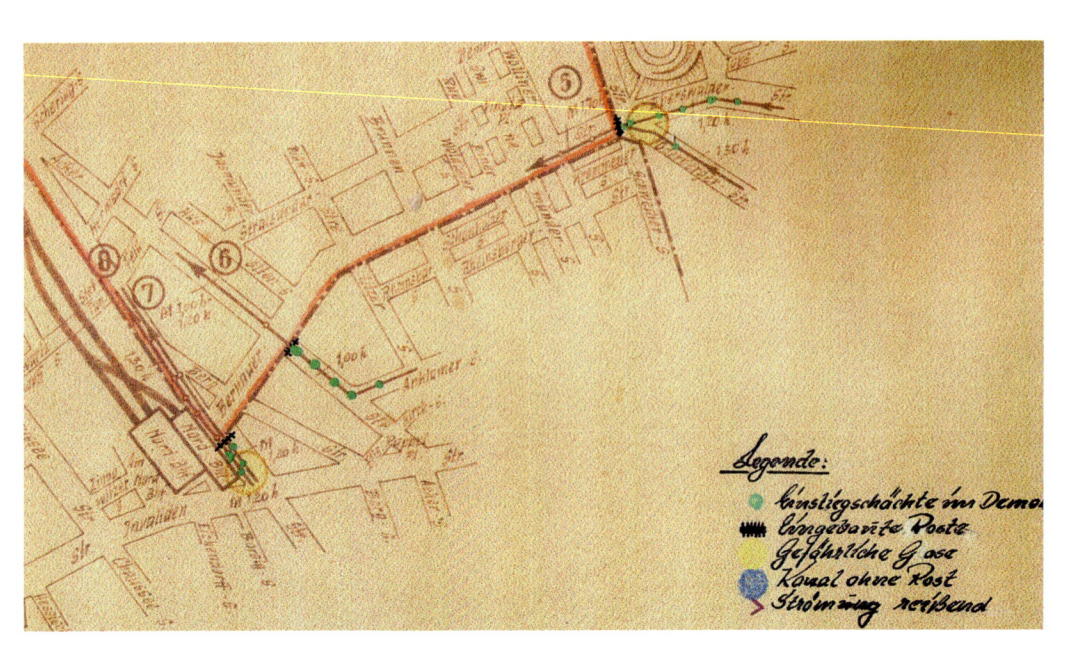

Map of the accessible sewage system, undated
Both the gully entrances and the gratings that were installed to prevent escapes are marked.
Border troops map,
Stiftung Berliner Mauer

"Barrier Breakers": Escaping through the Border Fortifications

The most common escape route, however, was still through the border fortifications. In the early years, people on Bernauer Strasse often fled across the grounds of the Sophien parish cemetery to side streets that ran into the Wall and then through open lots where buildings had been bombed out during World War II. The buildings on the border were torn down in the mid-1960s and replaced by a border strip with different obstacles. Watchtowers provided border guards with a good view of the border.

Although a few escapes were successful, most fugitives were discovered by the guards and arrested. Confronted with the border fortifications and surveillance, many fugitives became desperate. Klara E. asked border guards to "take pity on her" and allow her go to West Berlin. Heinz W. even asked some children if they knew of a good way to escape. H. offered the border guards 50 marks if they would let him cross the border. They were all arrested.

The border strip at the time of the escape
MfS photo, BStU

The buildings on the border were torn down in the mid-sixties and a border strip with various barriers was created in their place. Fleeing through the border fortifications became more dangerous and increasingly difficult, in part because the border guards had a better view of the border strip from their towers. Only a few people managed to successfully flee after that. The border guards arrested most of the fugitives and many of them were put in East German prisons. A man from Limbach tried to flee across the border fortifications on Bernauer Strasse in March 1970. He approached the border strip from Strelitzer Strasse (called Egon-Schultz-Strasse at the time), climbed over the inner wall and moved towards the Berlin Wall. He did not stop when ordered to halt. Border soldiers fired shots at him from a tower. The injured man was brought to a hospital and handed over to the secret police.

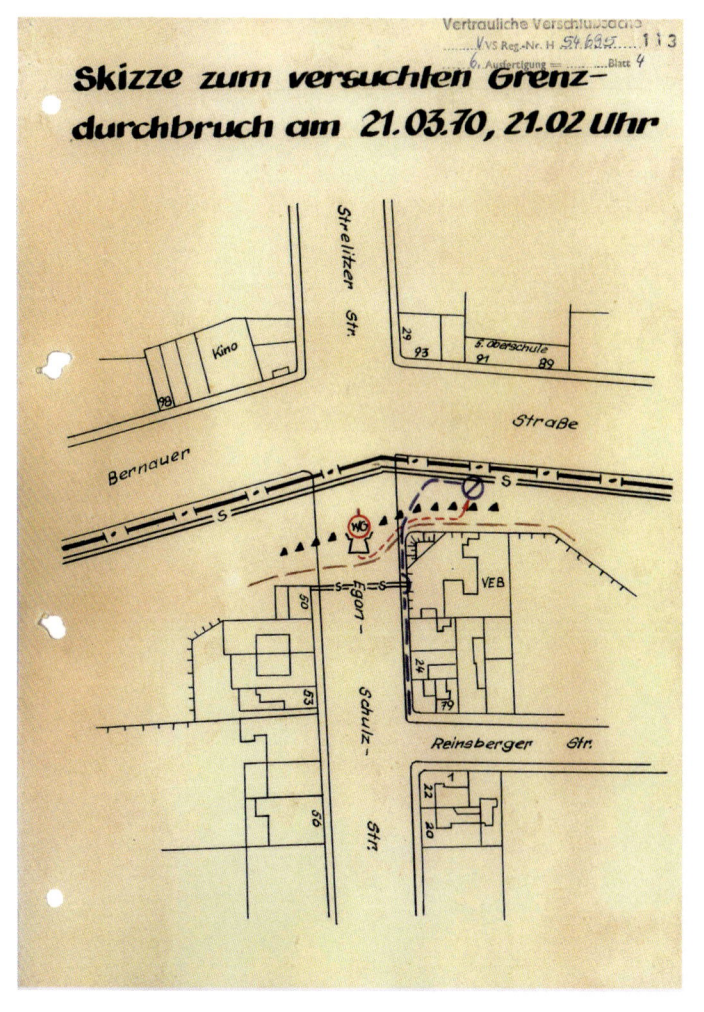

The fugitive's escape route and the site of his arrest
Border troop sketch of the crime site, Bundesarchiv-Militärarchiv

Exhibition theme: "The Wall on Brunnenstrasse," 2014
Berthold Weidner

Bernauer S...

1961

© Peter Leibing, Hamburg

1961 — Ende des franz. Sektors — 1963 — 1964

Straßensperrung verursacht durch die Schandmauer

© Peter Leibing, Hamburg

Exhibition theme: "The Wall on Brunnenstrasse," 2014
Berthold Weidner

5
The Victims

**Memorial for the victims
of the Wall on Eberswalder Strasse,
Sept. 20, 1985**

Brian Rose

The Victims
at Bernauer Strasse

Ida Siekmann

August 23
1902
–
August 22
1961

Rudolf Urban

June 6
1914
–
September 17
1961

Wreathes for Ida Siekmann, 1967
Klaus Lehnartz, ullstein bild

**Memorial sign for Rudolf Urban,
June 1962**
unknown photographer,
Polizeihistorische Sammlung Berlin

Ida Siekmann was deeply affected by the consequences of the closed border. Her sister lived in West Berlin. This unbearable situation led the 58-year-old woman to flee on the day before her birthday.

On August 21, 1961 the East Berlin police locked the front door of her apartment building that opened to West Berlin. It was probably then that she decided to flee. She had seen the West Berlin firemen catching neighbors who had jumped from their windows into rescue nets. Misjudging the danger, on the morning of August 22 she threw her bedding from her third-floor apartment onto the sidewalk below. For reasons that are not known, she jumped out the window before the firemen were ready with their rescue net. When she hit the ground, she was badly injured and died on the way to the hospital.

Ida Siekmann was the first person to die at the Wall. Her death sparked outrage. After the funeral several wreathes and flowers were placed in front of her apartment building. The Wedding district erected a monument in September.

Rudolf Urban and his wife witnessed the closing of the border and saw the first people fleeing in August 1961. Once they realized that the border barriers would be permanent, his wife wanted to flee. Rudolf Urban hesitated at first; he was reluctant to start over again at the age of 47. But when the front door of their building was nailed shut on August 18, the couple agreed to flee.

On August 19 the Urbans attached a rope to the window of their first floor apartment and slid down to the street below, but when they hit the pavement Rudolf Urban broke his heel bone. They were both brought to the nearby Lazarus Hospital where Rudolf Urban caught pneumonia and died on September 17.

Citizens placed wreaths and flowers at the entrance to the building after his death. A short time later a memorial sign was erected, where commemorative ceremonies were held. Later an inscription in the sidewalk and a white cross were added.

Olga Segler

July 31
1881
–
September 26
1961

Memorial and white cross for Olga Segler, 1979
Rolf Peter, Stiftung Berliner Mauer

When the border was closed, Olga Segler was separated from her daughter in West Berlin. Since August 13, 1961 she had lived in a building occupied by border police as if under siege.

Evacuation of the border houses on Bernauer Strasse began on September 24, 1961. The residents of the border houses were dragged out of bed early in the morning and had to quickly pack before their furniture and belongings were loaded onto trucks. Many people reacted by trying to flee, including Olga Segler. From the West Berlin sidewalk, her daughter encouraged her to jump. On the evening of September 25, the 80-year-old woman leaped into the firemen's rescue net from the 2nd floor of the apartment building at Bernauer Strasse 34. She was seriously injured and brought to the nearby Lazarus Hospital. The next day she died from her injuries.

In November a monument to Olga Segler was erected at the site where she jumped. Later an inscription in the sidewalk and a white cross were added.

Bernd Lünser

March 11
1939
–
October 4
1961

Students erecting a memorial cross for Bernd Lünser, October 1961
unknown photographer

Bernd Lünser studied at an engineering school in West Berlin where his father also lived. After the Wall was erected, the 22-year-old decided to flee so that he could continue studying in the West.

On October 4, 1961, Lünser climbed across the rooftops of houses on a side street to reach the roof of the border house Bernauer Strasse 44. He was going to slide down a rope, but the East Berlin police discovered him. Lünser got into a scuffle on the rooftop. He freed himself so that he could jump into the rescue net of the firemen. West Berlin and East Berlin policemen got involved in an exchange of fire, making it impossible for the firemen to position the rescue net exactly. Lünser jumped anyway, missed the net and hit the pavement. He died immediately.

The dramatic escape attempt and the shots fired at the Wall caused outrage in West Berlin. Fellow students erected a memorial cross for Lünser in October. Later an inscription in the sidewalk and a white cross were added.

Ernst Mundt

December 2
1921
–
September 4
1962

**Memorial sign for Ernst Mundt
at the Sophien Cemetery, after 1965**
Henry Ries, Deutsches Historisches Museum

Ernst Mundt, 40 years old, tried to flee to the West on September 4, 1962. One reason he objected to the wall was that his mother lived in West Berlin and he was only able to communicate with her through letters. Hence he decided to flee.

He rode his bike from his apartment in Prenzlauer Berg to the first border obstacle at Bergstrasse. He climbed on top of the cemetery wall of the Sophien parish cemetery and ran westwards on it. Two border soldiers who were patrolling the cemetery grounds discovered him. They called out to him to give up his flight. While they conferred with each other Mundt continued to run. Then two transport policemen from Nordbahnhof noticed him. One of them shot at Mundt, hitting him fatally in the head and causing him to fall off the wall.

Citizens of West Berlin erected an anonymous memorial sign to commemorate his death. A ground plate and white cross were added later.

Otfried Reck

December 14
1944
–
November 27
1962

**Memorial sign for Ottfried Reck
on Gartenstrasse, 1977**
Horst Siegmann, Landesarchiv Berlin

Ottfried Reck tried to reach the West through the S-Bahn tunnel on November 27, 1962. He had previously been imprisoned for protesting against the Wall at Gartenstrasse in September 1961.

Ottfried Reck and a friend tried to enter the underground S-Bahn at Invalidenstrasse near the skating rink by breaking through an emergency exit that had been welded shut. A border guard in the S-Bahn station heard them and gave the alarm. A search party found the fugitives who ran when they saw the border soldiers. Although they were quite a distance from the border grounds, an officer shot at them, hitting Reck in the back. He died in a hospital three hours later.

The shots were heard in the West. After learning of Ottfried Reck's death, West Berliners erected a monument and a white cross in his memory.

Heinz Cyrus

June 5
1936
—
November 11
1965

Memorial sign for the victims of the Wall at Bernauer Strasse, 1990
Hans-Peter Stiebing

Heinz Cyrus, who was just about to turn thirty, had already had a number of run-ins with the GDR state authority and had been imprisoned for political offenses. Threatened once again with prison, he decided to flee on November 10, 1965.

Cyrus tried to cross the Wall near Gartenstrasse. He was discovered by a watchdog and came under fire from three sides. Uninjured, he fled into the building at Gartenstrasse 85. The border soldiers pursued him and searched the building. Cyrus climbed out of a window on the fourth floor, apparently planning to lower himself from there, but he lost his balance and fell into the courtyard. He died of his injuries the next day.

Although people in the West heard the shots and watched as he was carried away, no one knew for sure whether the man they saw had died. This is why the death of Heinz Cyrus was not commemorated with an individual monument until 1989.

Commemorative column for Otfried Reck on Bernauer Strasse, 2013
Berthold Weidner

Central commemorative site
for the victims of the Berlin Wall:
Window of Remembrance, 2014
Berthold Weidner

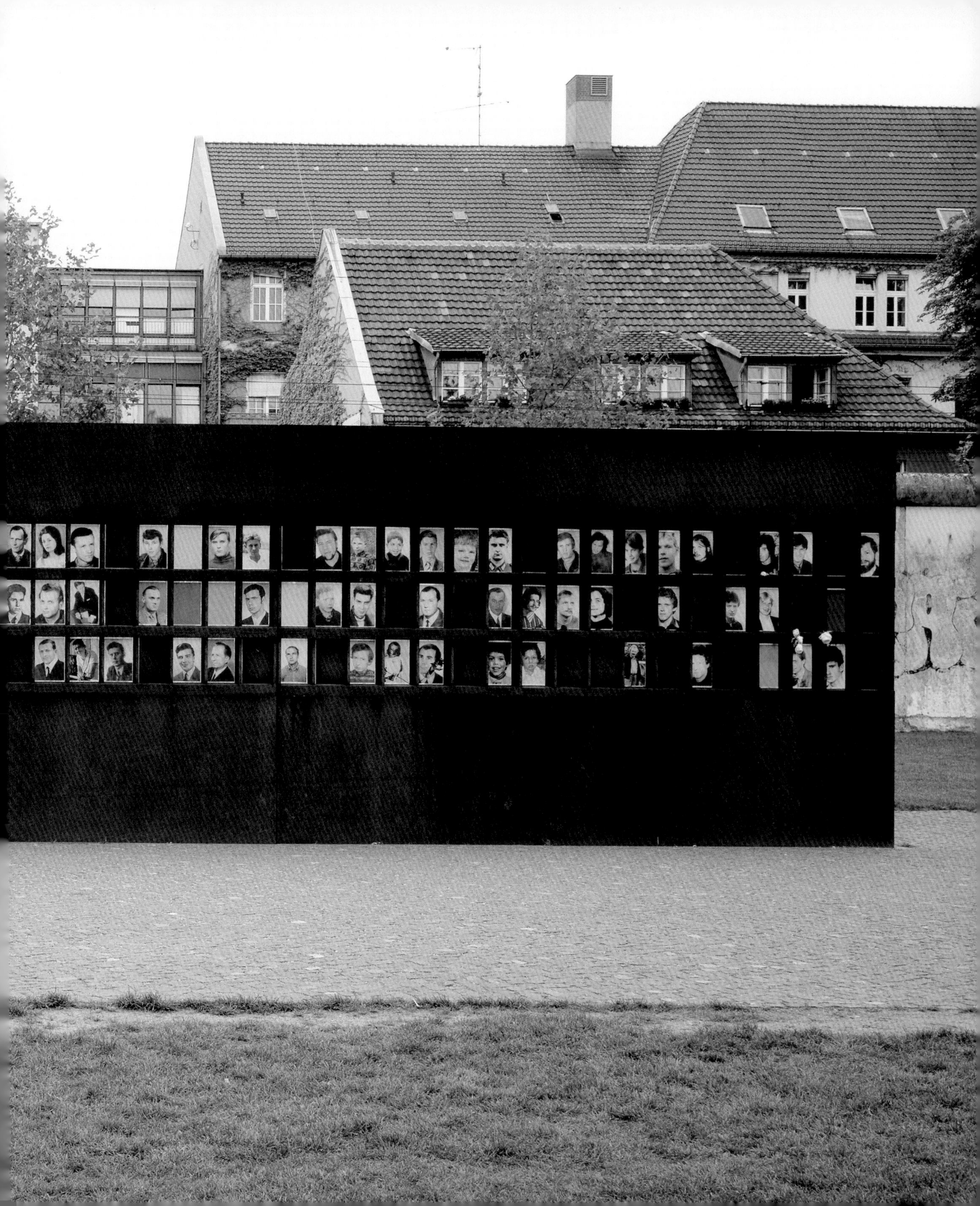

Maria Nooke

The Victims at the Berlin Wall

In the fall of 2012, a teacher from a suburb of Berlin visited the Berlin Wall Memorial with her class. While touring the grounds of the former death strip, the group paused in front of the Window of Remembrance, which presents the victims of the Berlin Wall with their names, birth and death dates, and a photograph.

When people look at this wall of more than a hundred names and faces, they recognize the magnitude and brutality of human rights violations that were committed in connection with the Berlin Wall border system. Each day, before being assigned to their border posts, guards were reminded: "Border violators are to be apprehended or exterminated." Anyone trying to escape, and anyone who inadvertently entered the border area from East to West Berlin, was to be stopped – if necessary with guns. The "integrity of the border" was the GDR leaders' highest priority. Human life, in contrast, had little value.

At least 100 people lost their lives trying to escape from East Berlin. Another 38 people who were not trying to flee also died at the wall. The photographs of victims presented in the Window of Remembrance show that it was primarily young men between the ages of 16 and 30 who were killed or who died in an accident while trying to escape. Only a few women, such as Dorit Schmiel and Marienetta Jirkowsky, risked undertaking a dangerous escape. They were both shot by border guards.

The photographs of children who lost their lives at the border are especially poignant. Jörg Hartmann was ten years old when he and his thirteen-year-old friend Lothar Schleusener tried to cross the border fortifications between Berlin-Treptow and Berlin-Neukölln in March 1966. They were planning to find Jörg Hartmann's father, who was living in West Berlin. Although shooting at women and children was forbidden, they died in a hail of bullets fired by the border guards.

The photographs of the men, women and children commemorated in the Window of Remembrance give the victims a face. Sometimes a photograph could not be found, in which case the window is left blank. The teacher approached one of the empty windows and was stunned to read the name and biographical dates of her own grandmother. She had known that her grandmother had drowned, but only then did she learn that the accident was connected to an escape attempt.

According to the most recent findings of the research project conducted by the Berlin Wall Memorial and the Center for Contemporary Research in Potsdam,[1] at least 138 people lost their lives at the Berlin Wall. Ninety-eight of them were shot. The victims include 100 people who were trying to escape and 30 people from both the West and the East who had no intention of fleeing. Eight border soldiers died while on duty.

Of the 100 people who tried to flee, including ten military deserters, 67 were shot and three took their own lives after their escape attempts failed. The Polish sailor Franciszek Piesik was the only non-German among them. He is one of the 30 people who died in an accident at the Berlin Wall. The people who died in accidents include those who drowned in the border waters of Berlin and those who crashed to their death while jumping from buildings on Bernauer Strasse in 1961.

The Window of Remembrance, April 2015
Berthold Weidner

Dorit Schmiel, ca. 1961
Dorit Schmiel died on February 19, 1962 after she was shot in the stomach while trying to escape at the sector border between Berlin-Pankow and Berlin-Reinickendorf
Polizeihistorische Sammlung Berlin

Marienetta Jirkowsky, undated
Marienetta Jirkowsky was shot and killed on November 22, 1980 while trying to climb over the Wall with a ladder at the border between Hohen Neuendorf and Berlin-Reinickendorf.
private ownership

Dieter Beilig
undated
BStU

Franciszek Piesik,
undated
Polizeihistorische
Sammlung Berlin

**Lothar Schleusener,
at the age of six,
ca. 1958**
private ownership

**Jörg Hartmann,
at the age of three,
ca. 1958**
private ownership

Twenty-two of the 30 people in the second group, which consists of those making no attempt to flee, were residents and visitors from West Berlin. Fifteen of them were shot, seven died in accidents. Those who were shot included four escape helpers and Dieter Beilig, who had become known for his acts of protest against the Wall in West Berlin. On April 2, 1971, he reached the Brandenburg Gate from the West side of the city and jumped down into the border area. The thirty-year-old man was brought to the border troops command station located near the Brandenburg Gate. A short time later an officer there shot him at close range. To support the "legend" of his death, the Stasi manipulated evidence and faked documents.

The seven West Berliners who died include five children from Kreuzberg, who were playing near the river at Gröbenufer (today May-Ayim-Ufer) when they fell into the border waters and could not be rescued. Eight East Germans were also shot in the border area although they were not trying to flee. One of them was 31-year-old Herbert Kliem. He took a wrong turn and accidentally drove into the border area. When he turned his motorcycle around to leave, two bullets struck him in the back and killed him. A third group includes the eight border soldiers who were killed while on duty. Border guards were responsible for securing the border and preventing escapes and were thus subjected to the dangers this entailed. In three cases, guards were killed by armed military deserters. In one case, the head guard in charge of a section of the border strip was mistaken for a fugitive and fatally shot by another guard. One border soldier was beaten by fugitives and died from his injuries. The other three border soldiers were shot, either intentionally or by accident, in connection with an escape attempt. One of them was Sergeant Egon Schultz. He was fatally injured by a bullet fired on the night of October 5, 1964 during an escape action through a tunnel that West Berlin students had dug from a bakery at Bernauer Strasse 97 to Strelitzer Strasse 55 in East Berlin.

The killings and murders that took place at the Berlin Wall, the inner German border, the Baltic Sea and the outer borders of the GDR represented the pinnacle of violence, which was a direct result of the GDR border security system. The SED leadership willingly accepted the killings and was well aware that these damaged its international reputation, which is why incidents at the border were supposed to be covered up. The border troops had to remove the injured or killed fugitives from the death strip immediately and take them to specific hospitals for treatment, or to the Forensic Medical Institute of the Humboldt University (Charité) or Bad Saarow Central Army Hospital for an autopsy. The fugitives were usually loaded onto the back of an army truck or "Kübel-Trabis" without being given any immediate medical attention. When they arrived at the hospital or forensic medical institute, the Stasi took over. [2] It alone decided what was to be done with the corpse and handled everything from the autopsy, to the issuing of a death certificate, to the transfer and cremation of the body, which was usually carried out in the Baumschulenweg Crematorium. Relatives were informed of the death, but usually were not given any details about the circumstances. They were instructed not to speak about the incident or were told to lie about it. Others relatives were lied to about the true cause of death. In the case of Jörg Hartmann and Lothar Schleusener, for example, the Stasi even created false evidence to support a fictitious cause of death. Relatives often did not learn the true circumstances until after the GDR archive was opened and criminal investigations against violent acts at the border were conducted in the 1990s.

When the Wall fell, the mother of Chris Gueffroy, who was the last person to be shot at the border, filed charges against the guard who had fired the fatal shots. Investigations of border guards began during the final months of the GDR and were continued after German reunification by public prosecutors in West Berlin. When the death had taken place on the outer ring around West Berlin, the investigation was carried out by Neuruppin's public prosecutor's office. A total of 112 charges were brought against 246 people in Berlin, both against the guards who fired the shots and against their military and political superiors. The Neuruppin public prosecutors brought another 21 charges against 39 border guards who had fired fatal shots and ten charges against their superiors – 12 commanding officers of the border troops. [3]

**Herbert Kliem,
ca. 1969**
Private ownership

Chris Gueffroy, 1985
Private ownership

Approximately half of the accused were acquitted. In some cases it could not be determined which guard had fired the fatal shots. In others, an intent to kill could not be proven. Some trials against border soldiers had to be discontinued because the accused was deemed unable to stand trial. The shots fired at military deserters were legitimized by the highest judicial authority because, according to the East German military law of 1962, military desertion was a crime. It was argued that killing a deserter was excusable since, in this "special case," the illegality of the marksmen's action could not have been evident to them." [4] A total of 151 of the accused received final sentences for various manslaughter offences – as direct or indirect offenders, as accessories, instigators or for aiding and abetting. Ten members of the SED leadership and National Defense Council were sentenced to prison terms ranging from three to seven-and-a-half-years; 54 members of the military leadership were sentenced to between six months and six-and-a-half years in prison. One hundred border soldiers were sentenced to between sixth months and two years in prison; most of these terms were commuted to suspended sentences. Only one border soldier was convicted of murder and sentenced to ten years in prison. [5]

When establishing a person's guilt and handing down punishment, the courts took into account subjective extenuating factors in favor of the accused, such as their integration into the hierarchy of a totalitarian system; the repression of justified doubts regarding state-given orders; the constant political indoctrination which corrupted their sense of what was right; the time that had passed since the crime; the young age of the accused at the time of the crime; and the advanced age of the accused at the time of sentencing, which increased their sensitivity to punishment.

Following the preliminary examination and after it had been established that the killing of a person was also a punishable offence in East Germany, the German federal courts applied West German law when passing verdicts and issuing sentences. With a few exceptions, this law was more lenient and, therefore, more favorable to the accused than the corresponding East German law. The courts' verdicts followed the jurisdiction of the Federal High Court, according to which the deliberate killing of unarmed fugitives cannot be justified, as it is "an obvious, unbearable offence against fundamental dictates of justice and against human rights that are protected under international law." [6]

Many found the number of acquittals too high and the punishments passed too lenient. From the perspective of legal prosecution, the suffering endured by many families and the injustice done to several generations of East Germans remain largely unatoned for. But it is thanks to the investigations and trials conducted by the criminal justice system that the human rights violations in East Germany and the crimes committed by the Communist Party are comprehensively documented.

Commemorating the victims of the GDR border regime is one of the central tasks of the Berlin Wall Memorial. Their biographies portray the everyday reality of life in a divided Germany and reveal an unwavering desire for freedom, which led many to risk dangerous escapes. Yet it is also important to remember the victims of the border regime who died although they had no intention of fleeing. When the design of the Window of Remembrance, as the central site to commemorate the victims, was under discussion, several questions and conflicts emerged: Is it right to have the border soldiers who died while on duty commemorated along side the others who died? Should they be considered perpetrators although they never used their weapons and were themselves killed by fugitives or deserters? Is it too much to ask relatives of the fugitives who were shot that they see photos of a killed border soldier presented next to portraits of their loved ones? Are we to make a distinction between dignified and undignified victims of the border regime? It was decided that the eight border soldiers who died on duty should not be included in the Window of Remembrance. Their names are instead presented on a separate column near the memorial. On the other hand, the fugitives and deserters who were responsible for the death of these border soldiers were included in the memorial. Those opposed to having everyone commemorated together were relieved by this historical-political decision; the families of the killed border soldiers were disappointed. The Berlin Wall Memorial continues to face many challenges in providing an adequate and suitable form of commemoration.

Central commemorative site for the victims of the Berlin Wall: Window of Remembrance

Smriti Pant, Stiftung Berliner Mauer

1
Hans-Hermann Hertle/Maria Nooke (eds.): *The Victims at the Berlin Wall 1961 – 1989. A Biographical Handbook*, edited for the Centre for Contemporary History Potsdam and the Berlin Wall Foundation, Berlin 2011.

2
On this and the following (MfS) orders for handling corpses, see o. O., o. J., in: BStU, MfS, HA IX Nr. 5134, pp. 10 – 16. Similar instructions existed for the inner German border.

3
On criminal investigations of cases of death at the Wall, see Henning Rosenau, *Tödliche Schüsse im staatlichen Auftrag: Die strafrechtliche Verantwortung von Grenzsoldaten für den Schusswaffengebrauch an der deutsch-deutschen Grenze*, 2nd edition, Baden-Baden 1998; Klaus Marxen/Gerhard Werle, *Die strafrechtliche Aufarbeitung von DDR-Unrecht. Eine Bilanz*, Berlin 1999; ibid. (ed.), Strafjustiz und DDR-Unrecht. Dokumentation, Vol. 2: *Gewalttaten an der deutsch-deutschen Grenze*, Berlin 2002; Toralf Rummler, *Die Gewalttaten an der deutsch-deutschen Grenze vor Gericht*, Berlin/Baden-Baden 2000; Karl Wilhelm Fricke, "'Grenzverletzer sind festzunehmen oder zu vernichten'. Zur Ahndung von Tötungsdelikten an Mauer und Stacheldraht," in: *Die politische Meinung*, No. 381/August 2001, pp. 11 – 17; Erardo C. Rautenberg, "Die strafrechtliche Aufarbeitung des DDR-Systemunrechts im Land Brandenburg aus staatsanwaltschaftlicher Sicht," in: Klaus-Christoph Clavée/Wolf Kahl/Ramona Pisal (eds.), *10 Jahre Brandenburgisches Oberlandesgericht*, Baden-Baden 2003, pp. 97 – 130; Roman Grafe, *Deutsche Gerechtigkeit. Prozesse gegen DDR-Grenzschützen und ihre Befehlsgeber*, Munich 2004; Hansgeorg Bräutigam, "Die Toten an der Mauer und an der innerdeutschen Grenze und die bundesdeutsche Justiz," in: *Deutschland Archiv* 37 (2004), pp. 969 – 976; Hanno Siekmann, *Das Unrechtsbewusstsein der DDR-"Mauerschützen,"* Berlin 2005; Klaus Marxen/Gerhard Werle/Petra Schäfter, *Die Strafverfolgung von DDR-Unrecht. Fakten und Zahlen*, Berlin 2007.

4
See the verdict of the German supreme court in the case against Rolf S. and Ernst R. in the death of Michael Kollender, Az. 5 StR 137/96, vom 17.12.1996, in: Klaus Marxen/Gerhard Werle (eds.), *Strafjustiz und DDR-Unrecht. Dokumentation, Vol. 2: Gewalttaten an der deutsch-deutschen Grenze*, Berlin 2002, pp. 277 – 281.

5
A detailed descripiton of the trial results is presented in: Hertle/Nooke, Todesopfer, pp. 24 – 25.

6
See the verdict of the German supreme court in the case against Karl-Heinz W. in the death of Manfred Weylandt, Az. 5 StR 167/94, 26.7.1994, in: Marxen/Werle (eds.), *Strafjustiz*, pp. 179 – 187, quote p. 182.

133

6

The Wall in the Cold War

State visits to the Wall were a routine part of political life in West Germany and West Berlin. Many well-known politicians attended vigils and memorial services for the victims of the Wall. Just days after the Wall was erected, the West Berlin Senate's Department of the Interior established a mobile information office. Everyday the "Studio at the Barbed Wire" broadcast appeals, music and news over the Wall to the police and border soldiers in the eastern sector. When East Germany reacted with its own loudspeaker vans, a serious battle of the loudspeakers ensued between the two sides. Posters were put up on both sides of the Wall to reinforce the messages. West Berliners demonstrated at the border to express their outrage over its closure. Some resorted to radical measures.

Loudspeaker confrontation, 1962
Alex Waidmann

Propaganda

On April 10, 1962, two boys from East Berlin climbed onto the roof of a border house at Bernauer Strasse 44. West Berlin firemen and police arrived to provide them with assistance. It was assumed that the boys were trying to flee. The nine-year-old Thomas jumped into the firemen's rescue net, but Bernd Schottka lost his courage and was taken down from the roof by East Berlin policemen. He was later placed in a juvenile home. A conflict reported by the press ensued between the East and West over Thomas' return: The West Berlin senator for youth affairs wanted to hand the boy over to his mother personally. The East responded by accusing her of kidnapping the boy. The western press reported that the East was not allowing the boy's mother to travel to the West to get her child. Following many weeks of haggling, Thomas was finally picked up by his mother and brought back to East Berlin on his 10th birthday.

Thomas Molitor, 1962
Jung, ullstein bild

Thomas Molitor jumping, April 10, 1962
unknown photographer, ullstein bild

**The Molitor affair in the news,
April / May 1962**
BILD, Der Abend, Neues Deutschland, Telegraf

"The point was that he had to be sent back, but they wanted to grant him a little freedom. That's why the press reported on his injuries and that he had to be treated first. That was basically a stalling tactic to keep him on the west side a little longer. But since he wasn't allowed to stay here at his age, he was handed over to the lawyer from over there."

The Malchows
Interview, Stiftung Berliner Mauer, 1999

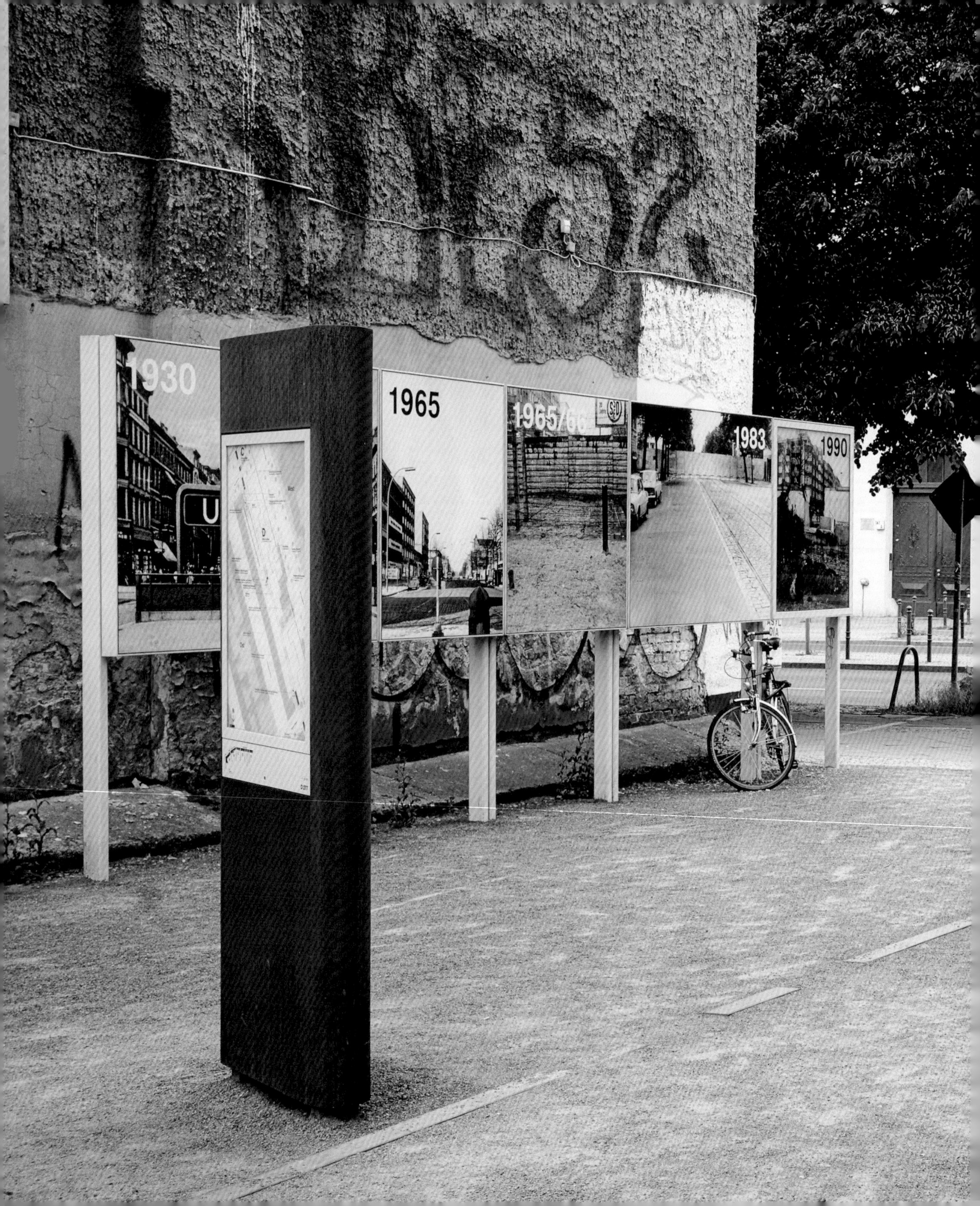
1930
U
1965
1965/66
1983
1990

Exhibition theme: "The Berlin Wall on Brunnenstrasse," 2015
Berthold Weidner

Battle of the Loudspeakers

The West Berlin Senate's "Studio at the Barbed Wire" provided information to policemen and border soldiers in East Germany. It encouraged them to flee and asked them not to shoot at fugitives. The border troop political division set up its own loudspeaker vans at the border to drown out western broadcasts with music. Sometimes border soldiers threw tear gas grenades. Both sides upgraded their equipment, adding more and stronger loudspeakers to their vans. In the mid-1960s, when the rapprochement began, this form of confrontation at the Wall came to an end.

Loudspeaker van of the "Studio at the Barbed Wire," 1961
unknown photographer, picture alliance

Border troops' loudspeaker van, 1962
Dieter Otto, ullstein bild

"Attention, Attention!
This is the Studio at the Barbed Wire speaking. Men of the National People's Army! Anyone who shoots at someone is committing murder. This murder cannot be justified morally or legally. Early yesterday, a member of the National People's Army bled to death very close to your border crossing. He was shot by one of your own comrades simply because he wanted to go from Germany to Germany. Anyone who is honored or praised for being a murderous sniper, remains branded, even to his comrades. This has been frequently confirmed by the 380 soldiers of the National People's Army who have fled since August 13, 1961. We have told you many times: Anyone who on orders from Ulbricht fires at defenseless people, who are simply trying to get from Germany to Germany, is committing murder! We have told you many times: Murder is murder. Even when it has been ordered."

Announcement from the "Studio at the Barbed Wire"
Heinz Gerull Collection, Oct. 7, 1965

Upgraded loudspeaker vans, 1963
Heinz O. Jurisch, ullstein bild

Upgraded loudspeaker vans of the "Studio at the Barbed Wire," 1963
Alex Waidmann

Observing, Helping, Protecting: The Western View of the Wall

Soldiers of the Western Allies patrolled at the Wall with the West Berlin police. The French were responsible for Bernauer Strasse. During routine duty at the Berlin Wall, police tasks were carried out primarily by the West Berlin police and customs officials. The police and customs officers were expected to demonstrate presence, document the border fortifications, support people who were fleeing and to take action in certain situations. They also tried to make contact with East German border guards.

During the first weeks after the Wall was built, western police forces were on duty at the Wall to help people who were escaping. They supported escapes, engaged in tear gas duels and an occasional exchange of fire with East German border guards. But they were only allowed to offer assistance after someone had reached West Berlin territory. They were permitted to fire their weapons only when shots fired from the East had struck West Berlin. Firemen on duty at Bernauer Strasse were equipped with rescue nets to catch people jumping from windows and rooftops. They had to operate as inconspicuously as possible so that border guards would not notice the escape.

Firemen preparing to use the rescue net, September 1961
Alexander Czechatz, ullstein bild

Documenting the enemy, August 1963
unknown photographer, dpa, ullstein bild

West Berlin police officers with drawn weapons provide cover during an escape and bring the fleeing family to safety, September 22, 1961
Wolfgang Braubach, ullstein bild

West Berlin police, French gendarmerie and a West Berlin customs official observe the situation behind the Wall, Bernauer Strasse, 1960s

Léon Herschtritt, La Collection (left)
Alex Waidmann (middle)
Deutsches Zollmuseum (right)

Position and movement of western police units during an escape attempt, January 15, 1966

Border troops map,
Bundesarchiv-Militärarchiv

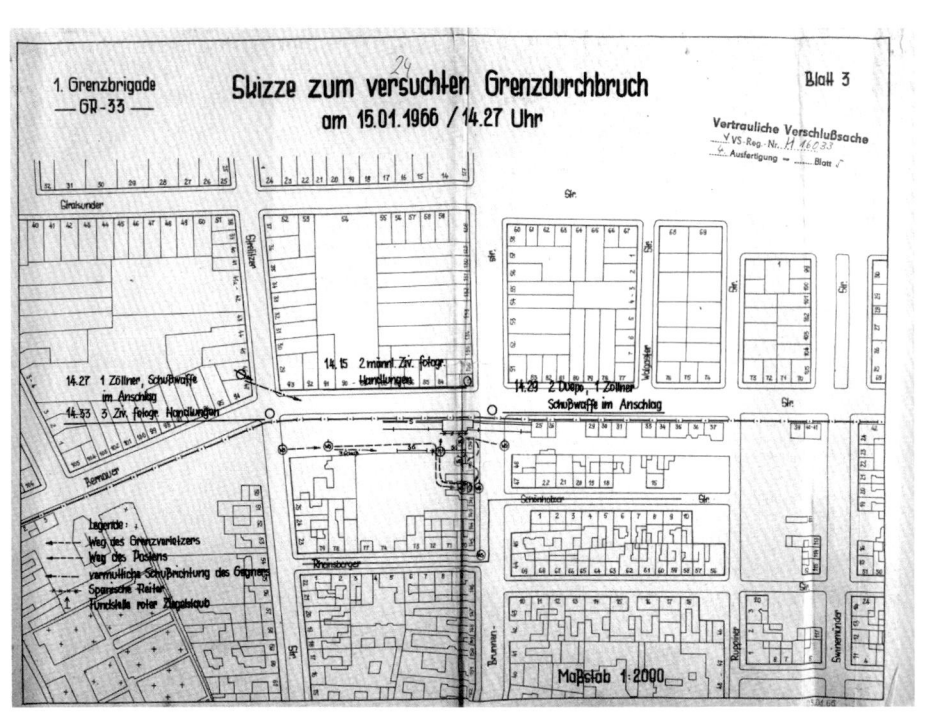

West Berlin police render harmless a tear gas grenade thrown over the Wall by border soldiers, September 24, 1961

unknown photographer, dpa, ullstein bild

143

Messages and Poster Propaganda

The SED hung posters at the Wall to convey catchy messages to the West. It justified the Wall as a blow against West German "aggressors." Some of the posters presented the SED's victory stance. Others attacked the West German political leadership, exploiting the fact that people who had served in politics and the military under National Socialism continued to fill these roles in West Germany after 1945.

The poster slogans from West Berlin changed over time. At first they focused on deterring guards from firing at fugitives, but when the policy of détente was introduced, they began promoting rapprochement and understanding.

Propaganda poster on Brunnenstrasse, 1965
Klaus Lehnartz, Photonet

Propaganda for the peace treaty, 1962
Dieter Otto, ullstein bild

Allegations against the West German president Heinrich Lübke, 1966
Ludwig Ehlers, Landesarchiv Berlin

Traffic sign in West Berlin, 1966
Fritz Eschen, ullstein bild

Poster on the "order to shoot," early sixties
unknown photographer,
Versöhnungsgemeinde Berlin-Wedding

Criticism of the ban against waving over the Wall, 1963
Alex Waidmann

Poster from the period of rapprochement, 1971
MfS photo, BStU

State Visits

The Wall symbolized the SED's inability to implement without coercion the political order it envisioned in East Germany. This was demonstrated to politicians from all over the world at the Wall. Many came to express their solidarity. But some, particularly from third world countries that had recently been liberated from colonial oppression, came to secure the goodwill of the West German government and the Western world.

Information minister T.O.S. Benson from Nigeria at the memorial for Bernd Lünser, 1963
unknown photgrapher, Bundesarchiv

Martin Luther King at Bernauer Strasse, 1964
unknown photographer, akg-images

Jacques Chirac, mayor of Paris, with Richard von Weizsäcker, 1983
Harry Hampel, ullstein bild

The Wall in West Berlin

Many West Berliners, including policemen, found it difficult to accept that they were helpless to do anything beyond feeling outrage about the Berlin Wall and the separation of East Berlin. The West Berlin police experienced daily the dramas taking place at the Wall. As the division of the city became permanent and there was no sign of the situation improving, some people resorted to radical measures. Hans-Joachim Lazai was one of them. In May 1962, he and his friends blasted a hole in the Wall as a symbolic gesture to draw international attention to Berlin's division. No one was harmed and the SED quickly had the hole repaired.

Berliners on both sides of the Wall had to get used to the Wall and being separated from friends and relatives. The West's policy of rapprochement towards East Germany that was introduced in the 1960s made it easier to establish personal contact. People on both sides of the Wall had to acknowledge the new reality and many came to accept it.

The effects of the explosion, May 26, 1962
unknown photographer,
Polizeihistorische Sammlung Berlin

Bricklayers under guard while repairing the hole in the Wall, May 26, 1962
unknown photographer, ullstein bild

West Berlin police on duty at a demonstration on Bernauer Strasse, August 13, 1963
unknown photographer,
Polizeihistorische Sammlung Berlin

Visitors at the Wall, 1965
Herbert Maschke, ullstein bild

**Children playing
in West Berlin, 1966**
Volkmar Hoffmann, picture alliance

**Boy playing at the Wall
in East Berlin, 1963**
Bernard Larsson,
Bildarchiv Preußischer Kulturbesitz

Boy at the Wall in West Berlin, 1963
Günter Zint, Bildarchiv Preußischer Kulturbesitz

7

The Fall of the Berlin Wall at Bernauer Strasse

On the evening of November 9, 1989, the East German government announced new travel provisions. Thousands of East Berliners rushed to the border crossings, forcing the Wall to be opened. The very same night thousands used this opportunity to move about freely on the west side of the city. To handle the large crowds of people, it soon became necessary to create additional border crossings. In November, excavators and other heavy machinery were still at work moving the position of the Wall at Eberswalder Strasse. In the night leading into November 11, border soldiers used this same equipment to break the first hole into the Wall. The first opening was cut through the Wall at Eberswalder Strasse to create a new border crossing.

**Break in the Wall at Eberswalder
Strasse, November 10/11, 1989**

Gabriele Fromm, ullstein bild

The first East Germans pass through the new border crossing, November 11, 1989
unknown photographer, picture alliance

East German border soldiers check passports at the new crossing, November 11, 1989
Günter Peters, ullstein bild

Reunited, November 1989
unknown photographer, imago

Demolition of the Wall, 1990
Klaus Lehnartz, Photonet

Demolition of the Wall on Ackerstrasse, June 1990
unknown photographer,
Versöhnungsgemeinde Berlin-Wedding

Incident markers along
Bernauer Strasse

Berthold Weidner

The Fall of the Berlin Wall at Bernauer Strasse
Brigitte Geschwind

*"In 1987 I was certain that the Wall would not go away in my lifetime. […] Then, when I arrived in Berlin, the first opening was being made on the northern end of Bernauer Strasse. […] And piece by piece, but very slowly and painstakingly […] it was taken down. Two, three, sometimes even four of those large T-shaped concrete blocks. Those things were extremely heavy […].
The next day I was there again and masses of people were coming over."*

Interview, Stiftung Berliner Mauer, 2012

Brigitte Geschwind was born in Berlin in 1947. She lived with her family near Bernauer Strasse on the sector border to West Berlin. As a schoolgirl before the Wall was built, she spent time on both sides of the border. Her father worked for a company in East Berlin. When the border closed in 1961, she saw people trying to escape and heard the shots fired by the border police. She was no longer able to contact her uncle and grandmother in East Berlin. When she got married, she intentionally moved to a different part of the city so she would not have to live "in the shadow of the Wall." Brigitte Geschwind eventually moved to Rheinland-Pfalz where she worked as a teacher

1961

Exhibition theme:
"The Cold War and the Media"
on Wolliner Strasse, 2014
Berthold Weidner

Photo documentation:
Expansion of the memorial site

Construction begins on
Gartenstrasse, August 2009
Jürgen Hohmuth, Stiftung Berliner Mauer

Ackerstrasse, 2010
Jürgen Hohmuth, Stiftung Berliner Mauer

Mounting the Window of Remembrance, April 2010
Jürgen Hohmuth, Stiftung Berliner Mauer

Construction work between Ackerstrasse and Strelitzer Strasse, 2010
Jürgen Hohmuth, Stiftung Berliner Mauer

Archaeological investigation and documentation of the border houses Bernauer Strasse 10, 10a and 11, 2010

Jürgen Hohmuth, Stiftung Berliner Mauer

Central planning team of the so-called workgroup implementation. 2010

Stiftung Berliner Mauer

Core area of the Berlin Wall
Memorial at night, 2015
Jürgen Hohmuth, Stiftung Berliner Mauer

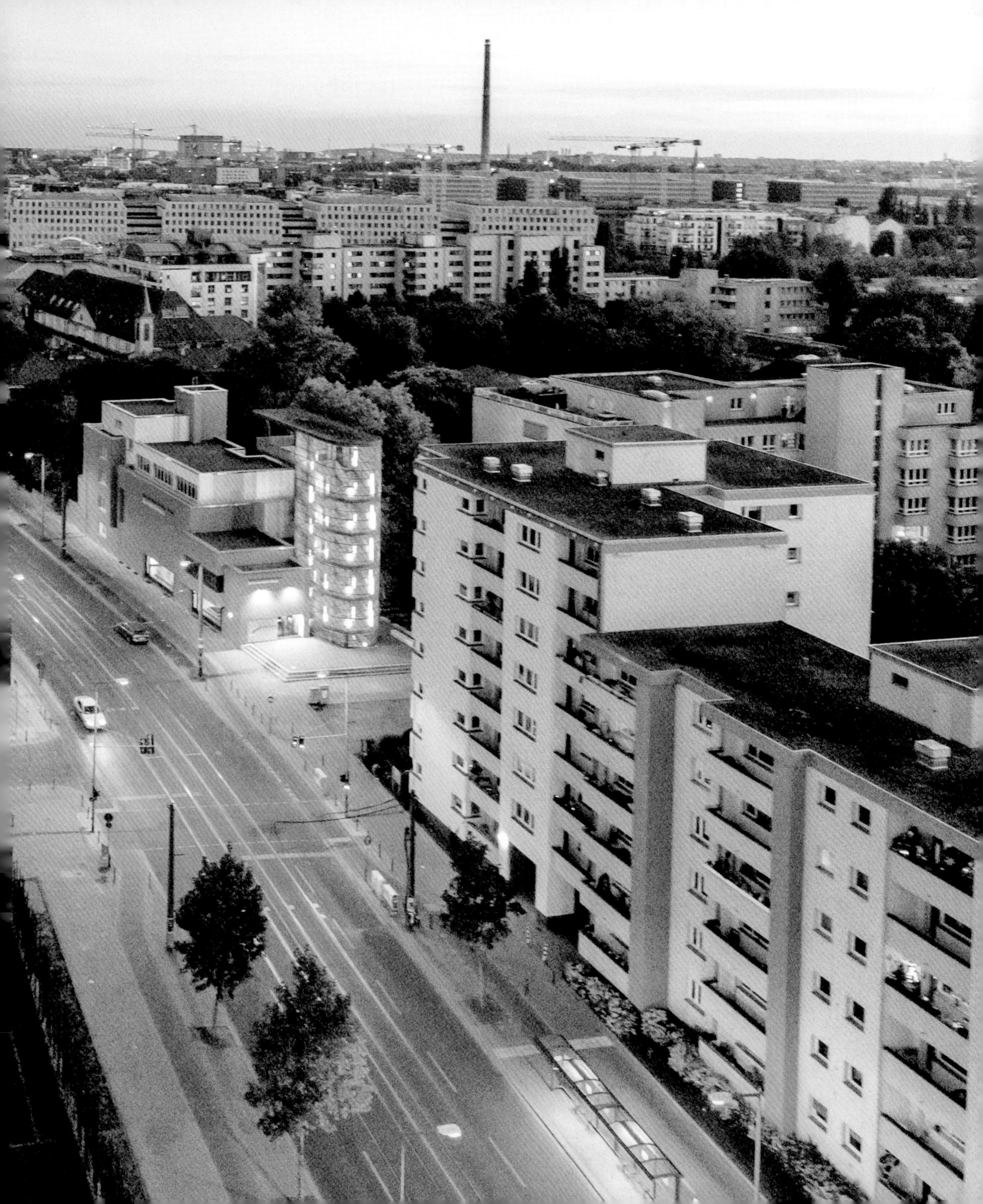

Günter Schlusche

This essay is dedicated to Pastor Manfred Fischer (February 7, 1948 – December 6, 2013).

From the Fall of the Wall to the Berlin Wall Memorial: How an Urban Commemorative Space was Created

Today, it seems perfectly natural that we commemorate the Berlin Wall and that more than a million people visited the Bernauer Strasse in 2014 alone to form their own impression of this monstrous structure. But this is misleading. The history of how the memorial was established makes very clear that a consensus has only existed for ten years or so. A long and painful controversial debate had to take place before the necessity of a memorial site to remember the second German dictatorship and its victims was recognized.

It all began with a resolution of December 29, 1989, initiated by the GDR interim government headed by Hans Modrow, which called for the immediate demolition of the border fortifications.[1] There were, however, other views. Willy Brandt argued as early as November 10, 1989 for "preserving a piece of this abominable structure […] as a memory."[2] A few weeks after November 9, the "Round Table of Berlin-Mitte" and a group of historical preservationists organized around the GDR general conservationist, Peter Goralczyk, presented a list of border areas it believed were worthy of special protection. One of them was the Bernauer Strasse.[3]

In August 1990, Peter Möbius from the GDR Museum for German History, Helmut Trotnow from the German Historical Museum (DHM) and Pastor Manfred Fischer from the Protestant Church of Reconciliation on Bernauer Strasse formed another group, which demanded "preserving the Berlin Wall and the border fortifications" at this site. The group proposed a concept for a "monument with a small museum."[4] But this initiative, along with the resolution passed by the East Berlin Magistrate on October 2, 1990 to protect this and other sections of the Wall as an historic monument, remained unsuccessful. Instead, following the first symbolic act of its demolition on June 13, 1990 on the corner of Ackerstrasse and Bernauer Strasse, efforts to tear down the entire Wall gained momentum.[5]

Given the more intuitive desire to tear the Wall down, which found expression in the slogan "The Wall must go," the Berlin Senate's resolution of August 13, 1991 to establish a memorial site at Bernauer Strasse and to reconstruct the many-layers of border fortifications that had been dismantled just a few months earlier, was also ineffective. Only through great effort and at the very last minute was it possible to hinder the border troops from carrying out their orders to demolish this already-damaged section of the border fortifications, and to stop "wall peckers" from causing further damage to the Wall. This was, above all, the achievement of members of the Reconciliation Church parish and their pastor, Manfred Fischer, who intervened several times.

It was at this point that new conflicts arose. One was the proposal from the Senate to have Bernauer Strasse integrated into the inner ring of bypass roads around the city center. But this would have meant expanding the Bernauer Strasse into a six-lane thoroughfare and tearing down the entire stretch of the border wall on the south side of the street. The plan was only partially retracted in 1995/96. Additionally, the neighboring Protestant Sophien parish demanded that the section of cemetery grounds, which had belonged to its parish before expansion of the border grounds led to its destruction, be reinstated as a cemetery. The parish also argued that graves from World War II, which had not been completely exhumed, were still protected by law, thus precluding the use of the grounds as a memorial.

In the midst of this extremely complex situation, the Berlin Monument Authority was in the process of re-wording the protection resolution from 1990. It repeatedly stressed that protecting the remaining border fortifications at this site was important, but that establishing a documentary exhibition and educational site was also crucial.

The neglected grounds of today's memorial at the border wall south of the building at Bernauer Strasse 111, 1997
Tobias Rücker, Stiftung Berliner Mauer

Art project "The furniture returns" by Boris Schwitalsky and Benita Joswig, presented on the former border strip at the corner of Bernauer Strasse and Strelitzer Strasse in November 1995 (standing at left: Pastor Manfred Fischer)
Dieter Schwertle, Versöhnungskirchengemeinde Berlin-Wedding

Remnants of the demolished border fortifications on the Sophien parish cemetery grounds, ca. 1997/98
Tobias Rücker, Stiftung Berliner Mauer

It was in the context of these diverging interests that an architectural and artistic ideas competition for establishing a Berlin Wall Memorial on Bernauer Strasse was held in 1994.[6] The competition description called for dividing the border strip between Ackerstrasse and Bergstrasse into two parts: "One section with the preserved segment of the former border fortifications and a connecting cemetery zone to contain a new memorial area."[7] This represented extremely fragile concessions.

The competition ended in a hard-won compromise: instead of a first prize, the jury awarded three second prizes, and acquired five others[8] – thereby throwing the problem back to the DHM and Berlin Senate for them to solve. By mid-1995, all parties had agreed on the design by the Stuttgart architects Kohlhoff + Kohlhoff, which called for strictly preserving – in its already damaged form – the 70 meters of the border grounds within the central area, and for adding two 6-meter-high steel walls that would enclose the space and reflect the interior. The plan also proposed establishing the western section that bordered Bergstrasse as a 140-meter-long cemetery area with a reconstructed cemetery wall.

This decision reinforced the inclination to divide the grounds into a core area and a cemetery area, in which the demolition of the landmarked border wall remained a possibility.[9] At the same time, the plan offered a very minor alternative to the positions held by the Sophien parish, which, having regained possession of its cemetery grounds, was feeling more confident. While the federal construction committee wrestled until April 1997 over how to pay for the 2.2 million DM construction costs of the Kohlhoff design,[10] the Sophien parish applied for the right to tear down the border wall along the 140-meter-long western section. Approval was granted by the district on April 16, 1997 and demolition began immediately,[11] causing two gaps, 14 and 18 meters long, in the border wall. Almost the entire back wall, where the Sophien parish believed collective graves from World War II still existed, was also torn down.

The Berlin Senate responded to this openly defiant violation of memorial protection rights by offering its clear support for preserving the border fortifications between Ackerstrasse and Bergstrasse. The Sophien parish suffered another setback after an expert opinion report determined that there were not any war or collective graves in this area of the cemetery after all.[12] Construction of the Kohlhoff design began in November 1997.

In this acute situation, the Reconciliation Church parish presented a new idea: it suggested that its parish community center, a building that had been erected in 1965, be used as a documentation center. It also proposed constructing a new structure, a "chapel of reconciliation" on the property where its church had stood before it was torn down in 1985.[13] This proposal reasserted the original connection between preservation and documentation/information that seemed to have been forgotten through the many controversies of the past years. It also expanded the urban space in which the planned memorial could be established. This new concept proposal, the consequences of which were only slowly grasped, elevated the planning to a standard that was on par with the commemoration of the Nazi past: it acknowledged that visitors today can only appreciate the authenticity of a site when it has been carefully interpreted and decoded through explanatory educational methods.[14]

The next conflict arose during construction of the Kohlhoff monument. This time it had to do with the dedication that was to be inscribed on the eastern outer side of the monument. Just days before the official opening of the memorial, several victim associations successfully appealed on the federal level to have the phrase "… and in commemoration of the victims of communist tyranny" added to the dedication text.

The Chapel of Reconciliation under construction in September 1999
Christian Jungeblodt
Versöhnungskirchengemeinde Berlin-Wedding

The former border strip between Bergstrasse and Ackerstrasse (now the core area of the memorial) in October 2007
Torsten Dressler, Stiftung Berliner Mauer

Around the time that the completed memorial was officially opened by Berlin Mayor Eberhard Diepgen on August 13, 1998, the "Berlin Wall Memorial Association," initiated by the Reconciliation Church parish, was established. It was difficult to acquire provisional start-up funding, but it was finally secured for a first exhibition presented in the former parish building at Bernauer Strasse 111.[15] A second exhibition titled "Berlin, August 13, 1961" opened on August 13, 2001. It focused on the period of the Wall's construction, addressing both the situation that led up to these events and the consequences that followed.

Given the limited church funds and the diminishing number of parish members, funding for the construction of the new Chapel of Reconciliation was a risky endeavor. Architects Rudolf Reitermann and Peter Sassenroth nevertheless succeeded in creating an impressive architectural design for the chapel, which respected both the existing remains of the older church building from 1894 and of the border fortifications. Furthermore, the single storey structure did not depend on height, nor did it call for historical reconstructions.[16] Construction began in 1999 and the completed chapel was dedicated the following year. Today the chapel continues to represent an unusual architectural concept that distinguishes itself from the architectural trends that dominate Berlin.[17]

The Berlin Wall Association moved forward with its plans to have the community center at Bernauer Strasse 111 partially remodeled by the architects Zerr/Hapke/Nieländer. Despite ongoing financial difficulties, a much-debated tower was built with a viewing platform which "congenially interlocks" the building with the Kohlhoff monument.[18]

The Sophien parish continued to insist on its right to unrestricted use of the cemetery on the western section of the grounds. It did this in what was often a very profane manner – storing huge mounds of compost, fragments of old headstones and debris from the border demolition at the site. The gradual but constant rise in the number of visitors to the site did nothing to alleviate the ongoing financial problems, nor did it lessen prevailing reservations about the location of the memorial. The entire area along Bernauer Strasse seemed to exist as an unfortunate mix of wasteland, soon-to-be-developed property and fringe space; the components of the memorial ensemble seemed strangely disparate among unattractive remnants of the border fortifications and evidence of urban development from before the construction of the wall.

This unfortunate situation was based on a deeper urban-planning conflict related to the "Planwerk Innenstadt." This referred to a general plan for Berlin's inner city, which was introduced by the Berlin Senate in 1996 and which called for both open spaces and traffic areas. It included the entire border strip, but allowed for building development based on the city's traditional block pattern construction.[19] This general plan was based on a very problematic understanding of history that ignored "urban development memory (of the time of division)" and regarded "evidence of the painful history of the dual-front city as a nuisance."[20] The Mitte district also designated the border strip within the residential block between Strelitzer und Brunnenstrasse as buildable land and approved requests until 2005 for building projects there. Fortunately, only one building was actually constructed.[21]

Outside views stimulated a change in opinion. Several national and international news reports and commentaries negatively viewed the dynamics of the inner-city transformation process. They also criticized the abandon with which important traces of the recent past were being swept aside and how the dramatic transformation taking place made it seem as if the city's division had never existed.[22] Moreover, visitors to Berlin were constantly asking where the Wall had stood. Ultimately, it was an installation initiated by Alexandra Hildebrandt, director of the museum "House at Checkpoint Charlie," which was presented as a "temporary art event" in 2004 that ended up having the biggest political impact. The installation consisted of 1,086 wooden crosses mounted behind a temporary reconstruction of the Berlin Wall at the former Checkpoint Charlie site.[23] Strongly criticized for its inaccurate calculation of wall victims, for its factual errors and questionable artistic quality, it was taken down after seven months, but by then it had succeeded in drawing attention to the problem.

In 2001, the Senate building administration took the first steps to remedy the situation by commissioning a comprehensive scholarly inventory of the remains and traces of the Berlin Wall. This investigation determined that the term "Berlin Wall" could not continue to refer exclusively to the border wall that faced the West, which reflected only a Western view. This term should also encompass the many spectacular findings that comprised the entire border fortifications.[24] The report showed that many more remnants and traces existed than had been previously thought. In some places, such as on Bernauer Strasse, these remains contained strong informative value.

It was up to the red-red Senate (SPD/Left party coalition) under Mayor Klaus Wowereit and Culture Minister Thomas Flierl to react to the change in mood and to respond to these new findings with a political initiative to address a general concept for dealing with the Wall and the division of the city. This concept, passed by the Berlin Senate in May 2006 and reinforced by a resolution of the German Bundestag, continues to be the foundation on which the completed Berlin Wall Memorial is based today.[25] The decentralized nature of the concept, which combined many different kinds of explanatory presentations, was important. It encompassed all the different sites in the city that commemorated the Wall and division, but granted a prominent role to the memorial site at Bernauer Strasse, allocating to it more than five hectare of urban space.

As these events unfolded, the Senate took a step forward with regard to urban development. In September 2005, the former border strip between Gartenstrasse and Schwedter Strasse was declared "a zone of exceptional urban-political significance" and a new building development plan was introduced. Its main aim was to "keep the former border strip free of construction" and "to remodel it into a commemorative landscape [...] in memory of the Berlin Wall."[26] This basic decision was modified for the area between Brunnenstrasse and Schwedter Strasse. Here construction was to be permitted on the edge of the border grounds bordering the street, but the strip of land along the almost continuous former patrol path was designated a memorial.

Thus, at the very last minute, the city took advantage of the opportunity to keep this area open and undeveloped and to preserve the many historic remnants and traces that still existed. In previous years, investors had expressed a strong interest in building along the border strip. In mid-2006 alone, four legally-valid building licenses were granted for the core area; several building requests were submitted and undeveloped plots of land changed ownership. The Senate had understandable reasons for wanting to link the extension of the grounds of the memorial east of the Brunnenstrasse with new building construction: in addition to wanting to lower its costs for the acquisition of this land, it was also concerned with meeting the demands for quality urban development.[27] In the following years, however, as the memorial was being built, this decision would prove problematic.

The general concept of 2006 was received positively by the public.[28] It became clear, however, that to realize it, each individual component of the project would have to have approved funding. As the tasks of the memorial continued to grow at a rapid pace, institutional backing also became increasingly important. In late 2008, a legally independent foundation was founded for this purpose.

The international open competition held in 2007 for the architectural and design implementation of the entire memorial extension project proved to be a challenge in many ways. Yet, in late 2007, the jury selected the design by three Berlin offices, Mola/Winkelmüller (architecture), "sinai" (landscaping) and "ON architektur" (exhibition design), which provided convincing solutions to almost all aspects of the project.[29]

Map of the entire Berlin Wall Memorial indicating the thematic focus of each section

sinai Landschaftsarchitekten

1. Chapel of Reconciliation
2. Monument (Kohlhoff + Kohlhoff)
3. Documentation Center with viewing tower
4. Visitor Center
5. "Window of Remembrance"
6. Remains of the Bernauer Strasse 10, a house on the border
7. Watchtower marker
8. Entry points with models

Bernauer Straße

Brunnenstraße
Ruppiner Straße
Swinemünder Straße
Wolliner Straße
Schwedter Straße

100 m

169

As the number of visitors rose and interest in the memorial's educational programs increased, it became important that a visitor center be added to the ensemble. The building erected on the corner of Bernauer Strasse and Gartenstrasse, a creative functional design by Mola/Winkelmüller, opened in late 2009. The "sinai" office's design of the former border strip did not reshape the grounds or create replicas of items that had been lost. Instead it called for a robust lawn and followed the "principle of remapping": The line of the border wall would be marked by steel poles mounted at varying intervals, which, from certain perspectives, provided the illusion of a wall, but which were actually open and passable. The most politically sensitive task was to create a site in memory of the victims of the Berlin Wall. Here the ON architecture office proposed a "window of remembrance" to be erected on the area of the Sophien cemetery grounds that had been converted into the death strip. It would consist of a framework of windows that presented each victim with his or her name, birth and death date and, if possible, a photo.

It was clear from the very beginning that the general design, which contained several complex individual components, would have to be realized in stages. The most difficult precondition was getting the Sophien parish to agree to having its cemetery grounds completely integrated into the memorial area. Following many years of negotiations, this was achieved in 2009, thanks to the emergence of a new younger generation of church council members and the commitment of new parish members. The next step was to purchase the plots of land needed to create the memorial extension.[30]

The completion date for the central area between Gartenstrasse and Brunnenstrasse was set for August 13, 2011, the 50th anniversary of the Berlin Wall – and the memorial was able to open on time thanks to an unusually successful cooperative and interdisciplinary effort. The exhibition "Border Stations and Ghost Stations in Divided Berlin" had already opened in October 2009 on the underground mezzanine level of the Nordbahnhof, an S-Bahn station that had remained closed until 1989.[31] In May 2010, the first section of the exhibition containing the "Window of Remembrance" was completed and included the reconstruction within the Kohlhoff memorial of the original watchtower that had been taken down in 1990.[32]

August 13, 2011 marks what by now has become the generally-accepted view that commemoration of the Berlin Wall and division is an essential and bipartisan part of the public consciousness. It also reflected a broad recognition of the design concept on which this modern and open urban memorial space was based. This concept chose not to include any reconstructions, instead placing emphasis on the unique character of the site – its emptiness in combination with carefully prepared relics that are left to speak for themselves. The design concept relies on empathetic visitors who, when provided with small amounts of information, are able to engage in independent reflection.

In the extended area between Brunnenstrasse and Schwedter Strasse, the design concept follows the same design principles. But here several problems arose during its implementation. The Senate's demand that the memorial in this area be limited to a ca. 4,500 square meter strip of land alongside the guard path and that housing construction be permitted on the northern edge of border strip led to a number of formal objections – mostly from residents and owners of the land south of the patrol path who felt that the concept was disadvantageous to their property. In response they demanded that the concept be revised before they would agree to sell the section of the land containing the patrol path.[33] These objections caused a considerable delay and led to a mediation process that ended in February 2012 with the recommendation that the concept include the condition that one story be eliminated to reduce the height of the new buildings.

The core area of the memorial between Gartenstrasse (bottom right) and the Visitor Center on Bernauer Strasse (bottom left), July 2010
Jürgen Hohmuth, Stiftung Berliner Mauer

Ownership structure in the core area of the memorial (between Gartenstrasse and Brunnenstrasse) in October 2008

Senatsverwaltung für Stadtentwicklung und Umwelt Berlin

Further delays were caused by the complex ownership structures within the border strip – the result of two German dictatorships. A number of properties had been expropriated from their original owners – in some cases from Jewish owners – before 1945. Unlike in West Germany, many of these cases had been left unsettled. Further property dispossessions took place after 1945. A claims law was passed in 1990 that called for property to be returned to its original owners. In the case of "wall property," however, complicated restitution conditions were set by a "wall law" of 1996 that included a repurchase right that was limited to 25 percent of the actual market value or equivalent compensation.[34] The original owners saw these conditions as discriminatory and as sanctioning the injustices of the GDR. This made it extremely difficult to reach an agreement that would allow the memorial to be extended. In a few cases in which restitution had already taken place, the owners had to be made to understand that the properties were not available for normal construction, but were instead to be sold to the foundation as land for the creation of a memorial – at a price based on the going rates for building plots. Other owners had established gardens on their plots of land, or they were using them as open space and were not willing to let them go – despite the fact that they had been informed of the memorial's extension by 2006 at the very latest.

Despite all these difficulties, with the exception of four small segments, all the necessary land was transferred to the foundation.[35] Several sections of the memorial were completed between 2012 and 2014. The documentation center underwent energy-efficient renovations and was redesigned to meet the demands of greater numbers of visitors. Inside, a new enlarged exhibition opened on schedule on November 9, 2014, the 25th anniversary of the fall of the Wall.

Thus an urban memorial space emerged along Bernauer Strasse that, with its open design and central location, signifies a new kind of memorial. It represents the central component of an open urban historical landscape on the grounds where the Berlin Wall had stood, beginning at the park at the Nordbahnhof S-Bahn station and continuing across the memorial to the "Mauerpark"; it is part of a "green ribbon" that runs from the city center all the way to Barnim, an approximately 160-kilometer-long historic Berlin Wall Trail that combines culture, nature and history.[36]

Berlin's urban development has been strongly marked by discontinuity, radical redesign and demolition. But this commemorative space, having resisted demands to build up, fill up, and reshape history, provides something novel. Here, where two bordering neighborhoods with very different social structures converge, a decision was made to cultivate change by creating a modern open space.

The green strip of land joining these two urban blocks now contains a unique memorial ensemble with a dual character: it functions both as an authentic historic and informative site and also as a site of commemoration and contemplation. It lends expression to the joy felt over the fall of the Wall and the peaceful end of German division. It also allows the very divergent experiences with the Wall in the East and West, in everyday affairs and private life, to be placed in a historical context and in relation to one another. The many people who visit Berlin sense that this is more than just a "popular tourist attraction." It is a space that subtly addresses the emotional and cognitive experience. Decades later, these kinds of sites, which confront German history by encouraging reflection and learning, and by imparting different perspectives, continue to fulfill a meaningful and reconciliatory function in society.

Core area of the memorial between Strelitzer and Ackerstrasse with preserved foundation walls of the former border building at Bernauer Strasse 10 A (right) and the Chapel of Reconciliation (left), 2014
Jürgen Hohmuth, Stiftung Berliner Mauer

1
Gerhard Sälter, *Der Abbau der Berliner Mauer und noch sichtbare Reste in der Berliner Innenstadt*, Berlin 2004, p. 7.
2
Peter Möbius/Helmut Trotnow (eds.), *Mauern sind nicht für ewig gebaut – Zur Geschichte der Berliner Mauer*, Frankfurt am Main/Berlin 1990, p. 13.
3
Deutsches Nationalkomitee für Denkmalschutz (ed.), *Tagung Mauer und Grenze – Denkmal und Gedenken*, (Vol. 76/2), Bonn 2009, pp. 53 f.
4
Möbius/Trotnow (eds.), *Mauern*, p. 12.
5
The inner wall, signal fence, some of the lamp posts and watchtowers in the section between Ackerstrasse and Bergstrasse had already been dismantled by September 1990. Parts of the watchtower were moved to the Allied Museum and remounted there in an altered form (see Ausschreibung Architektonisch-künstlerischer Wettbewerb Gedenkstätte Berliner Mauer in der Bernauer Straße, 1994, pp. 3 f.). Only the patrol path and border wall were still completely intact in this section. See also Ronny Heidenreich, "Eine Mauer für die Welt – Inszenierungen außerhalb Deutschlands nach 1989," in: Klaus-Dietmar Henke (ed.), *Die Mauer – Errichtung, Überwindung, Erinnerung,* Munich 2011, pp. 442 f.

6
Architektonisch-künstlerischer Ideenwettbewerb Gedenkstätte Berliner Mauer in der Bernauer Straße, Ausschreibung, p. 6 f.
7
Ibid., p. 27.
8
Ibid., Protokoll des Preisgerichts pp. 24 – 25. The winners were Susanne Winkler/Stefan Thiel (Berlin), Kohlhoff + Kohlhoff (Stuttgart) and Markus Antonius Bühren/Markus Maria Schulz (Allensbach).
9
Vorprüfbericht zum Wettbewerb, Beschreibung der Arbeit Nr. 90 (Kohlhoff + Kohlhoff) unpag.
10
Carola Rudnick, *Die andere Hälfte der Erinnerung*, Bielefeld 2011, p. 603.
11
Berliner Morgenpost, "In Gottes Namen – Abriss der Mauer an der Bernauer Straße," April 17, 1997.
12
Rudnick, *Die andere Hälfte*, p. 606 f.
13
Evangelische Versöhnungsgemeinde, Ensemble *"Berliner Mauer" – Vorschlag für einen Konsens*, unpublished manuscript, Berlin 1997; also informative: Gabriele Camphausen/Manfred Fischer, "Die bürgerschaftliche Durchsetzung der Gedenkstätte an der Bernauer Strasse," in: Henke (ed.), *Die Mauer*, pp. 367 f.

14
Volkhard Knigge, "Vom Zeugniswert der authentischen Substanz für die Gedenkstättenarbeit," in: Axel Klausmeier/Günter Schlusche (eds.), *Denkmalpflege für die Berliner Mauer*, Berlin 2011, pp. 65 f.
15
Verein Berliner Mauer (ed.), *Berliner Mauer – Gedenkstätte, Dokumentationszentrum und Versöhnungskapelle in der Bernauer Straße*, Berlin 1999, pp. 21 f.; Verein Berliner Mauer (ed.), *Die Berliner Mauer – Ausstellungskatalog Dokumentationszentrum Berliner Mauer*, Dresden, revised (2002).
16
Petra Bahr, *Die Kapelle der Versöhnung*, Berlin/Lindenberg 2008; Günter Schlusche, *Gedenkstätte Berliner Mauer Berlin*, Regensburg 2008, p. 15.
17
Philipp Oswalt, *Stadt ohne Form*, Munich 2000, pp. 190 f.
18
Thomas Flierl, "Einführung," in: *turm, Dokumentationszentrum Berliner Mauer – Zerr Hapke Nieländer*, Berlin 2004, (p. 2).
19
Beschluss des Berliner Senats vom 18. 5. 1999 zum Planwerk Innenstadt Berlin.

20
Harald Bodenschatz, "Planwerk Innenstadt Berlin. Eine Bestandsaufnahme" in: Architektenkammer Berlin (ed.), *Planwerk Innenstadt Berlin – Eine Provokation*, Berlin 1997, p. 111.
21
Bezirksamt Mitte von Berlin (ed.), *Rosenthaler Vorstadt – Zwischenbilanz und Ausblick*, Berlin 2005. Rahmenplan p. 33. The apartment building at Strelitzer Str. 28 was completed in 1999. It was built on the patrol path and has the protected legal right to remain standing. The property, however, is designated memorial grounds in the new development planning design 1 – 40 a.
22
See Konrad Jarausch, *Stellungnahme des Zentrums für Zeithistorische Forschung Potsdam zum Entwurf des Gedenkkonzepts Berliner Mauer*, 2005; other good examples include reports by Frédéric Edelman/Cengiz Bektas/Giorgio Muratore, in: *Stadtbauwelt 154* (Bauwelt 24), Berlin 2002.
23
Thomas Flierl, "Dokumentation, Information und Gedenken," in: Thomas Flierl, *Berlin. Perspektiven durch Kultur*, Berlin 2007, p. 131.
24
Axel Klausmeier/Leo Schmidt, *Mauerreste – Mauerspuren*, Berlin/Bonn 2005, p. 13.

25
Decision of the Berlin Senate, 3710/06, 20.6.2006, General Concept for the Commemoration of the Berlin Wall, Documentation Information Commemoration and Bundestag Decision, 30.6.2005 Printed matter 15/4795.
26
Decision of the Berlin Senate, 20.9.2005 und Senatsverwaltung für Stadtentwicklung, explanatory statement and development plan 1-40, Berlin 2007, p.3.
27
In the expert opinion report "Städtebauliche Studie für den Mauerstreifen Bernauer Str. zwischen Brunnen- und Schwedter Str.," compiled by the Senate in 2007, the concept by the Berlin architects Georg/Scheel/Wetzel was selected and used as the framework for fringe building development in the extended area.
28
The positive vote from the Sabrow Commission that the federal government established to investigate the SED dictatorship was influential. In the commission's final report, it recommended a special research focus on "division and border," assigning the Berlin Wall Memorial a central role in this. See Martin Sabrow/Rainer Eckert/Monika Flacke et al. (eds.), *Wohin treibt die DDR-Erinnerung? Dokumentation einer Debatte*, Göttingen 2007, pp. 17 – 19.

29
Senatsverwaltung für Stadtentwicklung, Resolution minutes of the open competition for realizing the building construction, open space and exhibition of the Berlin Wall Memorial expansion, Berlin 2008, p. 24.
30
The total costs to cover the purchase of property and leasing was 17.5 million euros. The open-air exhibition was paid for through 4 million euros from the federal and state program "Gemeinschaftsaufgabe Verbesserung der regionalen Wirtschaftsstruktur" and 5.6 million euros from the EU fund for regional development, the German federal government's memorial sites fund (BKM) and the state of Berlin (Stiftung Deutsche Klassenlotterie). The 2.45 million euros to build the Visitor Center was provided by federal and state funds. The remodeling of the Documentation Center was funded through 2.3 million euros from Berlin state funds. The new permanent exhibition was funded by ca. 0,75 million euros from the German federal government's memorial sites fund. The Foundation received special funding in 2009 to restore the preserved sections of the border wall and inner wall. The funds from Berlin came from the assets from the former "Party and Mass Organisations of the GDR" (PMO funds) – a certain irony of history.

31
Gerhard Sälter, Tina Schaller (eds.), *Grenz- und Geisterbahnhöfe im geteilten Berlin*, Berlin 2013.
32
It was not possible to secure the return of the watchtower that had been reassembled in a modified form from different watchtowers and erected at the Allied Museum in Zehlendorf because it had become an important, highly valued artifact of the museum. Instead, a watchtower of the same type that had stood in southeast of Berlin on the former radio operator barracks of the NVA in Spreenhagen was moved to Ackerstrasse.
33
Senatsverwaltung für Stadtentwicklung und Umwelt, Building development on Bernauer Strasse – Planning Information (Information brochure), Berlin 2012. The brochure describes the implementation of the building development concept created by the Berlin architects Georg/Scheel/Wetzel and revised following the mediation process. A design advisory board,of which the Berlin Wall Foundation is also a part, meets regularly and helps supervise the project.
34
David Rowland/Marc Hartmann, "Entschädigung im neuen Gewand," in: Aufbau New York, Vol. LXII, No. 24, 22. 11. 96, pp. 1 – 2.; see also: www. rowlandlaw.com.

35
This was possible on the basis of an administrative agreement between the federal government and the state of Berlin which also regulated the cooperation with the federal real estate agency in charge of federal properties. The necessary purchase of land was also supported by the real estate fund of the state of Berlin.
36
Grün Berlin GmbH, *Die Gedenkstätte Berliner Mauer und der Berliner Mauerweg*, Berlin 2013 (information brochure); Senatsverwaltung für Stadtentwicklung und Umwelt, Grünes Band Berlin, Berlin 2012 (information brochure); Michael Cramer, *Berliner Mauer-Radweg*, Rodingersdorf 2004 (bike tour book).

Model reflecting urban
development on Brunnenstrasse,
2013
Berthold Weidner

Pastor Manfred Fischer †

Pastor Manfred Fischer in the Chapel of Reconcilation, 2009
unknown photographer

"It is not the only wall in the world. It is a very extreme example of what exists throughout the world. Here one can see: It has to fail. What belongs together cannot simply be separated. A time will come when attempts to build a wall, to divide, become more common in a world that is drawing closer together. People should come here and take a look at this and learn: it has to fail."

DFF, Deutsches Rundfunkarchiv, 13.8.1990

Manfred Fischer studied Protestant theology in Frankfurt and at the Kirchliche Hochschule in Berlin and became pastor of the Reconciliation parish on Bernauer Strasse in 1977. He served in this position for more than 36 years. His congregation was separated from its church when the Wall was erected. Overnight the church found itself situated within the border grounds and inaccessible to the public. It was dynamited by the GDR border troops in January 1985. In the early 1990s, Manfred Fischer began campaigning to preserve the remnants of the Berlin Wall on Bernauer Strasse. For many years he served, first as deputy and later as chairman, on the board of the Berlin Wall Association, promoting the creation of a memorial site. From the outset, he was the guiding spirit of the Berlin Wall Memorial and played a pivotal role in developing the proposal for the memorial, which was passed by the Senate in June 2006. Under his direction, the Chapel of Reconciliation was constructed on the foundations of the razed church. Pastor Manfred Fischer died on December 6, 2013.

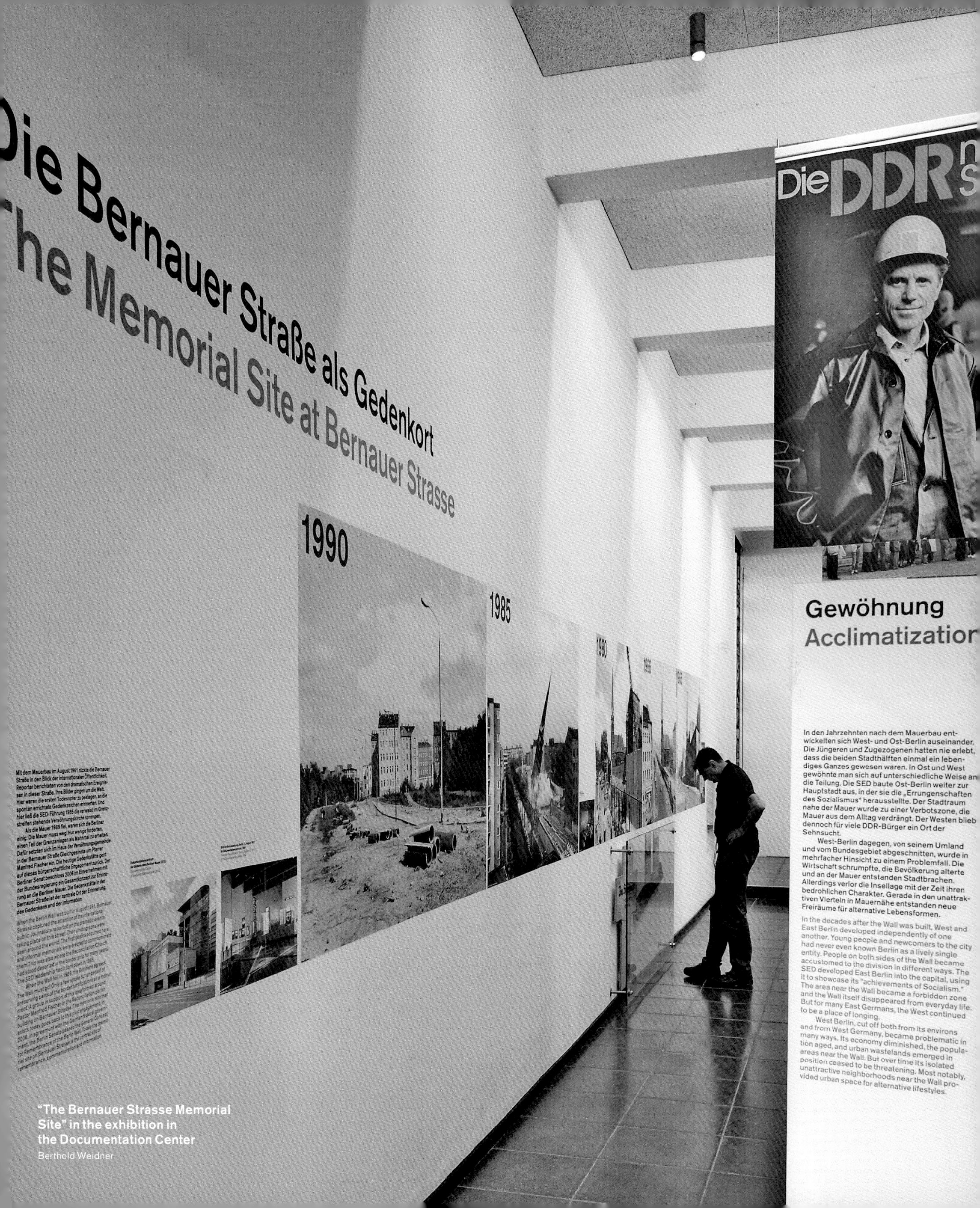

"The Bernauer Strasse Memorial Site" in the exhibition in the Documentation Center
Berthold Weidner

Monument and Documentation
Center on Bernauer Strasse, 2015
Berthold Weidner

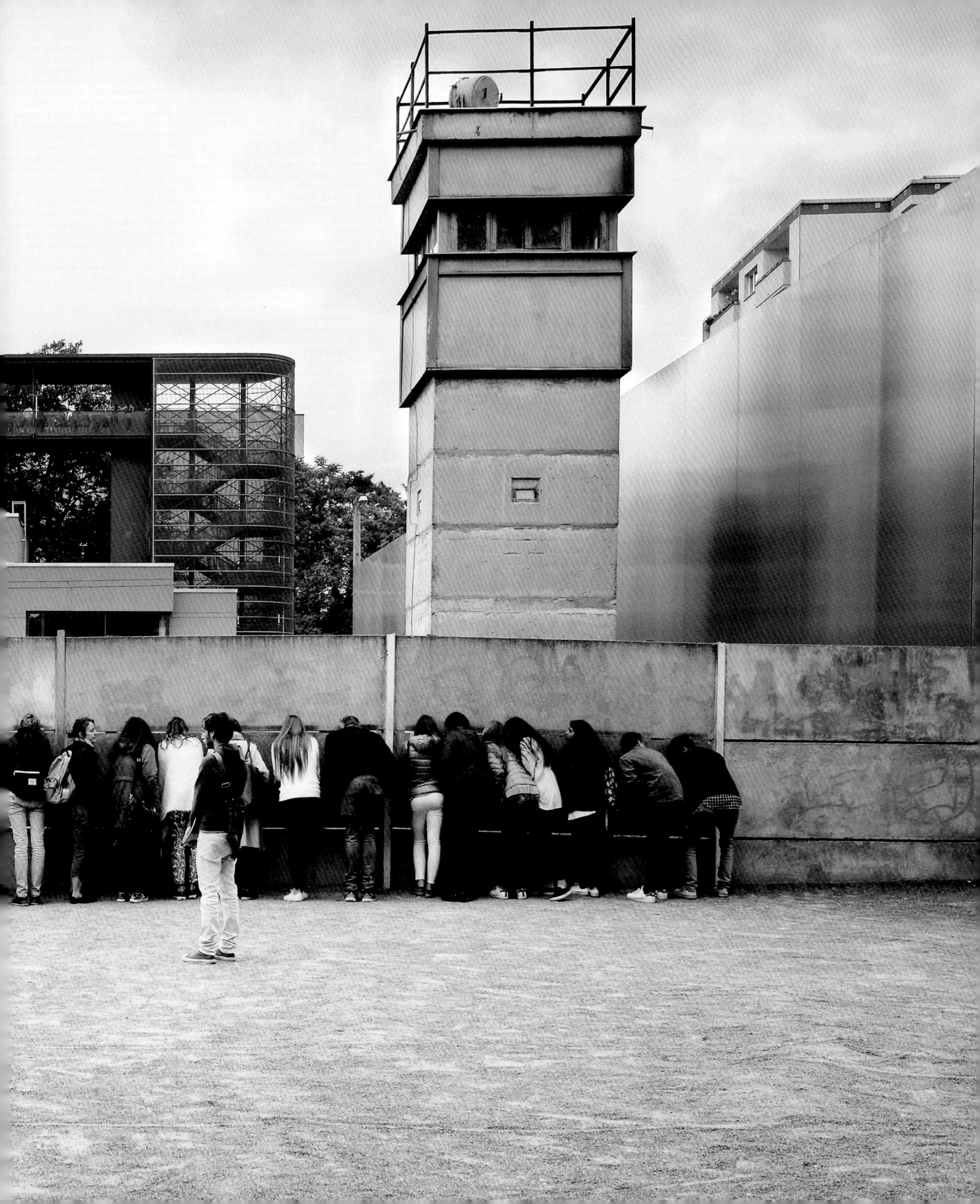

Permanent Exhibition in the Documentation Center on Bernauer Strasse 111

**"1961 I 1989 The Berlin Wall,"
exhibition in the Documentation
Center , 2015**
Christian Fuchs

Aufbegehren
Rebellion

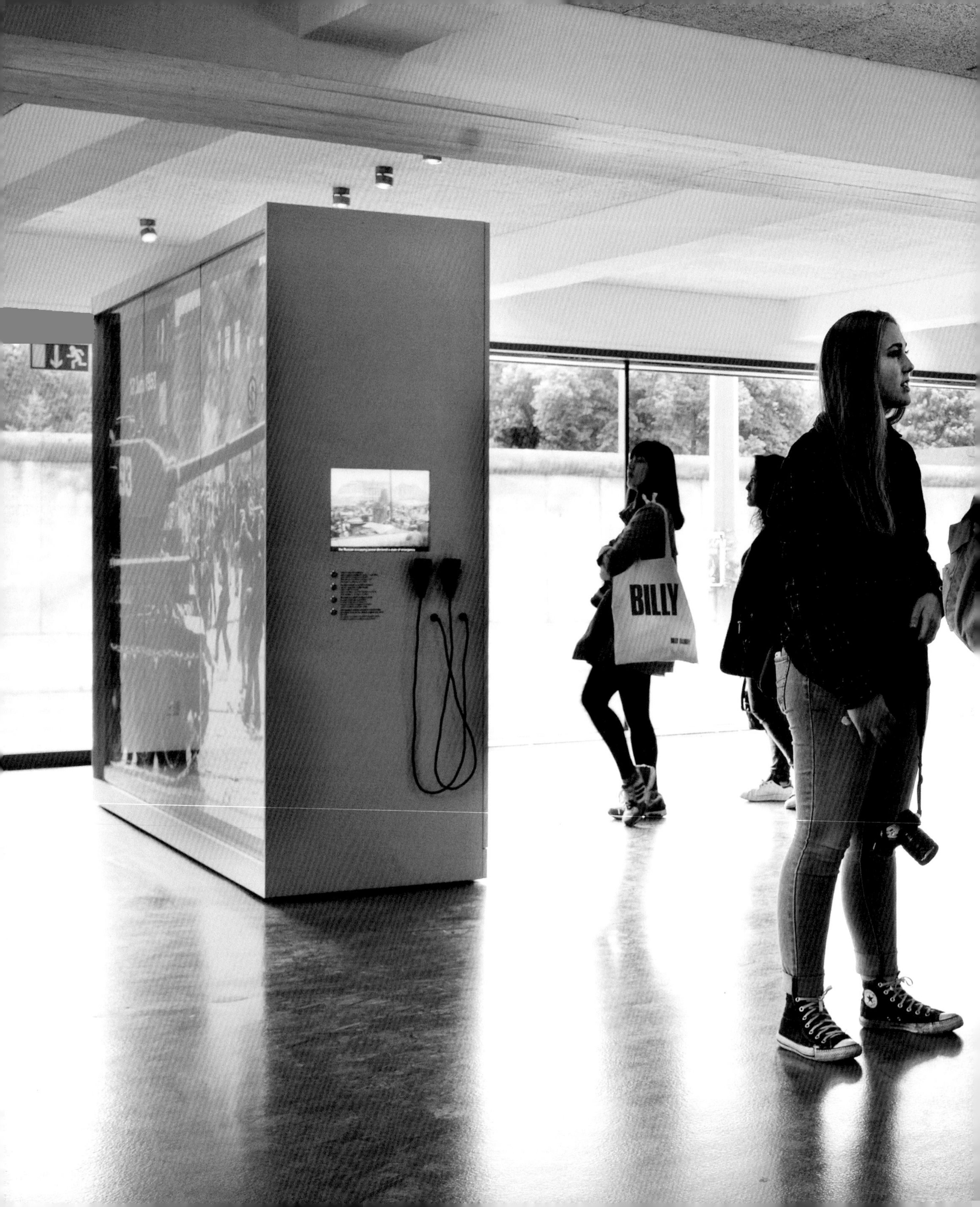
BILLY

West-Berlin, 1963

Visitors in the exhibition in the
Documentation Center, 2015
Berthold Weidner

1
Leading Up to the Berlin Wall

National uprising on June 17, 1953
Demonstrators throw stones
at Soviet tanks

Schirner, ullstein bild

Division of East and West

Berlin soon became a trouble spot of the Cold War. The Soviet Union tried to force the Western powers out of the city by blocking ground access to West Berlin in 1948/49. Although the blockade failed, it left Berlin politically divided. With the support of the Soviet military administration, the SED took over control of the eastern part of the city. The local parliament and city government were separated into East and West. East Berlin, the administrative center of the Soviet occupation zone, became the capital of the GDR in 1949. The Western Allies maintained sovereignty in West Berlin, which was situated like an island in the middle of the "east zone." It remained politically separate from the Federal Republic (West Germany), which was founded in 1949.

Ernst Reuter's speech in front of the Reichstag, September 9, 1948
unknown photographer, Presse- und Informationsamt der Bundesregierung

SED demonstrators block the city council, September 6, 1948
The Social Democratic Party (SPD) won the majority in the city council elections in 1946 and formed a government. After SED supporters made its work in the Soviet sector impossible, the city parliament moved to the British sector. At a rally in West Berlin, Ernst Reuter, soon to become mayor, appealed to the Western world not to abandon Berlin to the Soviets.
unknown photographer, ullstein bild

Shako with West Berlin police emblem, 1950s and shako with East Berlin police emblem, 1950s
Paul Markgraf, appointed chief of police in 1945, tolerated the arbitrary deportation of civilians by the Soviet occupying power. The city administration had him replaced in July 1948. But the Soviet occupying power refused to recognize Johannes Stumm as the new police chief. The division of the police force paved the way for the division of the entire city administration.
Stiftung Berliner Mauer

Everyday Life in the Occupied City

At first the political division of Berlin had little impact on everyday life in the city, but over time the municipal infrastructure was also divided: garbage collection in 1948, telephone lines in 1952, tram lines in 1953. Berliners, however, were still able to cross the sector border. The lingering connections between the two city halves were a frequent source of friction and conflict. The SED was particularly annoyed by the border crossers who commuted to work in West Berlin and earned western money. In preparation of building the Wall, a propaganda campaign targeted these so-called egoists and freeloaders.

East Berlin police check people crossing the sector border in Berlin-Kreuzberg, July 4, 1953
Before the Wall was built, crossing the sector border between West and East Berlin was not a problem. Checks were carried out on a random basis.
unknown photographer,
Polizeihistorische Sammlung Berlin

West Berlin poster against shopping on the east side of the city, 1950
As of 1950, West Berlin politicians and media began a campaign against buying goods in East Berlin. They didn't want the political opponent to benefit from the West German D-mark.
Bundesarchiv

Crowd in front of the border cinema "Camera" announcing a discount for "eastern visitors," 1950s
Border cinemas were located on the sector boundary in West Berlin and were very popular among East Berliners. Beginning in 1950, they showed German "Heimat" films and westerns that were not permitted in the GDR.
Stephanie Foss-Hoffstedde

Dictatorship and Mass Exodus

In the first and only democratic elections held in 1946 in the Soviet occupied zone and in Berlin, the democratic parties found themselves subjected to strong pressure. The SED fell short of an absolute majority. However, with the help of the Soviet occupying power, it was able to assert its autocratic rule nevertheless. In 1952, the SED leadership announced the "scheduled plan to build up socialism." This campaign brought with it greater expropriation of businesses, more disadvantages for the self-employed, a struggle against the church and the forced collectivization of rural agriculture. The intensified class struggle from above led hundreds and thousands of people to flee to the West. The mass exodus reached a peak after the failed national uprising on June 17, 1953. Refugees found shelter in several makeshift camps in West Berlin. The Marienfelde Refugee Center officially opened in 1953.

State of emergency declared by the Soviet commander in Berlin, June 17, 1953
An increase in work norms prompted a national uprising that quickly spread through the GDR. Demonstrators demanded that the government step down and free elections be held. The uprising was put down by Soviet tanks.
Landesarchiv Berlin

Miller Wolfgang Kuhn's escape suitcase, 1960
Approximately 2.6 million people fled to the West from the GDR between 1949 and 1961. One of them was the miller Wolfgang Kuhn. He went through the admissions procedure for East German refugees in the Marienfelde refugee camp in West Berlin. He was later flown to West Germany.
Stiftung Berliner Mauer

Propaganda panel on the total collectivization of Marxwalde, 1960
Beginning in 1952, the SED propagated the idea that farmers become part of agricultural production cooperatives (LPG). In 1960, the SED forced the remaining independent farmers into the LPG. That is when many farmers decided to flee. It was claimed that all the farmers in Marxwalde voluntarily joined the LPG within two days.
unknown photographer, akg-images

Dormitory room in the Siegfriedstrasse refugee camp, 1950s
unknown photographer, Stiftung Berliner Mauer

Leading Up to the Berlin Wall
Karl Wilhelm Fricke

"Yes, Berlin in the first half of the 1950s […], Berlin, naturally, was a focus of the Cold War. The mood within the population was also marked by the solidarity felt with the people in East Berlin; in the GDR […], the mood was also highly politicized."

Interview, Stiftung Berliner Mauer, 2012

Karl Wilhelm Fricke was born in 1929 and studied political science in the early fifties in West Berlin. He had already begun addressing the GDR in journalistic work at this time. In 1955 these articles led to his abduction to East Berlin by employees of the Ministry of State Security. They drugged him and drove him across the sector border. He was tried before the Supreme Court of the GDR and sentenced to four years in prison. Released to West Berlin in 1959, Karl Wilhelm Fricke worked again as a newspaper and radio journalist in Hamburg and Cologne. He continued to focus on the GDR and the political repression of the SED regime.

Kay Kufeke

Berlin Before the Wall
The Occupied City from 1945 to 1961

Germany's post-war era was marked by the defeat of National Socialism in World War II. The Allied powers – the United States, Great Britain, France and the Soviet Union – divided the country into four zones of occupation. Soon, however, important differences between the Western Allies and the Soviet Union became evident. The ensuing conflict grew into a "cold war" that ultimately divided Europe into two spheres of influence, the East and the West. The border between these two power blocs, which became permanent in the 1950s, ran right through Germany. Berlin, which had been separated into four sectors in 1945, was now divided into two halves and acquired a special role within this global political constellation. Everyday life in Berlin continued to be strongly influenced by the Cold War and the east-west conflict until 1989.[1]

The agreements made by the Allied powers in the London Protocol of September 1944 and at the Potsdam Conference in July 1945 set the foundation for Berlin's division. They called for the division of Germany into four zones of occupation and Berlin into four sectors. An Allied Control Council was responsible for making decisions on issues that concerned Germany as a whole; an Allied Kommandatura addressed matters pertaining to Berlin. Because the former Allies were unable to agree on a number of issues and all decisions had to be made unanimously, the decision-making process came to a deadlock in 1948. The Soviet representatives left both the Control Council and Kommandatura. In theory, Berlin's four-power status and the Allied government continued to exist until 1990. In truth, however, the city had been split into two separate parts: an East Berlin and a West Berlin. The sector boundaries became borders between two different political systems.[2]

The conflict between the three Western powers and the Soviet Union was also played out in Berlin. With help from the Soviet Military Administration, the Communist Party (KPD) took control of all power centers within the local government. As it became clear that the Communist Party was not going to achieve an absolute majority in the upcoming local elections for all of Berlin in October 1946, the Social Democratic Party was forced to merge with it to form the Socialist Unity Party (SED) in April 1946. But even with the newly founded SED, which only existed in the Soviet zone of occupation and in East Berlin, the Social Democrats (SPD) managed to win 48.7 % of the votes.[3] Through political pressure and repressive measures aimed at individual politicians, the SED forced all the bourgeois parties in East Berlin and in the Soviet occupation zone to fall into line with its political platform. In 1947, the Soviet occupying power rejected the city council's choice of Ernst Reuter (SPD) as mayor of Berlin. After the majority of the city parliament moved from the Soviet sector to the British sector in September 1948, the political division was complete. The municipal administrations soon separated as well.[4]

The political partition was followed by an economic division: in 1948, the Western Allies introduced a new currency into its three Western zones of occupation. At first the new German mark (D-Mark) remained invalid in Berlin. But after the four powers failed to agree on a jointly controlled currency for all of Berlin, the Soviet Union introduced a new currency in East Berlin for the Soviet zone. Henceforth the D-Mark, with a "B" printed on it, was also accepted in West Berlin.[5] The Soviet Union responded to the currency reform in the Western occupation zones and in West Berlin by blocking access routes to the Western sectors on June 24, 1948. The aim of the Berlin Blockade was to prevent food and coal from being delivered to West Berlin and to force the Western Allies out of the city. Instead, the Western Allies established an airlift to secure the provision of supplies to the city. The blockade that was maintained for almost an

Four occupation zones including Berlin, 1945
Stiftung Berliner Mauer

Berliners watching an airlift plane land, 1948
unknown photographer, ullstein bild

Border Police illustration of the "ring around Berlin," 1956
Stiftung Berliner Mauer

Banner on the sector boundary, 1949, "Here: democracy and the building of peace; There: dictatorship, war mongering, collapse."
Fiebig, Bildarchiv Preußischer Kulturbesitz

entire year failed and was lifted by the Soviets in May 12, 1949. The division of the city was now permanent. West Berlin was officially separated from the surrounding areas and economically dependent on the Federal Republic that had been founded in late May 1949. Politically, West Berlin was still under the control of the Western powers. East Berlin was declared the capital of the GDR in October of that year. The Soviet Union and the SED's attempt to gain control of all of Berlin had failed.

In the first decade after the war, the political and economic division of the city was followed by the gradual separation of garbage collection services, the electrical power supply, telephone lines and tram routes.[6] The S-Bahn commuter train service, which was operated by the GDR Reichsbahn, continued to run through all of Berlin without interruption. Additionally, both the inner-city sector boundaries and the outer-ring border between West Berlin and the Soviet Zone/GDR remained open and accessible. In May 1952, the GDR closed off the inner German border on the basis of the "decree on measures regarding the demarcation line between the German Democratic Republic and the Western occupation zones." The streets running between West Berlin and the Soviet zone were also blocked off and the number of checkpoints was reduced. West Berliners were no longer allowed to drive into the countryside without a travel permit. People leaving the Soviet zone and entering the eastern sector of Berlin were also subject to police controls. The GDR People's Police (later the border police) formed a "ring around Berlin," completely enclosing the city as of autumn 1948.[7] To end its dependence on railway connections running through West Berlin, the GDR began constructing an outer ring in 1950. The ring, completed in 1956, made it possible to completely circumvent West Berlin.[8]

The inner-city border remained open to passenger and goods traffic until August 1961 when the Wall was erected. Until then, it was still common for residents of East Berlin to attend musical performances in the "Sportpalast" in West Berlin or for West Berliners to spend an evening at the "Komische Oper," an opera house in East Berlin. The "border cinemas" located on the West Berlin side of the sector boundaries were also frequented by East Berliners. On the suggestion of the U.S. occupation administration, movie houses began featuring special films for East Berliners at reduced prices. It was hoped that news reports shown before the main feature would have a Western influence on the Eastern members of the audience. The Berlin Senate granted tax subsidies to twenty to twenty-five "border cinemas."[9]

There were West Berliners who worked in the East and East Berliners who worked in the West. It is estimated that shortly before the Wall was built, approximately 60,000 East Berliners crossed the border regularly to work in the West. The wages of these commuters were partially paid in D-Marks. In October 1960, these workers became the target of administrative discrimination and public denunciation. The SED regime accused them of putting their own interests before the good of the GDR economy, which was suffering a labor shortage. In 1961, shortly before the Wall was built, the GDR authorities prohibited commuter traffic to West Berlin and demanded that border commuters find work in the GDR.[10] Conflict also erupted in West Berlin over unrestricted east-west traffic. In a political campaign, the West Berlin media criticized West Berliners who bought their bread and other food in East Berlin, where it was cheaper. The rivalry of the Cold War even affected Berliners in their daily matters.[11]

But let us take a brief look back: Both the Federal Republic and the GDR were founded in 1949. The SED declared East Berlin the capital of the GDR; in West Berlin, however, the Western Allies maintained sovereignty. But the laws of the Federal Republic were often adopted in Berlin and Berlin delegates sat in the German Bundestag, albeit without the right to vote. Both sides of the city saw themselves in a "front position" on behalf of their political system: West Berlin was the "front city" in the struggle against communism; the East served as a thriving example of the advantages of socialism.[12]

193

Border patrol on the 10-meter security strip along the B173 (F173) near Ullitz
left: Customs border duty;
right: Two guards from the German border police, autumn 1952
Joachim Vollert,
Deutsch-Deutsches Museum Mödlareuth

The plan to "build up socialism" in the GDR, proclaimed by the SED in July 1952, caused a crisis. Since the end of the war, millions of people who had been expelled from their countries had been searching for relatives and work, especially in the Western zones of occupation. Those in possession of an inter-zone passport were permitted to travel, but most people simply crossed the "Green Border" without a passport. After the GDR was founded and the policies of the SED became increasingly repressive, large numbers of East German citizens immigrated to the West, setting off a mass exodus. A border police was established in 1946 to better control the inner German border between the Soviet occupation zone and the Western zones. In 1952, the GDR erected barbed-wire fences along the border. At the same time, the approximately 4,000 residents living within the border area were declare "unsafe" and forced to resettle in new areas away from the border.[13]

About a year later, on June 16 and 17, 1953, an increase in expected work output in the GDR led to a workers' protest that quickly escalated. Protestors demanded political reforms from the SED leadership. The SED Politburo sought protection within the headquarters of the Soviet occupying power and a state of siege was declared. The workers' protest, which had evolved into a people's uprising and had spread throughout the entire country, was put down with force. It was only with the help of the Soviet Union that the SED was able to reassert its power.[14] After the border was closed and the popular uprising suppressed, the SED began to systematically discriminate against farmers, craftsmen and independent professionals. This caused an exodus to the Federal Republic to flare up intermittently throughout the 1950s. A campaign to collectivize agriculture was introduced with the plan to have Agricultural Production Cooperatives (LPG) established by the spring of 1960. Within a very short period, the SED forced the remaining independent farmers to join the LPGs, once again setting off an exodus to the West.[15]

The SED initially regarded the exodus positively, believing it was getting rid of socialism's enemies. Over the course of the 1950s, however, it was forced to acknowledge that important groups of professionals and workers were leaving. By August 1961, approximately 2.6 million people – a sixth of the East German population – had fled. This was a growing problem that threatened the future existence of the GDR.

The crisis focused on Berlin: After the border fortifications were erected on the inner German border between the Federal Republic and the GDR, large numbers of East Germans used the inner-city border that was still open to flee to West Berlin. This led to an increase in the number of reception camps established for GDR refugees in West Berlin.[16] In late July 1961, as many as 2,000 refugees were arriving in West Berlin each day and they had no intention of returning to the eastern side of the city. The economic situation in the GDR had been in rapid decline since the spring of 1961 and the government was finding it increasingly difficult to provide basic supplies to its citizens. The GDR had been drained and there was no certainty that it would survive the crisis.

1
Michael Lemke, "Die Berlinkrisen von 1948/49 und 1958 bis 1963" in: Bernd Greiner et al. (eds.), *Krisen im Kalten Krieg*, Hamburg 2008, pp. 204–243, p. 204.
2
Wolfgang Ribbe, "Das gespaltene Berlin. Ein historischer Überblick (1945-1990)," in: Michael C. Bienert/Uwe Schaper/Hermann Wentker (eds.), *Hauptstadtanspruch und symbolische Politik*, pp. 33–97, pp. 33–35.
3
Helga Grebing/Siegfried Heimann (eds.), *Arbeiterbewegung in Berlin*, Berlin 2012, p. 105; see Kay Kufeke, "Kalter Krieg im Prenzlauer Berg. Die Durchsetzung der SED-Herrschaft 1945-1949," in: *Prenzlauer, Ecke Fröbelstrasse. Hospital der Reichshauptstadt, Haftort der Geheimdienste, Bezirksamt Prenzlauer Berg*, Berlin 2006, pp. 65–96.
4
Ribbe, *Das gespaltene Berlin*, p. 43–44; Michael Lemke, *Vor der Mauer. Berlin in der Ost-West-Konkurrenz 1948 bis 1961*, Cologne/Weimar/Vienna 2011, p. 53.
5
Ribbe, *Das gespaltene Berlin*, p. 50 f.
6
Lemke, *Vor der Mauer*, p. 59.
7
Gerhard Sälter, *Grenzpolizisten. Konformität, Verweigerung und Repression in der Grenzpolizei und den Grenztruppen der DDR 1952–1965*, Berlin 2009, pp. 38–40.
8
Axel Klausmeier, *Hinter der Mauer. Zur militärischen und baulichen Infrastruktur des Grenzkommandos Mitte*, Berlin 2012, p. 45.
9
Lemke, *Vor der Mauer*, pp. 495–496.
10
Frank Roggenbuch, *Das Berliner Grenzgängerproblem. Verflechtung und Systemkonkurrenz vor dem Mauerbau*, Berlin/New York 2008, pp. 347–349, pp. 365–367.
11
Lemke, *Vor der Mauer*, pp. 353–357
12
Ibid., *Vor der Mauer*, p. 37.
13
Inge Bennewitz/Rainer Potratz, *Zwangsaussiedlungen an der innerdeutschen Grenze*, 3rd edition, Berlin 2002, pp. 41–42.
14
Jens Schöne, *Volksaufstand. Der 17. Juni 1953 in Berlin und der DDR*, Berlin 2013, pp. 85–87.
15
Jens Schöne, *Frühling auf dem Lande? Die Kollektivierung der DDR-Landwirtschaft*, 2nd edition, Berlin 2007, pp. 194–196.
16
Manfred Wilke, *Der Weg zur Mauer. Stationen der Teilungsgeschichte*, Berlin 2012, p. 80, p. 252; Enrico Heitzer, "'Glücklich, dass wenigstens jeder Flüchtling in Berlin ein Dach über dem Kopf hat.' Notaufnahmelager für Flüchtlinge aus der SBZ/DDR in West-Berlin bis 1961," in: Henrik Bispinck/Katharina Hochmuth (eds.), *Flüchtlingslager im Nachkriegsdeutschland. Migration, Politik, Erinnerung*, Berlin 2014, pp. 164–189.

"Escape and Escape Assistance"
in the exhibition in the
Documentation Center
Berthold Weidner

Stabilisierung
The Situation Stabilizes

Auswirkungen auf West-Berlin
Consequences for West Berlin

Spaltung in Ost und
Division of East and

> # 2
> # Building the Wall

**Barbed wire is replaced by walls,
August 15, 1961**
Jung, ullstein bild

Escalation of the Crisis
By threatening to sign a separate peace treaty with the GDR in November 1958, the Soviet Union tried to force the three Western powers to withdraw from Berlin. But the Allies insisted on their rights and their presence in Berlin. The SED leadership was especially eager for the peace treaty, hoping to strengthen the GDR's national sovereignty. Given the mass exodus, it feared for the future of its country. When the Western powers remained firm, the Soviet leader Nikita Khrushchev and the GDR leader Walter Ulbricht agreed to close the border to West Berlin. In July 1961, Khrushchev gave the go-ahead for this momentous measure.

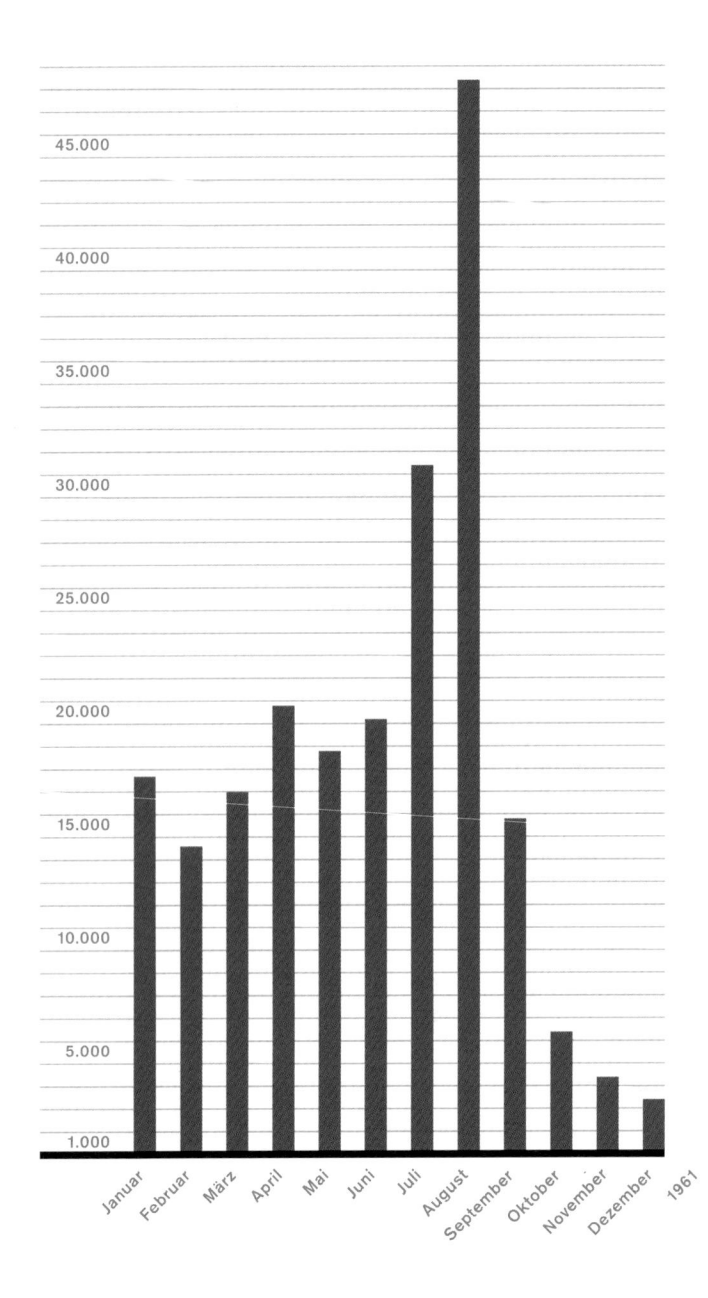

Refugee movement from the GDR in 1961
according to Wolle, Stefan: Aufbruch in die Stagnation. Die DDR in den Sechzigerjahren, Bonn 2005, Stiftung Berliner Mauer

Sealed Off

In the early morning hours of Sunday, August 13, 1961, the first steps were taken to close off the border to West Berlin. The East German police and worker militias erected barbed wire entanglements along the sector boundary. Most border crossings were made impassable. The operation was militarily charged: some distance from the border, units of the GDR national army were concentrated around Berlin; Soviet troops were placed on alert. The governments of East Berlin and Moscow wanted to be prepared both for a conflict with the Western powers as well as for an uprising.

People in East Berlin watch as Strelitzer Strasse is blocked off, August 14, 1961
Horst Siegmann, Landesarchiv Berlin

People in West Berlin watch as the border is closed near Potsdamer Platz, August 13, 1961
Schirner, Deutsches Historisches Museum

Reactions

The people in East and West Berlin watched in disbelief as the border was closed off. Crowds stood at the barriers, seeking contact with friends and family on the other side of the barbed wire fence. Only the West Berliners were able to vent their outrage openly. In East Berlin the SED suppressed all criticism, even from within its own ranks. The SED demanded the population's explicit approval. In the first days, several people ran hastily through the temporary barriers. There were some who hoped that the Western powers, in particular the Americans, would intervene militarily. But the position of the Allies in Berlin was not directly affected and they wanted to avoid a war, hence their action was limited to verbal protest.

Mass exodus at Potsdamer Platz, August 13, 1961
Hidden within the crowd, a few young men were able to cut through the border fence. Several East Berliners spontaneously decided to flee through the opening. But border guards quickly intervened.
Patrice Habans, Getty Images

An East Berliner swims across the Landwehrkanal to the West Berlin embankment, August 13, 1961
Lintow, ullstein bild

The East German police document the gatherings and protests by East and West Berliners at the border barriers, August 13, 1961
Landesarchiv Berlin

The East German border police use water canons to disperse protestors on the west side of the Wall, August 28, 1961
unknown photographer,
Zentralbild, Deutsches Historisches Museum

Building the Wall
Joachim Neumann

"In general I have to say that after the Wall was built – over a period of many weeks – the feeling kept growing: Now you are really locked up, now you are walled in."

Interview, Stiftung Berliner Mauer, 2012

Joachim Neumann was born in 1939 and studied civil engineering in Cottbus in the late 1950s. He was vacationing with friends on the Baltic Sea when the Wall was built. Thinking that the division of Berlin could not possibly be permanent, he returned to Cottbus. But the increased political pressure and his desire to evade serving in the National People's Army led Joachim Neumann to flee with a Swiss passport to West Berlin later that year. He continued his studies at the TU Berlin and had helped build several escape tunnels by 1964. He married in 1965. Since then he has built as many as sixty tunnels as a civil engineer.

"Archive of Memory" in the
Documentation Center, 2015
Berthold Weidner

3
Division Becomes Permanent

**The border strip
on Harzer Strasse, 1972**
MfS photo, BStU

The Situation Stabilizes

In August 1961, the SED leadership began to replace the temporary border barriers with walls. The border fortifications formed a broad corridor through the city. The Berlin Wall affected the entire GDR. It stabilized SED rule since people could no longer leave the country. This increased the pressure on the population to acquiesce to the dictatorship. The SED more strongly prosecuted deviant behavior. Feeling its power secure, it soon introduced a compulsory military service. It also initiated reforms in its domestic and economic policies. But the tentative liberalization of culture and youth policies in particular was short-lived.

A bricked-up border house on Harzer Strasse, June 18, 1964
Klaus Lehnartz, Photonet

Brandenburg Gate in East Berlin, 1962
Fritz Eschen, ullstein bild

Demolition of border houses on Bernauer Strasse, 1965
Buildings in the border strip were vacated and torn down to provide East German border troops with an unobstructed view and clear "field of fire." Residents of border houses on Bernauer Strasse had to vacate their homes in the fall of 1961. Demolition began in 1965.
Schütt, ullstein bild

Potsdamer Platz, 1965
Günter Zint

Consequences for West Berlin

The Berlin Wall caused a major rupture in the lives of all Berliners. Before the border was closed, many people crossed the sector boundary to work in the other part of the city, visit friends and relatives, shop, attend movies and go to the theatre. That was over now. It was hard to keep workers and companies in West Berlin. The population decreased, the number of pensioners grew and the economy stagnated. West Berlin continued to be heavily dependent on subsidies from the West German government.

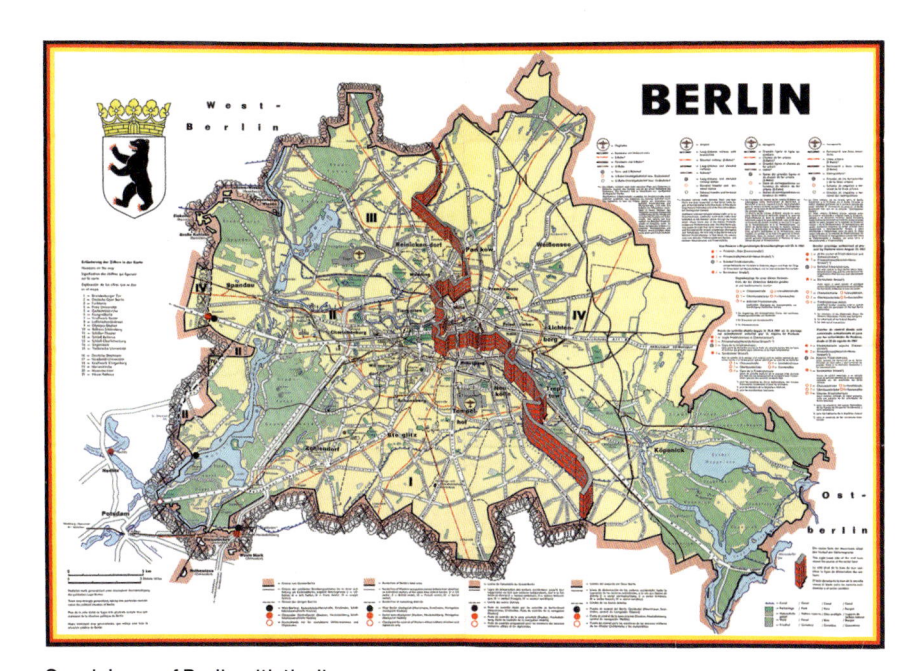

Special map of Berlin with the line of the Wall clearly marked, 1962
Presse- und Informationsamt Berlin /
Stiftung Stadtmuseum Berlin

West Berlin advertises in national newspapers to win commissions for businesses in the city, August 10, 1962
The Berlin Sales Organization (BAO) was founded in 1950. It aimed to prevent business losses in the West Berlin economy. The Berlin Wall made it more difficult to entice business to Berlin.
Christ und Welt, Staatsbibliothek zu Berlin – Preußischer Kulturbesitz

Politics with the Wall

When the Wall was built, the Berlin question was defused and the Berlin crisis ended for both world powers. The Soviet Union refrained from signing a separate peace treaty with the GDR. The United States pursued a policy of détente in Europe. In the global Cold War, other trouble spots came to the fore. West Germany had to adjust to this new reality. Hence, in 1963, the SPD began campaigning for rapprochement policies towards East Germany: its aim was to make "the Wall more permeable." The SED was able to stabilize its rule and emphasized the GDR's national independence. It justified the Wall as a measure to secure peace, declaring it an "anti-fascist protection rampart."

Face-off of tanks at Checkpoint Charlie, October 27, 1961
The tensions in Berlin intensified in October 1961 when the SED leadership restricted the Western Allies' access to East Berlin. American and Soviet tanks pulled up to the sector boundary in a face-off. Both powers withdrew their tanks following negotiations.
unknown photographer,
Bildarchiv Preußischer Kulturbesitz

Parade in East Berlin on the fifth anniversary of the Berlin Wall, August 13, 1966
unknown photographer, AP, ullstein bild

U.S. President John F. Kennedy at the Brandenburg Gate, which the SED had covered for the occasion, June 26, 1963
U.S. President John F. Kennedy's visit to West Berlin was a sign of his commitment. The people in West Berlin gave him an exuberant welcome. Soviet leader Nikita Khrushchev visited East Berlin at about the same time, but was unable to arouse the same enthusiasm.
unknown photographer,
AKG, dpa Picture-Alliance

Escape and Escape Assistance

The SED leadership had hoped that by building the Wall it would put a complete stop to the movement to leave the GDR. Although it did cause the flood of refugees to peter out, people in East Berlin continued to search for ways to get to the West – in a race against the rapid expansion of the border fortifications. They received assistance from escape helpers in West Berlin. With fake passports, converted vehicles and escape tunnels, East Germans persistently succeeded in escaping the SED dictatorship. But they took great risks: The border soldiers had orders to fire at fugitives in extreme circumstances. Those wishing to escape and those who helped them were willing to put their lives at risk.

East German border guards carry the fatally-injured Peter Fechter out of the border strip, August 17, 1962
The escape attempt by the 18-year-old Peter Fechter ended in front of the border wall. He was shot down by border guards without warning. He cried in vain for help. Fifty minutes passed before the border guards carried his lifeless body away.
Wolfgang Bera, ullstein bild

Escape attempt at the Invalidenstrasse border crossing, May 12, 1963
Eight young East Berliners tried to break through the border fortifications in a bus. They were seriously injured by 138 shots fired by the border guards. The fugitives were arrested and sentenced to long prison terms.
unknown photographer, UPI, dpa Picture-Alliance

Hubert Hohlbein digging "Tunnel 57" on Bernauer Strasse, 1964
In November 1963, the 21-year-old Hubert Hohlbein swam at night through the Jungfern Lake to West Berlin. He made some of the diving gear himself. In West Berlin he helped build an escape tunnel through which 57 people were able to flee in October 1964. One of them was his mother.
Donated by Hubert Hohlbein, Stiftung Berliner Mauer

Harry Seidel

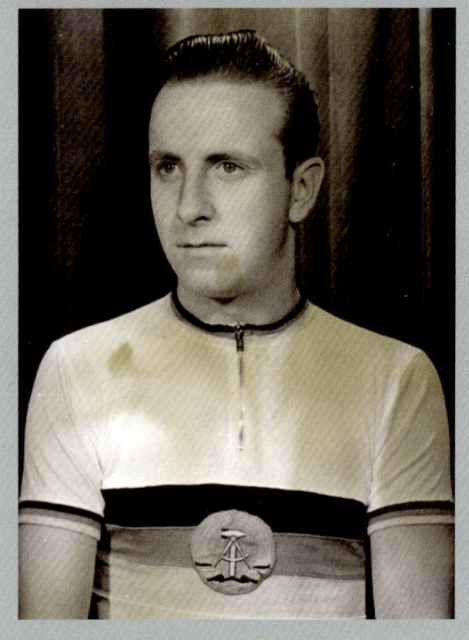

Harry Seidel, 1960
Harry Seidel

1938 Born in Berlin
1961 Escape from East Berlin
1962 Arrest for escape assistance
1966 Release from an East German prison after ransom was paid by the West German government

Harry Seidel was a successful racing cyclist in the GDR, but he was not permitted to participate in the 1960 Olympics. He fled to West Berlin soon after the border was closed. He later crossed the border fortifications several times to help others escape. He was able to get his wife and baby through the barbed wire entanglement. In 1962, he helped dig several escape tunnels. During a tunnel escape in March 1962, he just barely avoided an ambush by the secret police. Heinz Jercha, another escape helper, died from a gunshot wound. In November 1962, the secret police was waiting at the entrance to an escape tunnel again. This time Harry Seidel was arrested. Just six weeks later he was sentenced to life in prison. He had succeeded in bringing 100 people over to the West.

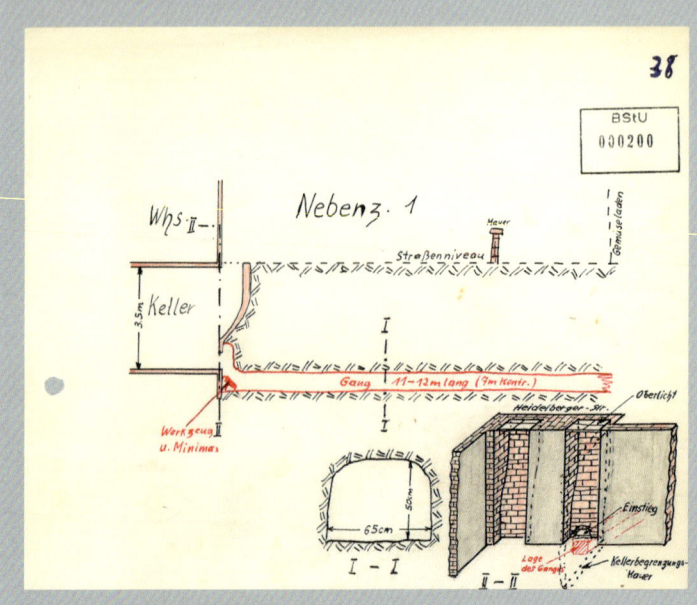

Sketch of the betrayed escape tunnel on Heidelberger Strasse, March 1962
BStU

Siegfried Uhse
IM "Hardy"

Siegfried Uhse, ca. 1961

1940 Born
1958 Escape from East Berlin
1962 Agrees to work as an informant (IM) for the secret police
1977 Breaks off contact with the secret police

Siegfried Uhse, a hairdresser, had lived in West Berlin since 1960. He came into contact with the secret police during a border check at the Friedrichstrasse station in September 1961. After he was recruited as an informant (IM), he established contact with escape helpers in West Berlin. He convinced them that he was looking for an escape route for a girlfriend and her mother. This is when Harry Seidel's and Siegfried Uhse's paths crossed. By the end of 1963, Uhse had betrayed five escape tunnels and other escape plans to the secret police. He played a role in the arrest of 89 refugees and escape helpers. After that the secret police feared he might be exposed, and he gradually withdrew from the group of escape helpers. He continued to serve as an IM until 1969. Contact remained sporadic after that and eventually ended.

The secret police pay IM "Hardy" a bonus for betraying the escape tunnel, October 17–18, 1962
BStU

213

Protests

Immense outrage over the construction of the Wall was felt on both sides. In East Berlin, the SED regime quickly stifled any protest that flared up. The East German police dispersed all gatherings. West Berliners protested in large numbers. Later, protests usually erupted on the anniversaries of the day the Berlin Wall was built or when a person died trying to escape. Fearing riots in 1962 and 1963, the West Berlin Senate had the police stand guard at the border. The mass protests died down in the sixties. But resentment remained. Border soldiers were verbally attacked and assaulted with stones and bottles. There were even a few isolated bomb attacks on the Wall.

Demonstration in West Berlin on the first anniversary of the Berlin Wall, August 13, 1962
Robert Lackenbach, Getty Images

May demonstration in front of the Reichstag in West Berlin, May 1, 1963
Heinz O. Jurisch, ullstein bild

Holding on to Connections

Families, friends and neighbors were separated by the Wall. But many people did everything in their power to stay in touch with one another. Letters and packages served as a substitute for meeting in person. Many Berliners tried to get a glimpse of each other over the Wall and wave. On the East Berlin side, all efforts to establish contact were prohibited, even waving silently. The situation eased considerably after the entry permit measures were introduced. With the approval of the West German government and the Western powers, representatives of the West Berlin Senate under Mayor Willy Brandt and the GDR negotiated four Entry Permit Agreements between 1963 and 1966. They allowed West Berliners to enter East Berlin to visit close relatives during specified time periods. The farewells following these visits were difficult, particularly since the next meeting remained uncertain.

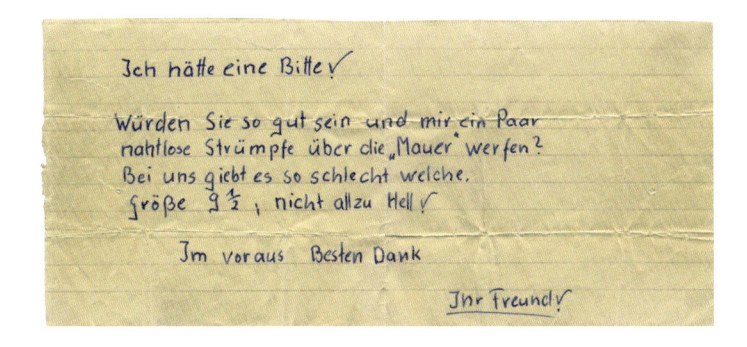

Correspondence between a border soldier and a West Berlin resident of Bernauer Strasse, 1960s
It was strictly forbidden for border soldiers to have contact with West Berliners. But the occasional conversation or correspondence over the Wall did take place.
Donated by Christa Arndt, Stiftung Berliner Mauer

An East Berlin woman greets her daughter and grandchild at the Oberbaum Bridge border crossing, 1964
unknown photographer, AP, ullstein bild

Jürgen Radischewski | Hartmut Richter | Elke Rosin | Konrad Weiß

Repression, Haft und Schießbefehl
Repression, Imprisonment, Order to Shoot

"Archive of Memory"
in the Documentation Center, 2015
Berthold Weidner

Susanne Muhle

Building the Berlin Wall and Life in Divided Berlin

Contact across the barbed wire was still possible in the first few days, August 13, 1961
Gert Hilde, ullstein bild

On Sunday, August 13, 1961, when the residents of Berlin woke up to discover that the border had been closed during the night, they had no way of knowing the profound effect that this would have on their lives. Many people went to the sector boundary to get a look at the closed border. Some went there hoping to meet relatives and friends on the other side of the barbed wire fence. People were deeply shocked; there was a strong feeling of insecurity.

Before August 13, 1961, East and West Berliners were able to travel to the other side of the city with little difficulty to visit friends and relatives or to work or shop. Despite the administrative and political division, in the minds and everyday life of many residents, Berlin was still one city. But the wall cut off almost all connections between the two halves of the city and between West Berlin and its environs. Families and friends were suddenly separated from one another. Many had hoped that the barbed wire barrier would be temporary. It seemed unthinkable that Berlin might be permanently divided. Given Berlin's four-power status, many thought that the Western occupying powers would intervene. The atmosphere was tense in the divided city during those days in August. The population felt both shocked and concerned, but these feelings were also mixed with a sense of outrage over the brutal measures taken by the SED regime and over the restrained response from the West German government and Western Allies.

In East Berlin the SED leadership carefully monitored the reactions of the Western powers. The memory of the national uprising in 1953 had led the SED leadership to fear widespread protests or another revolt. It therefore organized a broad propaganda campaign to accompany the border construction measures and to exert influence on public opinion from the very beginning. It claimed that the "anti-fascist protective rampart" would protect the GDR from "war mongers," "agents," "human trafficking" and would "secure peace." SED functionaries held assemblies in factories, clubs and neighborhoods during which participants – often under great pressure – were expected to sign similar, pre-formulated statements of solidarity. The SED also intensified its repressive measures to demonstrate its newly-acquired power. Political opponents were arrested in large numbers, and non-conformist behavior of any kind was prosecuted.[1] The East German police broke up large crowds that had formed at the border and prevented protests from taking place. The state did not tolerate people's contacting one other across the barbed wire fence. According to an order from the East Berlin chief of police, "Any form of contact – waving, greeting, exchanging letters or presents, etc., is to be prevented in the entire area of the state border."[2]

Fearing the situation might escalate, West Berlin police also kept people on the West side away from the border. But they were unable to stop citizens from gathering and protesting loudly. When people threw rocks, the GDR police responded with water guns and tear gas. Hundreds of thousands of demonstrators participated in a protest rally in front of Schöneberg's town hall on August 16, during which Mayor Willy Brandt appealed to the angry West Berliners, whose outrage he shared, to remain calm. A few demonstrators holding posters reading "You can't stop tanks with paper!" criticized the Western Allies for doing no more than sending letters of protest to the Soviet Union. In his speech, Mayor Brandt strongly condemned the border closure, criticizing the inaction of the Western Allies and stressing his solidarity with the people, particular on the eastern side of the city, but he also called for prudence.

Hundreds of thousands protest against the Wall in front of Schöneberg's town hall, August 16, 1961,
Schirner, Deutsches Historisches Museum

Bethaniendamm, 1968
Klaus Lehnartz, Photonet

Trying to make contact from the West Berlin side of the Wall at Leuschnerdamm, 1963
Max Scheler, Max Scheler Estate

Various measures were taken to calm the angry public in West Berlin. These efforts were often ineffective, but did serve to channel the anger and protest. Many people, for example, followed the Confederation of German Trade Unions' call to boycott the S-Bahn, which was run by the Reichsbahn, the East German railroad company. To demonstrate its support, the United States government reinforced its armed forces in West Berlin and dispatched General Lucius D. Clay, the city commander who had organized the airlift in 1948, to West Berlin. Two years later, West Berliners welcomed American President John F. Kennedy enthusiastically and cheered his statements of solidarity. But both East and West Berliners recognized that while the Western powers stood up for West Berlin's freedom, they were not willing to engage in countermeasures or risk a war over Berlin's unity.[3] On March 10, 1962, seven months after the border was closed, an East Berliner wrote to the RIAS radio station in West Berlin: "It has irked me for a while, always hearing about how the freedom of West Berlin must be preserved no matter what. Yet no one speaks about the freedom of East Berlin. It shouldn't be a surprise then, when, despite all assurances, we soon give up our hope for freedom."[4] By then the city's division had become permanent: powerless, the people in the East and West could only watch as the SED regime replaced the barbed wire with walls and fences, physically walling in West Berlin. As the border fortifications were expanded, successful escapes became less frequent. During the first weeks and months after the Wall's construction, many people managed to flee to West Berlin, sometimes under dramatic circumstances. Some escape attempts ended with imprisonment, a few even with death. In 1962, more than 2,300 people escaped across the border to Berlin. In 1965, only 259 succeeded and, in 1968, the number had dropped down to 46.[5] Throughout the 1960s, the GDR government continued to expand its border fortifications, creating a border strip that was enclosed on each side by a wall or fence and that cut through the center of the city.

As the border fortifications were continually expanded, Berliners were forced to accept this new reality. The population in East Berlin and the GDR was left little opportunity to act freely and was forced to come to terms with living under a dictatorship. In the words of Ilko-Sascha Kowalczuk, they were compelled "to seek normality under abnormal circumstances."[6]

West Berliners, in a different way, also had to get used to the situation created by the Wall. Public protests occasionally flared up when a person was shot at the Wall or on the anniversary of the day the Wall was built. On the Wall's first anniversary and after Peter Fechter died at the Wall in August 1962, protests were so great that the West Berlin Senate had the West Berlin police stationed at the Wall to prevent conflict. The fervor, however, soon settled. Several memorial sites were established along the Wall to commemorate the people who had died there. West Berliners continued to feel the impact of the Wall, sometimes painfully, in their daily lives. Completely cut off from their environs and far away from West Germany, many of these "islanders" felt that it was they who were actually walled in. Only West German citizens were permitted to travel to the eastern side of the city. West Berliners continued to be denied this privilege throughout the 1960s. Families and friends who were separated by the Wall could only stay in touch through letters and packages and by making dates at the Wall where they could see one another from a distance. The telephone lines between East and West Berlin had been cut off in 1952 and were not reestablished until 1971.

Personal meetings were only possible through the four travel permit agreements that the West Berlin Senate negotiated with the GDR government between 1963 and 1966. In possession of a travel permit, West Berliners could enter East Berlin to visit close relatives on holidays such as Easter, Whitsun and Christmas. Such permits were extremely important to the people in both Berlins. The existence of the Wall made West Berlin Mayor Willy Brandt determined to "ease human relations." He wanted to "make the Wall permeable" in order to "hinder the German people on the two sides from growing apart."[7] The close bond that still existed between East and West was demonstrated by the first travel permit agreements at Christmas time in 1963: approximately 725,000 West Berlins – a third of the West Berlin population – took advantage of the

Blocked-off border crossing at Heerstrasse in Berlin-Staaken, 1965
In April 1965, the GDR government temporarily blocked off all transit traffic. The reason: The German Bundestag was convening in West Berlin.
unknown photographer, Berlin-Bild, ullstein bild

opportunity to see relatives again after two years of separation. Many of them travelled to East Berlin on several different occasions. At the same time, nearly half a million people from the GDR came to East Berlin to meet their West Berlin relatives there. The four travel permit agreements facilitated a total of 5.4 million visits to East Berlin, thereby undermining the SED government's policy of isolation.[8]

When negotiations over a fifth travel permit agreement failed in 1966, the Berlin Wall once again became impassible to most West Berliners for several years. But in the early 1970s, following a new policy of détente, it gradually became more permeable, at least from West to East. In the Berlin Agreement passed by the four occupying powers, the Soviet Union guaranteed unhindered civilian traffic from and to West Berlin. A transit agreement between the two German states eased travel through the GDR and an agreement between the West Berlin Senate and the GDR government allowed West Berliners to travel to East Berlin and the GDR on a permanent basis. Tensions had eased in the walled-in city: The economic situation in West Berlin remained problematic and it continued to be strongly dependent on federal subsidies. But the Wall had become less frightening to the West Berlin population. Only when someone died at the Wall were people reminded of its horror.[9] Opportunities for private, cultural and academic exchanges between West and East increased, creating 'holes' in the Wall. Because of the West's policies of rapprochement, the SED, which had tried to isolate the GDR by building the Wall and asserting its policy of confinement, was unable to stop this development.

1
See Gerhard Sälter/Manfred Wilke, *Ultima Ratio: Der 13.8.1961*, Sankt Augustin/Berlin 2011, pp. 81–91.
2
Order from the East Berlin chief of police, August 28, 1961. Cited in Hans-Hermann Hertle, *Die Berliner Mauer. Monument des Kalten Krieges*, Bonn 3 2009, p. 41.
3
See Hermann Wentker, "Der Westen und die Mauer," in: Klaus-Dietmar Henke, *Die Mauer*, Munich 2011, pp. 196–210, here pp. 197–198.
4
Special RIAS radio program during which letters from East German listeners were read, 13.8.1962, Deutschlandradio.
5
See Hertle, *Die Berliner Mauer*, p. 57.

6
Ilko-Sascha Kowalczuk, "Es gab viele Mauern in der DDR," *Deutschland-Archiv* 1/2012, URL: http://www.bpb.de/geschichte/zeitgeschichte/deutschlandarchiv/61489/viele-mauern-in-der-ddr (Accessed: January 2015).
7
Cited in Hermann Wentker, "Der Ort des Mauerbaus im Kalten Krieg und in der deutsch-deutschen Geschichte," in: *Deutschland Archiv* 11+12 (2011), URL: http://www.bpb.de/geschichte/zeitgeschichte/deutschlandarchiv/53150/der-ort-des-mauerbaus (Stand: January 2015).
8
See Roger Engelmann, "Die Mauer durchlässiger machen." Die Politik der Reiseerleichterungen, in: Henke, *Die Mauer*, pp. 211–226, pp. 215–216.

9
See Hans Georg Lehmann, "Mit der Mauer leben? Die Einstellung zur Berliner Mauer im Wandel," in: Aus Politik und Zeitgeschichte Vol. 33–34 (1986), pp. 19–34; Rolf Heyen (eds.), *Die Entkrampfung Berlins oder Eine Stadt geht zur Tagesordnung über*, Hamburg 1972; Wilfried Rott, *Die Insel. Eine Geschichte West-Berlins 1948–1990*, Munich 2009.

Division Becomes Permanent
Renate Werwigk-Schneider

"But the real motivation to flee didn't actually become acute until after the Wall was built, when suddenly the gate to good old West Berlin was no longer open. […] There, where you could read […] and visit the cinema and theatre and concerts. That this gate to the so-called free world had simply closed […] I was supposed to join the party […] They expected me to become a socialist doctor. That was not my dream."

Interview, Stiftung Berliner Mauer, 2012

Renate Werwigk-Schneider was born in 1938. In 1961, when the border was closed and the Wall was built, she was studying medicine at the Humboldt University in East Berlin. Her brother managed to flee to the West in 1963. He built a tunnel with other students from West Berlin that his sister and parents were supposed to escape through. But the tunnel was betrayed to the police and the family was imprisoned. Renate Werwigk-Schneider was released in 1965. She tried to escape again two years later using a false passport. She was arrested in Bulgaria and sentenced to three years in prison in the GDR. In 1968, the West German government paid money for her release and she moved there to work as a doctor.

"Dictatorship of Borders"
in the exhibition in the
Documentation Center, 2015
Berthold Weidner

Thomas Onißeit

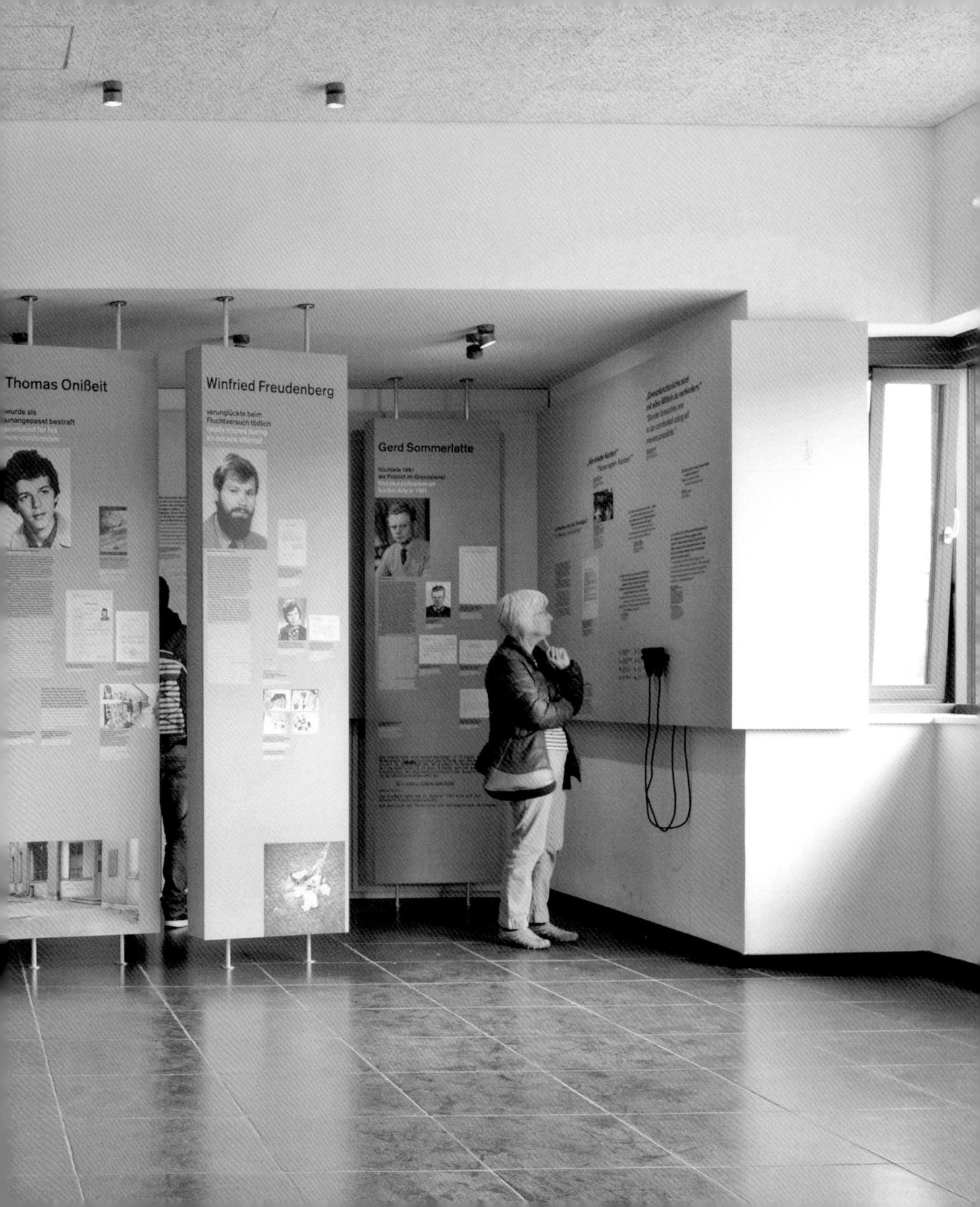

wurde als unangepasst bestraft
punished for his non-conformism

Winfried Freudenberg

verunglückte beim Fluchtversuch tödlich
fatally injured during an escape attempt

Gerd Sommerlatte

flüchtete 1961 als Polizist im Grenzdienst
fled as a policeman on border duty in 1961

4
Dictatorship of Borders

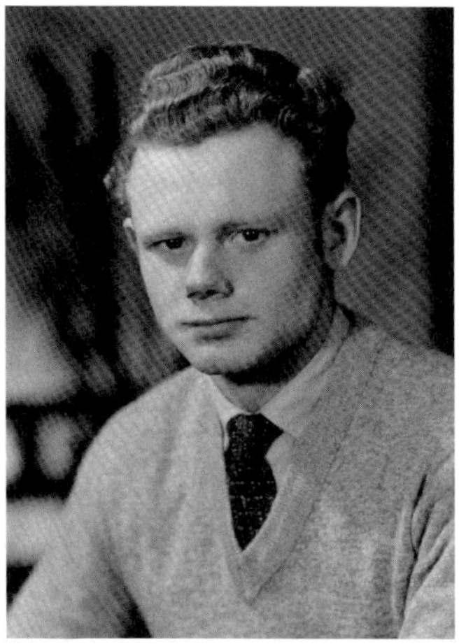
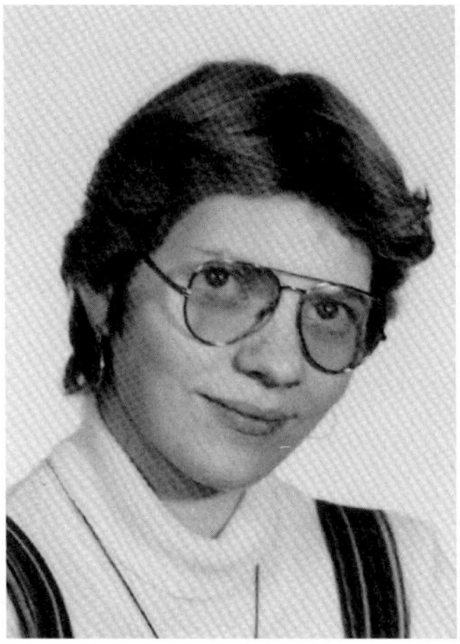
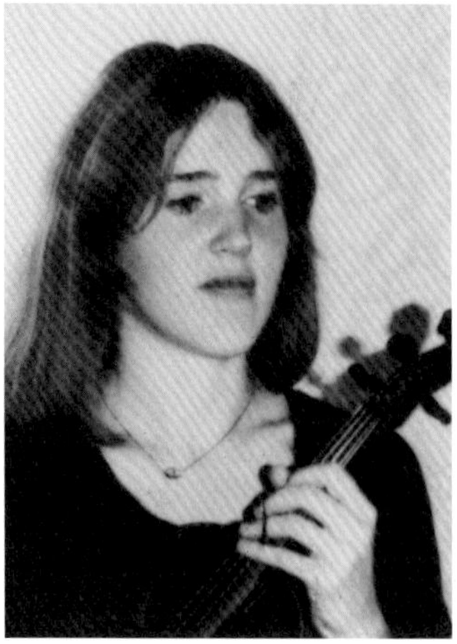
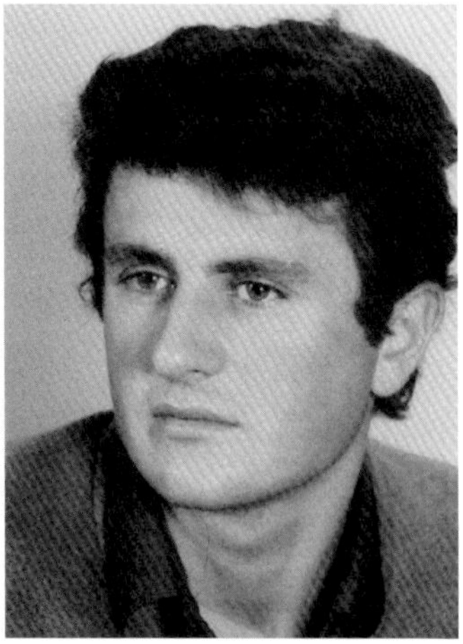
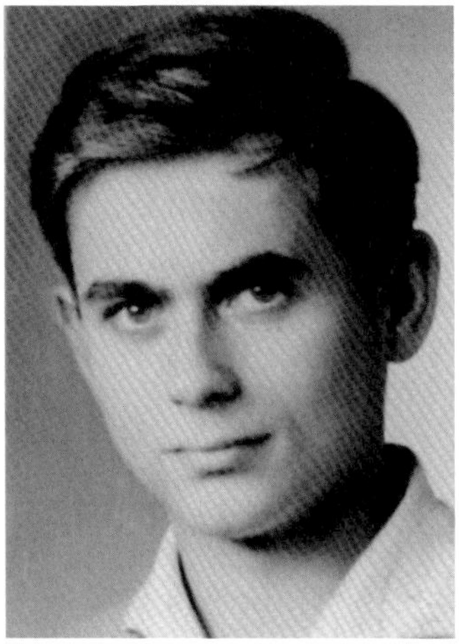
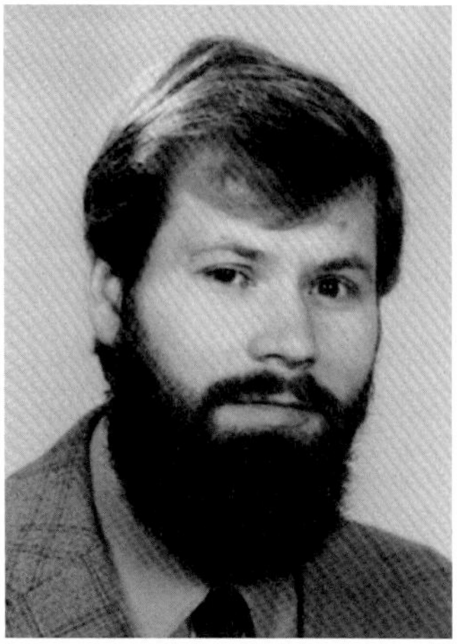
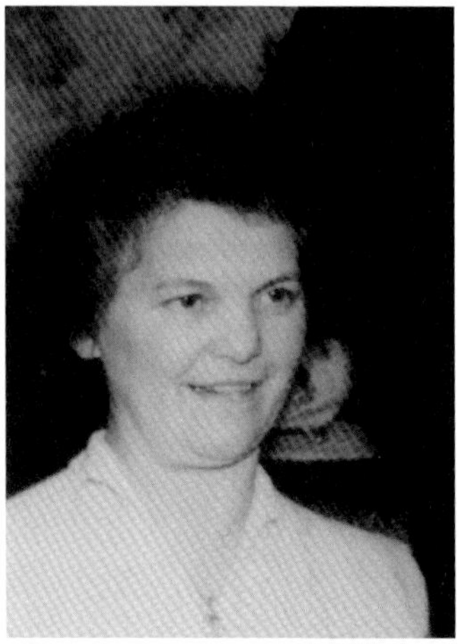

Escape from the GDR: A Criminal Offense
The right to move about freely, in particular the freedom to leave the country, did not exist in East Germany. People who wanted to flee to the West were criminalized by laws forbidding escape from the GDR. As of 1954, anyone caught preparing or attempting an escape risked severe punishment. Having knowledge of this "criminal" act was also prosecuted.

"(1) Whoever illegally crosses the state border of the German Democratic Republic [...] will be punished with a prison sentence of up to [...] two years. (3) In serious cases the perpetrator will be punished with a prison sentence of between one and eight years."

Article 213 of the GDR penal code, 1979

Manfred Redlich
sentenced as an accomplice

Manfred Redlich, ca. 1965
Manfred Redlich

Manfred Redlich was born in September 1946 in today's Poland. His family moved to the Vogtland in 1963. Redlich began working there as an automobile mechanic for the VEB Motor Traffic of Rodewisch in 1966. At a party in November 1970, the 24-year-old met Hans-Rolf W., a young man his age who wanted to flee to the West. He asked Manfred Redlich if he was interested in joining him. Redlich turned down the offer with the words "I'm going to stay a bit longer." He was unaware that W. was serious about his plans. This would have consequences for him in April 1971. Unable to gain a foothold in West Germany, W. returned to the GDR. During interrogations with the secret police, he incriminated Manfred Redlich as a tacit accomplice. Redlich was prosecuted for not having reported his knowledge of the escape plans. But because he was a diligent and conscientious worker, he was given only a two-year suspended sentence. His work brigade had to agree to support his "development of a socialist personality." For the next two years Manfred Redlich was not allowed to leave his home district or change his place of work. Even after the sentence had expired, the certainty that he was being watched and controlled continued to disturb him until 1989.

"The defendant is required [...] to prove through reliable work that he has drawn the right conclusions from his sentence. The guarantee from the factory workshop of the business in question has been confirmed."

Judgment of the Auerbach/
Vogtland district court, July 9, 1971

Winfried Freudenberg
fatally injured during an escape attempt

Winfried Freudenberg, 1980s
BStU

Winfried Freudenberg was born in 1956 in the Harz, directly on the border to West Germany. His parents were independent farmers, but as part of forced collectivization, were required to give up their farm in 1960. After completing an apprenticeship, he acquired his high school degree and served his basic military duty with the East German army. In February 1985, he graduated from the Illmenau Technical College with a degree in information technology. He was assigned a job in the VEB Steremat "Hermann Schlimme." Winfried Freudenberg was annoyed by this state interference in his life. He changed jobs several times, but was unable to fulfill his professional goals. Frustrated with this lack of career prospects, he began planning his escape to the West. He and his wife, a chemist, hoped to establish a new life there. For weeks the couple secretly taped a balloon together out of plastic sheets in their apartment. They avoided family and friends so as not to put them in danger. They planned their takeoff for March 7, 1989, but at the last minute Freudenberg's wife decided not to flee. Winfried Freudenberg managed to steer the balloon over the border to West Berlin, but he lost control and died when he crashed down in Zehlendorf.

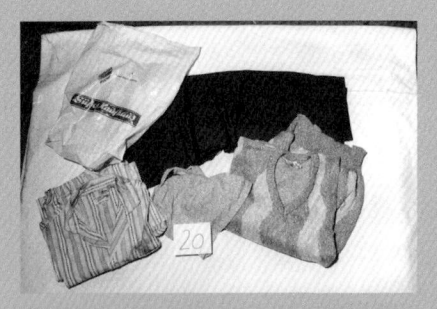

Photographs of the things that Winfried Freudenberg had attached to the balloon, March 8, 1989
In a large area around the site where Winfried Freudenberg's balloon crashed, the West Berlin police found chemistry textbooks, music cassettes, undergarments and other items that he had brought along for his wife and himself. The items were photographed by the police.
Polizeihistorische Sammlung Berlin

"Economic Crisis in the GDR" in the exhibition in the Documentation Center, 2015
Berthold Weidner

Werner Coch
tried to escape twice

Werner Coch, 1965
Werner Coch

Werner Coch was born in 1941 in Upper Lusatia. As a child and teenager, he often visited his grandparents and other relatives in West Germany. When he was a student in 1961, Coch traveled through southern Europe during the semester break. He was on his way home when he learned that the Wall had been built. He returned to Dresden anyway and soon noticed an increase in political pressure. All students were now required to serve military duty with the East German army. Werner Coch began searching for a way out. His first attempt to flee through the Swedish consulate in Warsaw in October 1962 failed. A second attempt was also unsuccessful: Coch was arrested by the secret police while planning an escape through a tunnel. He was sentenced to 21 months in prison in August 1963. After his release in November 1964, he worked in the Synthetic Fiber Production Plant in Premnitz. He kept his imprisonment secret from most of his colleagues. The University of Dresden was reluctant to let him resume his studies, but he managed to study again in September 1965. His criminal record was cleared in March 1970, but the authorities remained suspicious of him. When a friend from West Germany visited him in the mid-1980s, Werner Coch again became a target of the secret police. Suspecting him of engaging in espionage, they created a large investigative file on Werner Coch, his friends and his colleagues.

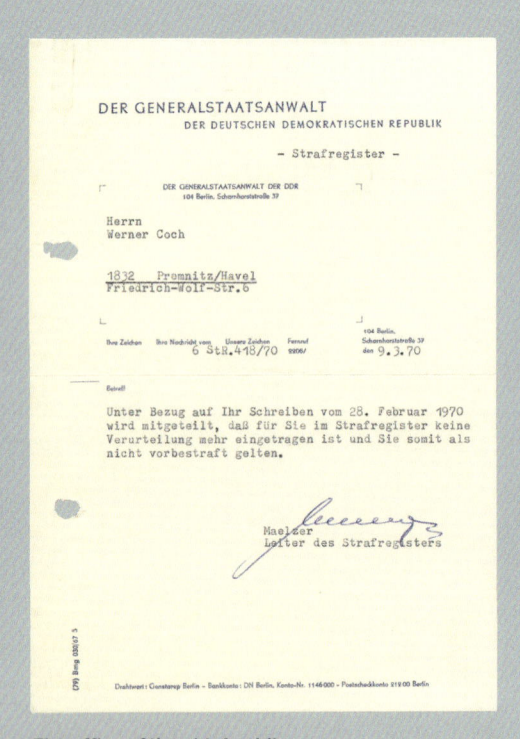

The office of the chief public prosecutor in the GDR confirms that Werner Coch's criminal record has been cleared, March 9, 1970
Werner Coch

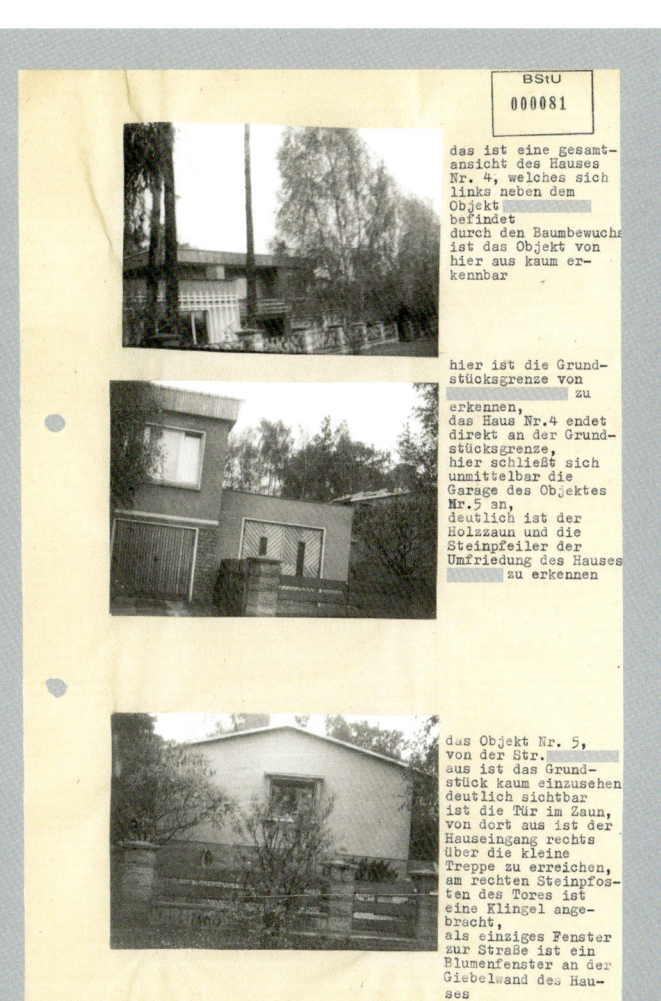

The secret police observes the
Coch family's house, 1988
MfS documentation, BStU

> "Your son conducts himself in a disciplined manner and performs good work, but has yet to give up his thoughts about leaving the GDR. If, however, he tries to get to a capitalist foreign country through legal channels and later reach the Federal Republic, then this attests to the fact that he has yet to develop a firm connection to our German Democratic Republic. For this reason it remains necessary to use the remaining term of penalty for the best possible re-educational process."

The public prosecutor rejects Werner Coch's early release in a letter to Werner Coch's father, July 21, 1964
BStU

Dorothea Ebert
tried to flee via Bulgaria

Dorothea Ebert, ca.1980
Dorothea Ebert

Dorothea Ebert and her brother Michael, 1978
Dorothea Ebert

Dorothea Ebert was born in 1960 and raised in an educated bourgeois family. She learned to play the violin; her brother Michael played piano. Her mother used her music lessons to justify her daughter's absence from pioneer events. As a teenager, Dorothea Ebert performed in the Soviet Union; in the summer of 1980 she had a concert in Paris as well. This trip made her dramatically aware of how limited her life was in the GDR. She found it increasingly difficult to accept the state's intervention in her life. For example, despite her excellent final grades, she was expected to become a music teacher, not a soloist. She confided her distress to her brother, her husband and a friend. In summer 1983, they planned their escape in the apartment they shared in Dresden. They travelled through Hungary and Rumania to Bulgaria, looking for a place to flee. But everywhere they went, they found the border impassable. They were eventually arrested on the border between Bulgaria and Yugoslavia and extradited to the GDR. On January 18, 1983, Dorothea Ebert was charged with "attempted escape from the republic" and sentenced to two years and eight months in prison, which she served in the Hoheneck prison for women. In December 1984, West Germany paid ransom for her release and she was brought to West Germany. Her brother joined her a short time later.

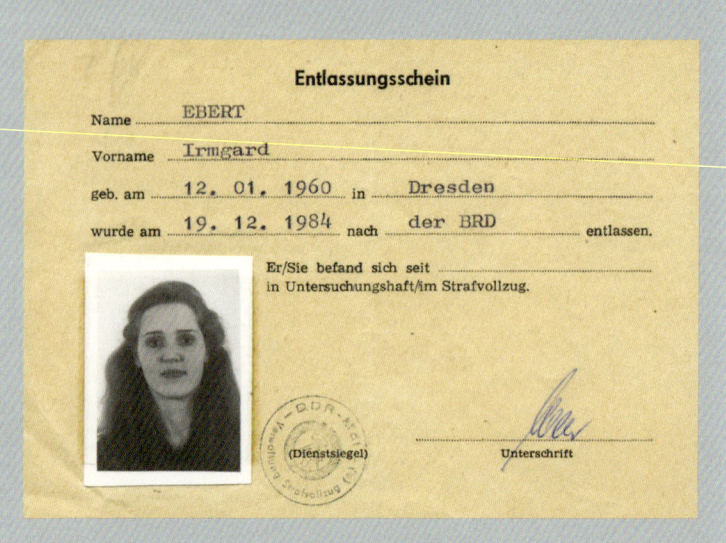

Prison release certificate, December 19, 1984
Dorothea Ebert

Margarete Hohlbein
escaped through a tunnel to West Berlin

Margarete Hohlbein, 1959
Hubert Hohlbein

Processing slip from the Marienfelde refugee camp in West Berlin, 1964
Hubert Hohlbein

Margarete Hohlbein, daughter of the businessman Eugen Krebs and his wife, was born in 1912 in Berlin-Adlershof. She already had a daughter when she married Hubert Hohlbein. In 1942, their son Hubert was born. After 1945, the couple established a new livelihood for themselves with a transport company. This is why they did not consider fleeing to the West, even when the SED regime increased pressure on private businesses. Only after her husband died did Margarete Hohlbein begin seriously thinking about fleeing. But after August 13, 1961, there were hardly any opportunities for someone her age to escape. Her son Hubert was able to flee to West Berlin in the fall of 1963. Once there, he began looking for an escape route for his mother. He built a tunnel with other students that Margarete Hohlbein and 56 other people were able to escape through to the West in October 1964. At the age of 53 she was able to find work as a sales clerk. But it tormented her to be separated from her daughter, whose escape had failed. She followed her son to Bavaria in the 1980s, so as to have at least one child nearby. She had to wait until the spring of 1989, when her daughter entered retirement, before they could meet in West Berlin. Margarete Hohlbein died in 2003 in Munich.

The Krebs family's colonial goods store, 1930s
Hubert Hohlbein

Heike Wilke
lived in the restricted area at the border to West Berlin

Heike Wilke, late 1970s
Heike Wilke

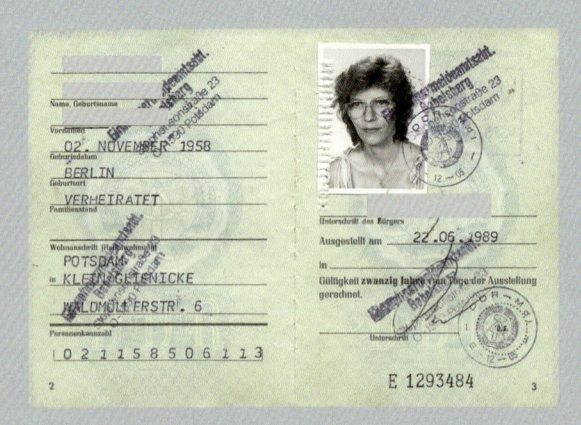

Heike Wilke's identity card with the restricted area entry, 1989
Heike Wilke

Heike Wilke was born in East Berlin in 1958 and lived with her parents in Potsdam. She trained to become a nurse and met her first husband there. Since his parents' apartment was too small for the young couple, they looked for their own apartment. They found one in the restricted area in Klein Glienicke in 1978. They hoped that through a planned exchange of territory they would soon be assigned an apartment in town. Heike Wilke found the constant controls at the entrance to the restricted area stressful. She was also unhappy that only close family members were permitted to visit. Every vehicle that drove into the restricted area, without exception, had to be accompanied by border soldiers. This concerned her when she became pregnant again after a miscarriage. She worried that the doctor would be unable to reach her in time, particularly since she did not have her own telephone line. She therefore decided to spend the last weeks before the birth at her mother's home outside the restricted area. Although the Wall was an everyday presence in the family's life, they were not allowed to photograph it. After November 9, 1989, Heike Wilke took snapshots from her kitchen window. They show the close proximity of the border fortifications to her apartment.

Map of the restricted area Klein Glienicke, 1980s
The blue circle marks the building where Heike Wilke lived.
Staatsbibliothek zu Berlin – Preußischer Kulturbesitz/Stiftung Berliner Mauer

Mandated Silence

At least 138 people died at the Berlin Wall. The SED regime tried to cover up the deaths of fugitives; some families did not learn the true circumstances under which their relatives died until after the GDR collapsed. The death victims were vilified as criminals and social deviants. Relatives often had to refrain from having an official funeral service. But these methods failed in February 1989: Chris Gueffroy's violent death at the Wall and his funeral could not be kept secret.

Statement of sworn secrecy signed by the mother of Christian Peter Friese, who was shot at the Wall, January 7, 1971

When the Western media reported on the fatal shots at the Berlin Wall on the first day of Christmas 1970, Christian Peter Friese's mother had no idea that the dead fugitive was her son. The secret police informed her that her son had committed a crime and pressured her to sign a statement, in which she agreed to speak of his death as an accident. Since he had officially died in a car crash, a life insurance policy was paid out to her as part of the cover up. The actual circumstances of the young man's death did not become known until 1990.
BStU

Preventing Escapes

The GDR government tried to stop escapes when they were still in the planning stage. The closely interwoven surveillance by the secret police, the police and other authorities served this aim. Police patrols and "voluntary assistants" checked anyone suspicious in the border area. The technical infrastructure of the border fortifications was also constantly expanded and improved.

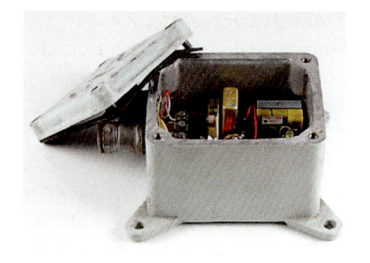

Lecture notes by a student of the college of the secret police in Potsdam on the topic "Attacks on the state border to the GDR," June 26, 1987
The student took detailed notes on the tasks of all the institutions involved in securing the border – the police, SED district leadership, "voluntary assistants to the border troops," secret police and border troops. They were to work jointly to prevent escape attempts at the earliest moment possible.
BStU

"The comrades of the 'Unity' brigade have drawn the correct consequences from the 2 escapes that took place from their collective, by having […] 3 colleagues agree to serve as border patrol assistants for the protection of our state (and hence our factory as well)."

Protocol of the factory party organization of the SED in the VEB Motor Vehicle Maintenance Factory of Berlin-Treptow, 1964
Landesarchiv Berlin

Motion detector to prevent escape attempts from the VEB Motor Vehicle Maintenance Factory of Berlin-Treptow, 1980s
Stiftung Berliner Mauer

To Shoot or not to Shoot?

Harsh drills and severe punishments were aimed at preparing the border soldiers to shoot at fugitives. Most of the soldiers hoped that no one would try to flee in their section of the border when they were on duty. Some were determined to intentionally miss if they had to fire. Others waited to see what would happen in a confrontation with a fugitive. Some were ready to pull the trigger without hesitation – after all, "an order is an order." The everyday life of the conscripts was dominated by monotony and alcohol consumption. Most of them yearned for the end of their military service. Those who were up for discharge counted the remaining days with a tape measure.

Border soldiers on Friedrichstrasse in East Berlin, 1987
The candidates who are up for discharge pose with tape measures that show that their term of service is almost over. This is how the soldiers expressed their frustration about border duty.
Carsten Gennert, Stiftung Berliner Mauer

"U. submitted his petition for discharge to the company's political deputy on Nov. 6, 1975. Although U. did not provide any explanation for his petition, it has to be assumed that it is connected to the incident. U. is politically stable."

Situation report of the secret police, November 6, 1975
In November 1975, border soldiers shot and killed the 21-year-old Lothar Hennig, mistaking him for a fugitive in the border area. In a situation report the secret police recorded how members of the border company felt about the killing.

"It is the dead man's own fault [...]. It really angers me personally since I now have to clean up the filthy car."

Border soldier, who transported the fatally-wounded Lothar Hennig to the army hospital

"I've been a KP guard in Sacrow for a long time. I would have done the same. No one has to complain to me. I'm acting on behalf of the GDR and the law is on my side."

Border soldier deployed as a controller (KP)

"What a bummer that we shot an innocent person."

Staff sergeant of the border troops, squad leader

Gerd Sommerlatte
fled as a policeman on border duty in 1961

Gerd Sommerlatte, 1965
Gerd Sommerlatte

Gerd Sommerlatte was born in 1943 near Dessau. In the spring of 1961, at the age of 17, he enlisted with the East German police. After the Wall was built, his unit was transferred to border duty in Berlin in September 1961. Gerd Sommerlatte was expected to prevent escapes to the West, and to use his weapon if necessary. Instead he decided to flee at the first chance available. On September 10, when no one was watching, the young man jumped over the Wall at the Brandenburg Gate. In West Berlin he first lived in the Marienfelde refugee camp where he underwent intensive questioning by the Western intelligence agencies. He was scheduled to be flown out to West Germany on October 2, but this never happened. On the evening of September 30, two men abducted him to East Berlin. The secret police took him directly from the Heinrich-Heine-Strasse border crossing to the remand prison in Lichtenberg. The district court of Frankfurt/Oder sentenced him to ten years in prison on February 20, 1962. The court gave him an aggravated sentence because he was believed to have encouraged other border guards to desert. Sommerlatte served his sentence in the secret police prison work camp X in Berlin-Hohenschönhausen and in Brandenburg. After the West German government paid ransom for his release in October 1965, he was able to begin a new life in West Germany.

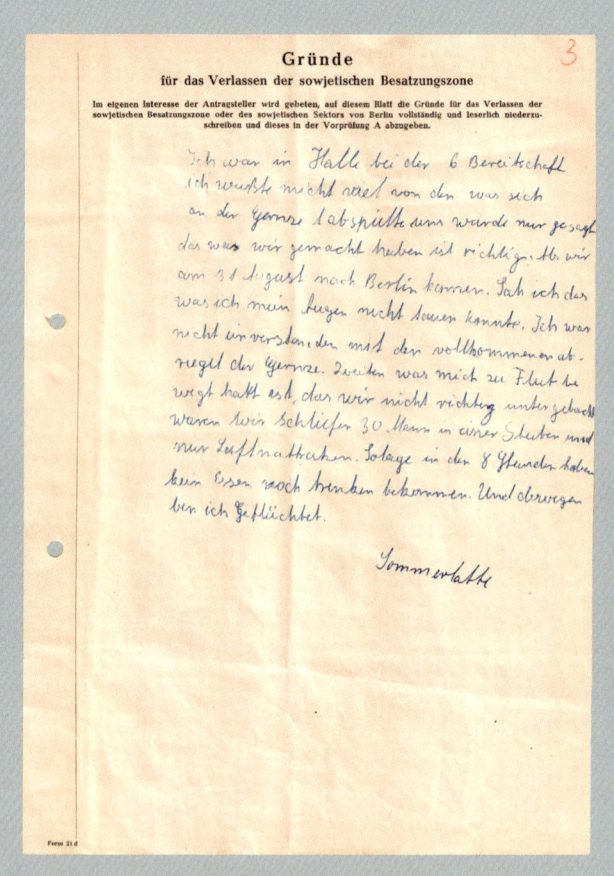

Gerd Sommerlatte's statement on his motives for fleeing, provided during the admissions procedure in West Berlin, September 10, 1961
Bundesverwaltungsamt Gießen

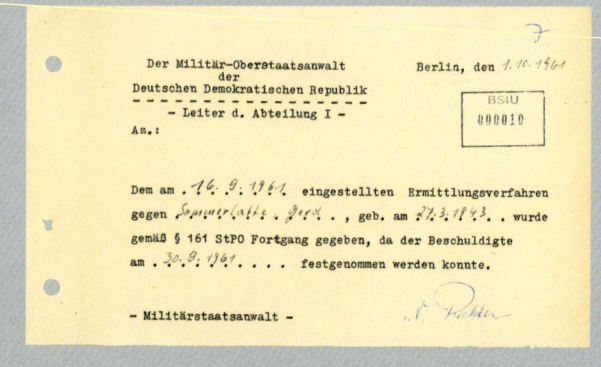

Note from the military senior prosecutor on Gerd Sommerlatte's arrest, October 1, 1961
BStU

Elke Kimmel

Dictatorship of Borders

Until its very end, the GDR's survival as a state depended on the existence of its borders, a fact demonstrated by the rapid collapse of the regime after the Berlin Wall fell. But the leaders of the GDR had also secured their power by imposing widespread restrictions on everyday life in the GDR. Nearly every area of society was dominated by the SED, the ruling party in the GDR. It rewarded those who were loyal to it and punished those who tried to evade its influence. To ensure that set boundaries were not crossed, authorities were set up within subgroups of society:[1] these included the State Security Service, the People's Police, and political and social functionaries, who included party group organizers and union workplace representatives, as well as teachers, work supervisors and colleagues. One had to be a member of the SED and its affiliated organizations to be a successful part of East German society and achieve profession goals. Living with these conditions in a government-controlled society, East Germans were constantly pressed to seek out new areas where they could enjoy a degree of freedom. Many felt this pressure in their daily lives, even those who succeeded in partially realizing their life plans (which depended on the prevailing political situation).[2] Quite a few came to accept that the internal and external borders set by the state were unalterable.

For lack of any other alternatives – especially after 1961 – the majority of East Germans felt they had no choice but to adjust to these new conditions. But during the later phase of the GDR, the general willingness to adjust diminished. Increasing numbers of citizens could no longer tolerate the limitations placed on their individual freedom and the impositions created by surveillance, controls and heteronomy. Until well into the autumn of 1989, the state continued to severely punish any conduct that overstepped boundaries.

The power of the SED reached its own limits, however, when strong-willed citizens opposed it through resistance and a struggle to achieve freedom in a dictatorship of borders. The most radical and dangerous way to escape the demands of the state was to flee the GDR, an expression of total disregard for the borders. A few personal examples of this behavior are presented below.

Winfried Freudenberg was one of 100 people who died while trying to flee at the Berlin Wall. The state had interfered in his life on several occasions prior to his escape attempt: He had been hindered from acquiring an *Abitur*, the secondary school degree that would have qualified him to attend university. Only later was he able to obtain the degree by attending evening classes. He was also initially prevented from studying the subject of his choice. His second attempt to do so was successful. After graduation he was assigned a job by the state. Only later was he able to freely choose his place of work.[3] Weary of forever being told what to do, he decided to risk a dangerous escape over the border in a self-made balloon. He died on March 8, 1989 when the balloon crashed in West Berlin.

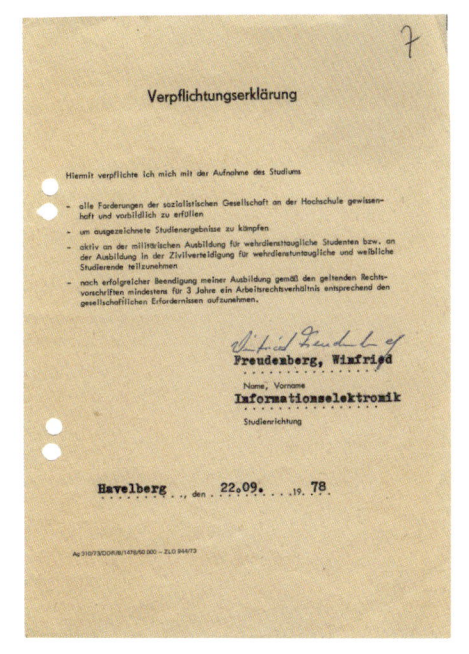

Winfried Freudenberg's consent to accept a job assigned to him by the state after graduation, Sept. 22, 1978
Technische Hochschule Ilmenau

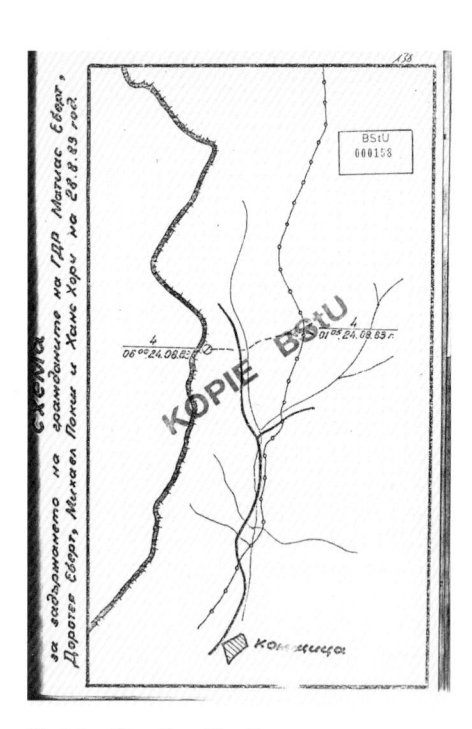

Sketch of Dorothea Ebert's escape route drawn by the Bulgarian state security, 1983
BStU

Dorothea Ebert's professional plans were also thwarted by the state,[4] which had expected her to become a music teacher, not a concert pianist. For Dorothea Ebert, this was the final straw: She had previously been denied a suitable apartment with the argument that she could practice piano in her parents' home. She consequently ended up living "illegally" in a run-down apartment in Dresden's Neustadt. But this time, with no easy way to avoid the demands of the state, the young woman decided to flee to West Germany by way of Bulgaria. When she was arrested at the Bulgarian-Yugoslavian border, the Bulgarian border guards confiscated her violin and handed it over to the GDR State Security: it was not returned to her when she was released from prison and deported to the West a year later.

The state interfered drastically in Rudolf Bahro's life on a number of occasions[5]: until the early 1960s, Bahro, a committed socialist, appeared undisturbed by this. After working in Brandenburg and Mecklenburg, he got a job as an editor at *the Forum*, a progressive FDJ magazine – but this did not last very long. After publishing a drama that was critical of the regime, Bahro was transferred against his will to the "production" department. He continued to pursue his scholarly studies after work, but ten years later his completed dissertation was rejected, apparently for political reasons.[6] Bahro took the SED dictatorship to task in his book *The Alternative*, but he knew the chances of having it printed in the GDR were slight. Instead he smuggled it to the West for publication in 1977. The state punished him severely for this: he was charged with betraying state secrets and sentenced to eight years in prison in June 1978.

Young men had to decide early on between conformism and resistance: if one opted to serve as a construction soldier instead of joining the military, he was denied the chance to acquire an *Abitur* degree and study at university. Admission to university was granted foremost to young men who had committed themselves to serving three years in the National People's Army (NVA). Thomas Onißeit,[7] a young man from Weimar, was eager to study, and therefore made an early commitment to military service. Later, he began causing trouble in school; the school board found him to be enthusiastic about the "wrong" things, for example the Dada and punk movements. When he withdrew his agreement to serve three years in the military, the Stasi began interrogating him at school. Thomas Onißeit had to leave school after 11th grade without an Abitur degree; he began training as a male nurse instead. His inclination to form his own opinions earned him the label "negative-decadent teenager," which caused him further harassment by the state authorities. A few nights before the GDR's anniversary celebration on October 7, 1983, Thomas Onißeit and his friends vented their resentment by spraying graffiti on buildings in Weimar's city center. There slogans included "make cucumber salad out of the state," and "the country needs new men." The second one was Thomas

Rudolf Bahro on trial before the municipal court of Berlin, June 30, 1978
He was represented in court by attorney Gregor Gysi (front right).
BStU

Onißeit's own idea. Someone betrayed them and the teenagers were arrested within a few days. Thomas Onißeit was sentenced to six months in prison in the spring of 1984. Even after his release, he continued to be harassed by the state. His identity card was revoked and he was prohibited both from travelling to East Berlin and from going to Czechoslovakia to visit his brother, who lived in the West. Denied any viable future, Thomas Onißeit also applied to immigrate to the West. Recognizing that he could not be shaped into what the SED regarded as a "good citizen," the State Security allowed him to leave.

Many people in the GDR experienced similar or other kinds of state meddling in their lives. Most of them chose to adapt to the circumstances because their lives were rooted in their country through family, friends and work and they thought of the GDR as their home. Some accepted the conditions in the GDR as they were; others tried to improve them. Most people never considered escaping to the West, feeling it was too dangerous. Many did not feel that the West offered a political alternative to the GDR. They often found ways to get around or manipulate the unreasonable demands of the state and make them bearable. The SED was, after all, also dependent on the participation of "its people" and it wanted to assert its claim to power.[8] In the end, however, conformism, a form of self-distortion that many GDR citizens were forced to engage in, also left scars, even when the people did not experience reprimands or punishment.

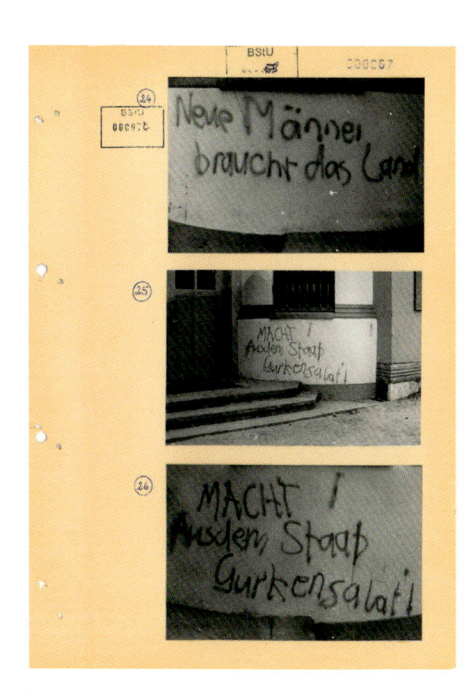

Thomas Onißeit's graffiti in Weimar, documented by the secret police, 1983
MfS documentation, BStU

1
See Thomas Lindenberger, "In den Grenzen der Diktatur. Die DDR als Gegenstand von 'Gesellschaftsgeschichte,'" in: Rainer Eppelmann/ Bernd Faulenbach/Ulrich Mählert (eds.), *Bilanz und Perspektiven der DDR-Forschung*, Paderborn 2003, pp. 239 – 245, here: pp. 243 – 244.
2
On the idea of dictatorship as social practice, see Thomas Lindenberger, "Die Diktatur der Grenzen. Zur Einleitung," in: Thomas Lindenberger (ed.), *Herrschaft und Eigen-Sinn in der Diktatur. Studien zur Gesellschaftsgeschichte der DDR*, Cologne/Weimar/Vienna 1999, pp. 11 – 44, here pp. 21–23.
3
See for example: Ilko-Sascha Kowalczuk, *Geist im Dienste der Macht. Hochschulpolitik in der SBZ/ DDR 1945 bis 1961*, Berlin 2003.
4
On Dorothea Ebert's biography, see Dorothea Ebert/Michael Proksch, *Und plötzlich waren wir Verbrecher. Geschichte einer Republikflucht*, Munich 2010.

5
On Rudolf Bahro's biography, see Guntolf Herzberg, *Rudolf Bahro – Glaube an das Veränderbare: eine Biographie*, Berlin 2002.
6
See Rudolf Bahro, Plädoyer für eine schöpferische Initiative. *Zur Kritik von Arbeitsbedingungen im real existierenden Sozialismus*, Cologne 1980.
7
See Ulrich Jadke/Holm Kirsten/Jörn Luther/Thomas Onißeit, Macht aus dem Staat Gurkensalat. *Eine andere Jugend. Weimar 1979 – 1989*, Berlin 2011 and Anne Hahn/Frank Willmann (eds.), *Der weiße Strich. Vorgeschichte und Folgen einer Kunstaktion an der Berliner Mauer*, Berlin 2011.
8
See Richard Bessel/Ralph Jessen, "Einleitung. Diktatur der Grenzen," in: Bessel/Jessen (ed.), *Die Grenzen der Diktatur. Staat und Gesellschaft in der DDR*, Göttingen 1996, pp. 7 – 24, here pp. 14 – 15.

5

Leading Up to the Fall of the Berlin Wall

Illegal flyers from East Berlin, 1988
BStU

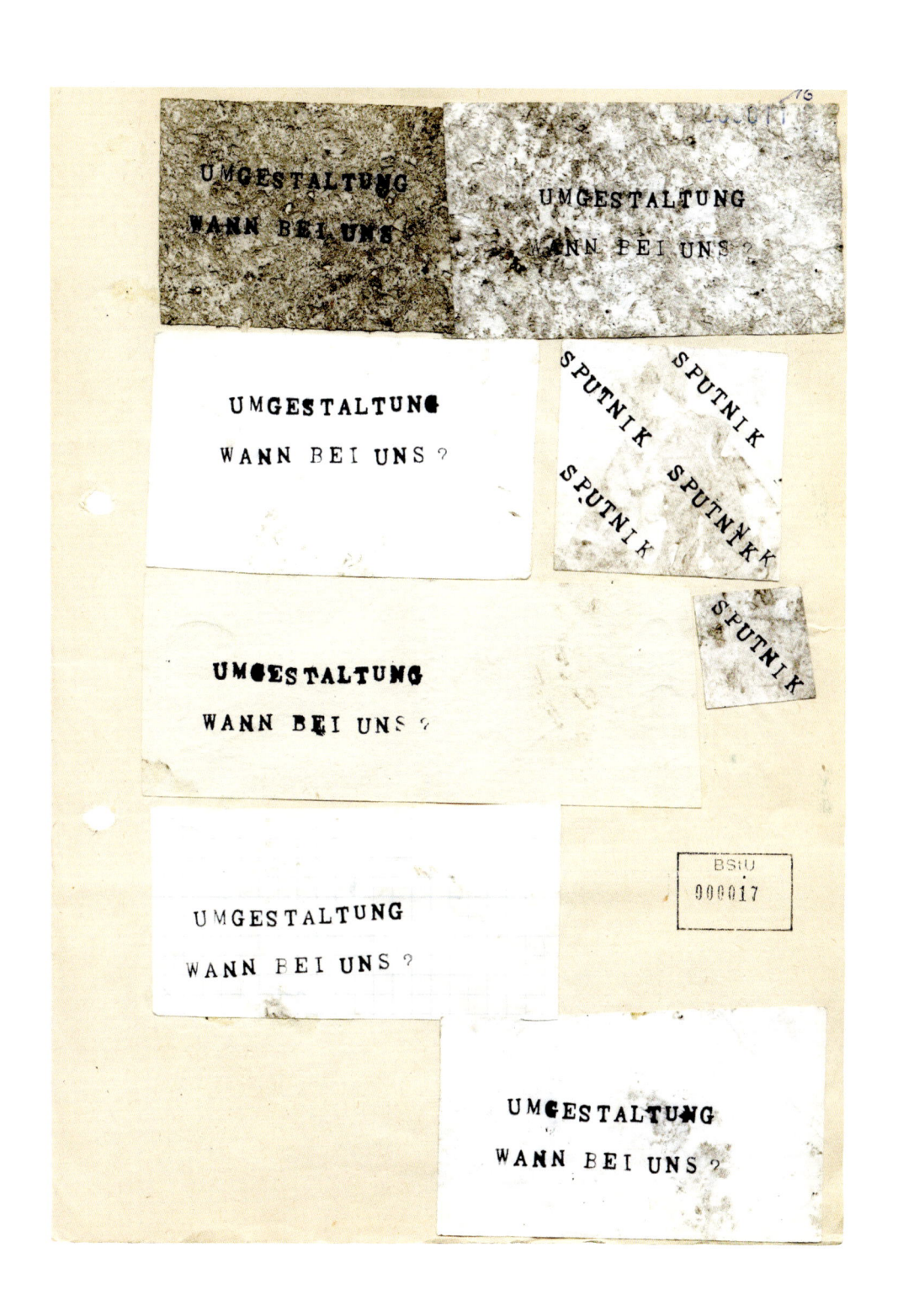

Acclimatization and Rapprochement

Pedestrians at Bethaniendamm in Berlin-Kreuzberg, 1985
Müller-Preisser, ullstein bild

Leading Up to the Fall of the Berlin Wall
Roland Jahn

"Based on my personal experience in the GDR, I knew how important it was that we be able to learn about the poor conditions in the GDR from the Tagesschau [West German television news] […] So I began making contacts […] and collecting information about what was going on in the GDR and I passed this information on to the radio and television stations. The editorial teams worked them into news reports […] that were broadcast back into the GDR."

Interview, Stiftung Berliner Mauer, 2013

Roland Jahn was born in Jena in 1953. In 1975 he began studying economics. After Jahn protested against Wolf Biermann's expatriation in 1977, he was forced to leave the university. He worked as an unskilled laborer and joined the GDR opposition. In 1982 he was sentenced to 22 months in prison for expressing open support for the Polish trade union Solidarność. Protests in West Germany led to Roland Jahn's release, but he was expatriated in 1983. He worked as a journalist in West Berlin and supported the opposition in the GDR. Since 2011, Roland Jahn has served as Federal Commissioner for the Records of the State Security Service in the former GDR.

West Berlin: The Walled-in City

In the decades after the Wall was built, West and East Berlin developed independently of one another. Young people and newcomers to the city had never even known Berlin as a lively single entity. People on both sides of the Wall became accustomed to the division in different ways.

In West Berlin the Wall became its trademark and eventually a tourist attraction. The city, which was heavily subsidized by the West German federal government, began attracting large numbers of young West Germans in the 1970s. Urban milieus developed parallel to mainstream culture, providing alternatives to young people. West Berlin's subculture was characterized by individualism, artistic diversity and distance to the state. The Wall ceased to represent a threatening political issue. For most people it inevitably became normal.

The "Märkische Schweiz" garden allotments in Berlin-Neukölln, 1989
The Wall became normal to people living in West Berlin. Their sympathy with the fate of their neighbors in East Berlin and the GDR faded into the background. They adjusted to life on the island. Some people created their own idyllic sites or used the area for recreational activities. The Wall became normal to people living in West Berlin.
Rolf Kißling

Demonstration in West Berlin against the arrest of deserters from the West German armed forces, July 31, 1969
West Berlin did not belong to West Germany. Due to its special status as a demilitarized city, it had no compulsory military service. Young West Germans moved here to avoid serving in the military. In 1969, the West Berlin "War Resisters International" demonstrated against the extradition of deserters from the West German armed forces.
Wolfram Beyer, Archiv der Internationale der Kriegsdienstgegner/innen" (IDK e.V.)

Guests in "Café Kranzler" on Kurfürstendamm, 1984
West Berlin was a diverse city full of contradictions. Bourgeoisie and anarchy, provincialism and urbanism existed side by side. All these qualities exemplified West Berlin's image in the shadow of the Wall.
Jens Schumann, ullstein bild

East Berlin: Capital of the GDR

East Berlin was the SED party's center of power and its showpiece. Officially declared the "capital of the GDR" in 1949, it became the window of the East with large new housing areas and highly visible symbolic structures such as the television tower and the "Palace of the Republic." Although the border fortifications were visible at many places in the city, they were meant to be inconspicuous. That is one reason why neighborhoods close to the border territory were declared restricted areas and the Wall became taboo. Many East Berliners tried not to think about the fact that they were locked in. They avoided the border and learned to ignore the Wall in their everyday lives.

Often, apartment buildings extended all the way to the border strip. Registrations, constant ID checks and surveillance were a routine part of everyday life here. Visitors had to have an entry permit and register their visit in a "house book".

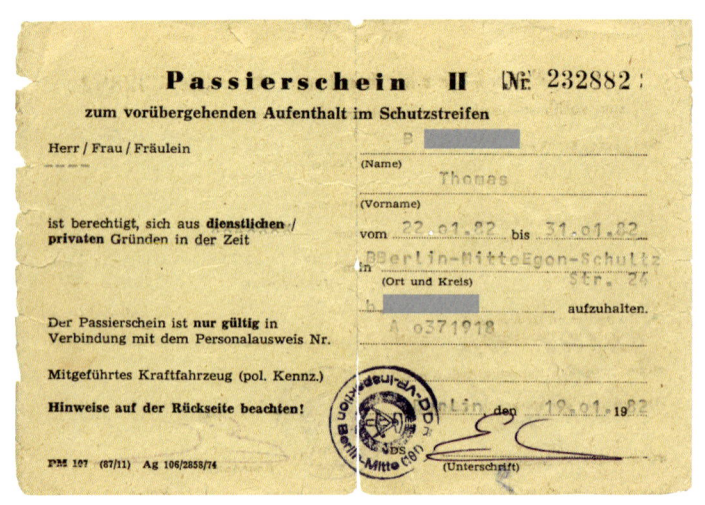

Permit to enter the border area, January 19, 1982
Stiftung Berliner Mauer

Excerpt from a "house book" in the border area, 1953 – 1980
Stiftung Berliner Mauer

View into the border strip on Bernauer Strasse, 1980s
Christine Bartels photographed the border strip from her apartment. Taking pictures of the border fortifications was strictly forbidden and could be construed as military espionage or preparation of an escape. Hence, there are very few personal photos showing the Wall from the East Berlin side.
Christine Bartels

Family photo in front of the "Palace of the Republic," August 28, 1976
The "Palace of the Republic," completed in 1976, was one of the GDR's symbolic structures. It was supposed to manifest the SED state's concern for the people and the political consensus between the SED and the populace.
Christoph Eckelt, Caro Fotoagentur

Sunbathing in front of the Wall, 1987
Jürgen Hohmuth, Stiftung Berliner Mauer

Rapprochement

The policies towards the East pursued by West Germany's social-liberal government led to several treaties with Eastern bloc states in the early 1970s. One of them was the Four Power Agreement on Berlin in 1971, which regulated traffic between West Germany and West Berlin. That same year West Germany and the GDR agreed on the details of the Transit Treaty. Beginning in June 1972, West Berliners were allowed to travel to East Berlin or the GDR without having to explain the purpose of the trip. Increasing numbers of West Berliners and West Germans took advantage of the eased travel restrictions.

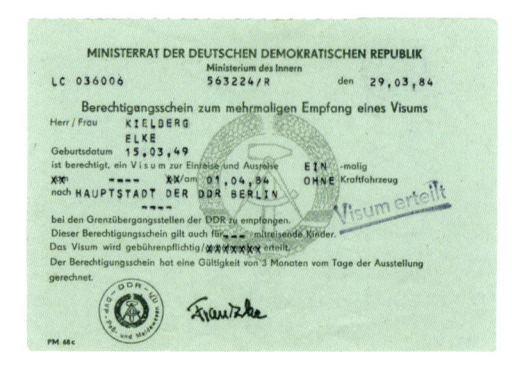

Authorization to receive a visa to enter East Berlin, March 29, 1984
Stiftung Berliner Mauer

Teenage tourists at the Brandenburg Gate in East Berlin, May 15, 1974
When travel restrictions were eased, West German schools organized significantly more class trips to West Berlin. A day trip to East Berlin was a must.
Klaus Morgenstern, akg-images

Leading Up to the Fall of the Berlin Wall
Hartmut Richter

"Well, I always say, you can't be afraid when you are doing something like that. But the payoff is just so nice. You get to experience the joy felt by the people you bring together […] And I detested the regime. I understood why the people wanted to get out. But clearly, each trip was an incalculable risk."

Interview, Stiftung Berliner Mauer, 2012

Hartmut Richter was born in 1948 and had already come into conflict with the GDR political system as a schoolboy. The SED had no tolerance for beat music and long hair. He completed vocational training as a factory and transport railroad worker. His first escape attempt failed in 1965. The following year Hartmut Richter fled across the Teltow Canal and reached West Berlin. In 1972 he began helping other GDR citizens flee to West Germany by hiding them in his car. He brought them over the border on the transit road between West Germany and West Berlin. He was arrested by border troops in 1975. Hartmut Richter was sentenced to 15 years in prison. He came to the West in 1980 after the West German government paid for his release.

Transit under Control

The rise in transit traffic posed a challenge to the GDR. Vehicle inspections were only admissible when there were concrete grounds for suspicion. The more permeable border provided East Germans with new ways to escape. The secret police continually expanded its control and surveillance measures along the transit routes. It monitored both the travelers and the people they contacted throughout the country.

Surveillance camera at the transit autobahn near Magdeburg, 1980s
MfS photo, BStU

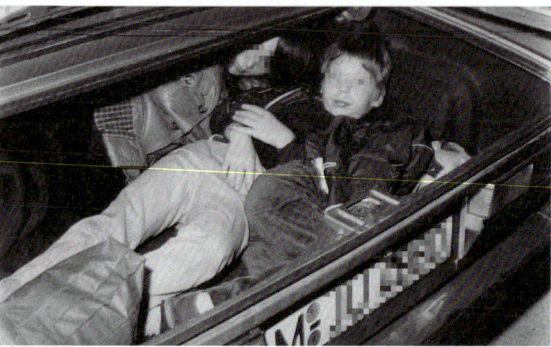

Failed escape attempt, September 12, 1983
The BMW was inspected at the Marienborn checkpoint and the passengers were arrested. The secret police made the escapees reenact how they had hidden in the escape vehicle. The young woman was given a four-year prison sentence. The escape helper was sentenced to five years and six months in prison. The two children were placed in a children's home.
MfS photo, BStU

Forbidden Ways

Veronika Schneider

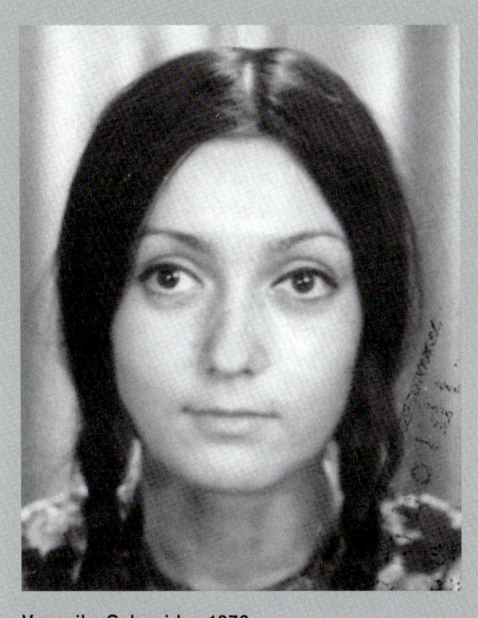

Veronika Schneider, 1970
Veronika Schneider

1952 Born in East Berlin
1970 Study at the Humboldt University in East Berlin
1973 Escape to the West

Veronika Schneider grew up in Berlin before the city was divided. She got her high school degree in East Berlin and planned to study costume design. But the school director pushed her to study cultural science instead. When, as a student, she was expected to join the SED, she requested to leave the university. Her boyfriend at the time was planning to flee to the West. Since Veronika Schneider saw no future for herself in the GDR, she decided to flee too. A friend from the West helped smuggle them across the transit route to West Germany in 1973. They hid in the trunk of an Audi 100.

After her escape, Veronika Schneider visits her uncle in Munich, 1973
Before the Wall was built, her uncle, while serving as a young border soldier, fled across the inner German border. In 1973, he smuggled his sister and her husband to West Germany in the trunk of his car.
Veronika Schneider

Veronika Schneider (left) while visiting her cousin in Karlsruhe in West Germany, 1957
Veronika Schneider

Beyond Borders: Radio and Television

In most regions of the GDR, people had access to television and radio programs from the West. The SED leadership saw a threat in having information available that it had no influence over. After the Wall was built, it tried unsuccessfully to block the reception of Western media. In the 1970s, East German television had far fewer viewers during prime time than did West German channels. The SED leadership's efforts to make national television programming more appealing in the 1980s were mildly successful. But for East Germans, Western media remained the more credible information source, especially when it related news about their own country.

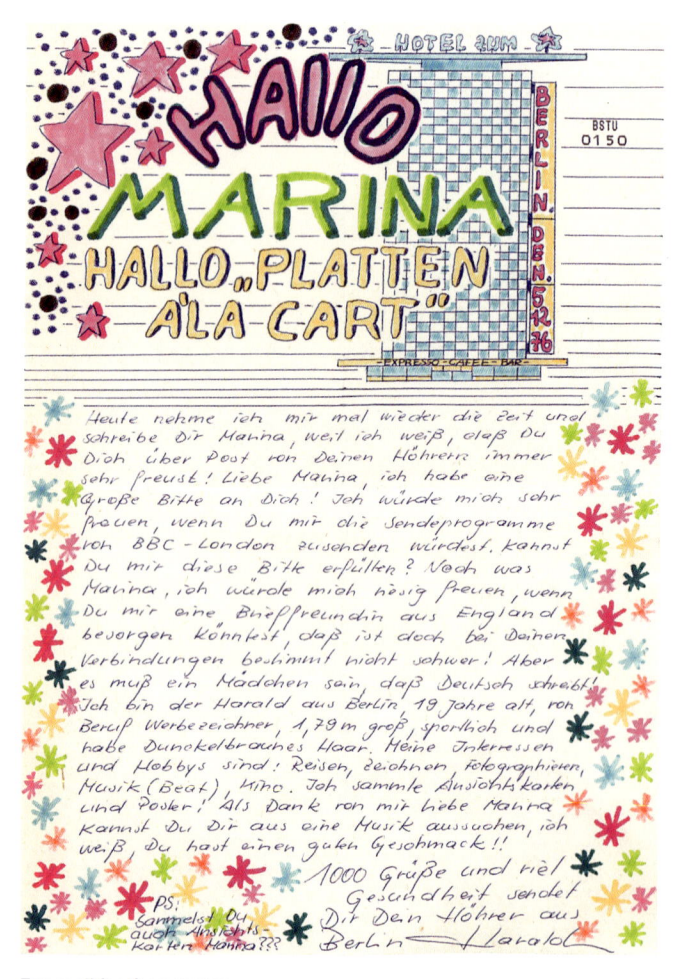

Fan mail for the program "Records à la carte" on BBC, December 5, 1976
The radio program "Records à la carte" was very popular with teenagers in the GDR. Full-length songs were played during the show. The listeners could record the songs on tape and listen to them repeatedly. In his fan letter, Harald asks the BBC to send him a copy of the program and to provide him with an English pen pal.
BStU

Detlef Matthes

Detlef Matthes, 1967
Detlef Matthes

1968 Born in Eberswalde
1987 Arrested
1988 Emigrates from the GDR

Detlef Matthes grew up near Berlin. He enjoyed listening to western rock and pop music. On the weekend of Whitsun, 1987, a major rock festival took place in front of the Reichstag in West Berlin with David Bowie, Eurythmics and Genesis. Detlef Matthes and thousands of other young people went to the Brandenburg Gate so that they could at least hear their idols from the other side of the Wall. The situation escalated when the East German police tried to push the teenagers back. Detlef Matthes described this in a letter he sent to the West German TV program "Kontraste." He was arrested, but thanks to an amnesty, was released by the summer of 1987. He submitted an application to emigrate and left the GDR in February 1988.

Teenagers at the Brandenburg Gate listening to the rock concert in front of the Reichstag, June 7, 1987
Detlef Matthes

Camera EXA 1b from the Ihagee company in Dresden, 1970s
Detlef Matthes received this reflex camera on his confirmation. He used it to document the protests at the Brandenburg Gate and to secretly photograph the Wall from the East Berlin side.
Detlef Matthes

Stagnancy

**Fruit and vegetable shop in Erfurt,
April 1, 1985**
Peter Seyfferth, ullstein bild

Political Impulses from the East

When Erich Honecker took office as head of the SED in 1971, many East Germans shared a hope for political change. But they were disappointed. Political reforms failed to emerge and the SED leadership continued to crack down on critics. They were persecuted, arrested and sometimes expatriated. At the same time, new political movements were emerging in the neighboring Eastern bloc countries, such as the "Charta 77" in Czechoslovakia and the Solidarność trade union movement in Poland in 1980. The SED leadership watched these developments with growing suspicion. There were people within the population who felt strong sympathy for them.

Strike-leader Lech Walesa speaks at the entrance to the Lenin Shipyard in Danzig, August 25, 1980
In summer 1980, Polish workers rose up against the communist government and founded "Solidarność," an independent trade union. In December 1981, the Polish government declared martial law and forbid the work of the trade union. Solidarność was not tolerated again until April 1989. The dictatorship in Poland came to an end a short time later.
unknown photographer, AFP, Getty Images

Illegal flyers from East Berlin, August 26, 1981
The unidentified authors used a simple stamp set to create flyers with the slogan: "Do it like the Poles." They distributed them in East Berlin. The secret police's search for the authors remained unsuccessful.
BStU

State-prescribed Stagnancy Instead of Glasnost

On March 11, 1985, Mikhail Gorbachev became General Secretary of the Communist Party in the Soviet Union. Soviet politics soon underwent fundamental change. Economic and political problems had put the leading power of the Eastern bloc in a precarious situation. The solution, Gorbachev believed, resided in a policy of openness ("Glasnost") and restructuring ("Perestroika"). Gorbachev also embarked on a new foreign policy course. Until then the Brezhnev Doctrine had codified the Soviet Union's claim to power over the Eastern bloc. Gorbachev wanted to grant these friendly governments more independence. This fed the East Germans' hope for political change.

The slogan "Glasnost Now" scrawled on a building in the East Berlin district of Prenzlauer Berg, 1989
Volker Döring, BILDART

Patch with hammer and sickle on a handbag, 1989
The symbols of the Soviet flag became very popular among young people in the GDR when the Soviet Union embarked on a political change of course.
Volker Döring, BILDART

Economic Crisis in the GDR

Erich Honecker's new economic and social policies were supposed to significantly improve the living standard and availability of goods and raise tolerance of the regime. For this same reason, the subsidy for basic needs was increased: food prices, rents, heat and electricity costs remained constant over years. Although this course strongly overtaxed the GDR's economic capacity, the SED leadership adhered to its policies, plunging the country into a deep crisis.

"Our 2nd youth collective [...] is not able to work optimally because the machinery [...] is technically and morally worn out. A three-shift operating schedule is not feasible given the frequency of break-downs. Only limited general repairs are carried out in the republic. [...] My employees have no more tolerance for these conditions, given that twice a day new, higher demands are placed on them. A degree of resignation is apparent."

Petition submitted by a member of the SED to the Chemical Industry Ministry, October 23, 1986

Berlin satirical magazine "Eulenspiegel," 1984
"The day will come when the goods we produce are of such good quality that we will have to conduct security checks at the gate."
Heinz Behling

Espenhain lignite refinery plant, May 5, 1989
Rising oil prices forced the GDR to use domestic brown coal as its main energy and raw material source. Old industrial plants were still operated although they were highly susceptible to breakdowns.
Jansson, ullstein bild

Tom Sello protests with a gas mask against the air pollution in the GDR, July 4, 1982
The SED leadership tried to conceal the true extent of environmental damage. Young people used an unauthorized bike demonstration to draw attention to the growing pollution.
MfS photo, BStU

Pre-war buildings in the East Berlin district of Prenzlauer Berg, 1988
In the city centers of the GDR, neighborhoods with old buildings fell increasingly into decay. Since the 1970s, a large amount of resources were put into creating building areas constructed of prefabricated concrete slabs. But the GDR's economy was not strong enough to meet the growing needs for new housing.
Harald Hauswald,
OSTKREUZ - Agentur der Fotografen

Prefab housing estate Neuberesinchen in Frankfurt/Oder, 1988
Thomas Kläber, akg-images

Exhibition in the
Documentation Center, 2015
Berthold Weidner

Cornelia Thiele

The Last Years of the Wall

Despite a few isolated acts of protest,[1] the final years of the Wall were characterized by stability and normality. The Wall that stood during this period was more effective than ever before and, from the perspective of those on both sides, its existence had become a normality. Although the two halves of the city had grown apart during the 25 years since the Wall had been built and their residents had adjusted and grown accustomed to it in very different ways, the border had not become any less brutal or dangerous over the years. Deaths still occurred at the Wall and the arbitrarily granted travel visas did little to make the Wall more permeable to East Berliners and GDR citizens. So what made a "normalization of the abnormal" in the people's daily lives possible and what did it mean?

When the Wall was built in 1961, Berliners in the East and West vented their anger over the Wall and the city's division, and engaged in public protests. But such protests soon died down. On both sides a sense of powerlessness to change "world politics" had set in. West Berliners became used to life with the Wall. Some of them moved away from neighborhoods that were situated near the Wall and avoided streets that led up to it. For others, walking along the Wall on their way to work became routine.

In the early 1970s, the new policies towards the East that were introduced by the Social Democratic government in West Germany led to several East-West agreements that further eased the situation for West Berliners. New transit regulations made leaving West Berlin relatively easy and its island-like situation lost its menacing character. West Berliners even began to recognize the benefits of having a Wall: children could play at the Wall without having to worry about traffic. After the Wall was built, some properties that had once been situated on busy streets were now on quiet streets at the city's edge. In 1988, when an exchange of territory was negotiated with the GDR that would have altered the position of the Wall on the Lohmühlen Bridge, people in Berlin-Neukölln protested to keep the Wall where it was. Residents feared that the bridge would become a busy thoroughfare.

The Wall also became a West Berlin trademark and tourist attraction. Nothing like it existed elsewhere in the world. "A trip to Berlin is worth it!" went the slogan – especially because of the Wall. It became the symbol of the inhumanity of the SED dictatorship, which is why the West German government sponsored educational tours to Berlin. On tours of the city, buses stopped at the viewing platforms set up along the border. Street vendors sold beverages and sausages along with postcards and souvenirs of the Wall. The Wall was a lucrative business.[2]

Through its unusual island-like situation, West Berlin developed into a unique socio-cultural "biotope" that differed strongly from West Germany.[3] These differences were created by many circumstances, in particular by the de-militarized special status of West Berlin. Unlike West Germany, there was no compulsory military service in West Berlin. In response to America's engagement in the Vietnam War, young West Germans came to West Berlin both to avoid compulsory military service and to protest against militarism and imperialism. Berlin evolved into the center of the student movement headed by Rudi Dutschke. The half-city of West Berlin, surrounded by a wall, attracted many young people striving for individuality and alternative lifestyles. The cheap neighborhoods near the Wall provided space for a diverse urban subculture: "Our concern is not always about world revolution," Heinrich Dubel wrote. "Sometimes we spend entire nights at the cinema or strive to achieve alternative lifestyles that are situated somewhere between the end of time and the rejection of consumerism, between housing battles and queerness, between punk and new wave."[4]

"The Wall must stay." Graffiti on Lohmühlen Bridge in West Berlin
Hans-Peter Stiebing

Postcard of the Berlin Wall, 1980s
Stiftung Berliner Mauer

The gay movement's first political group in Germany was founded in West Berlin. Here: A demonstration by "Homosexual Action of West Berlin," June 9, 1973
unknown photographer, Schwules Museum*

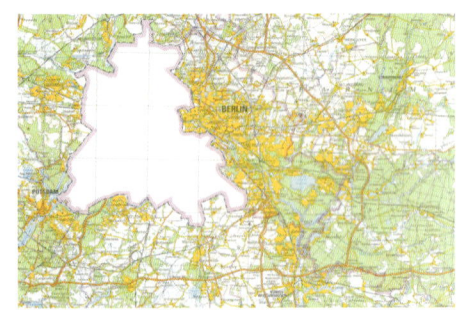

West Berlin: A "white spot on the map," GDR city map, 1988
digitalised, Zentral- und Landesbibliothek Berlin (ZLB), Spezialbereich Berlin Studien

Photograph of the border fortifications taken secretly from a highrise on Leipziger Strasse, 1986/1987
Detlef Matthes

Life in the walled-in city had "normalized" by the late 1980s. West Berlin was a city of diversity and contradictions: a co-existence of the bourgeois lifestyle and anarchy, of provincialism and urbanity. For this reason, bringing an end to Germany's division in 1989 seemed like the "old jokes we had hidden away in the back corner of the bottom drawer a long time ago."[5]

Over time the Wall in West Berlin became an integral part of the city's identity. The SED government, on the other hand, used repressive measures and taboos to make the Wall seem normal and accepted. When demonstrators in East Berlin protested against the closed border, the SED leadership took harsh action against them and many people were arrested and imprisoned. East Germans were not allowed to approach the border or to wave or call out to people on the West Berlin side. The personal connections between the two city halves were to be severed once and for all. The area near the border was declared a restricted area that could only be entered with authorization or a resident's permit. The people living directly along the border were under constant surveillance. Despite these conditions, many East Berliners learned to forget about or ignore the Wall in their everyday lives. Lutz Rathenow recalls: "I was struck in the beginning by how unfazed East Berliners were by the peculiarities created by the border. An example: a trip on the S-Bahn from Schönhauser Allee to the Pankow station ran directly along the border. The border planners thus felt compelled to build a wall on both sides of the track. One glided through as if in a transit tunnel. [...] On every subsequent ride, the observer could recognize the visitor by his confused, curious glance out the window. The border-resistant East Berliner never raised his eyes from the newspaper."[6]

The close proximity of East Berlin to the West posed a special challenge to the SED leadership. East Berliners were not supposed to show any interest in the Wall or even be aware of the West's existence. The GDR tried to block out West Berlin by printing official Berlin maps that portrayed West Berlin as a blank white space.

The SED leadership made East Berlin the "capital of the GDR." Through city planning and propaganda, it thus served to counterbalance West Berlin, the "showcase of the West." East Berlin's special role allotted it several privileges that other cities in the GDR did not enjoy, such as a better supply of consumer goods. The redesign of the city centre around Alexanderplatz also played an important role. The Palace of the Republic, for example, was built as a GDR prestige building. The government held its mass events on Alexanderplatz with its World Clock and "Fountain of International Friendship." The large square was a busy and popular meeting place both for East Berliners and tourists. To young people, East Berlin in the 1980s represented a big city that was less insular and offered more opportunities than the small towns in rural areas of the GDR. The neighborhoods in Prenzlauer Berg and Friedrichshain, with their decaying pre-war buildings, also provided space for alternative lifestyles, but not without drawing the attention of the State Security.[7]

And yet, the Wall and the taboos associated with it were not enough to seal off the East Berlin population and establish East Berlin as an independent city. For many East Berliners, including Detlef Matthes, the taboos and bans had their own fascinating appeal. When Matthes was a child his father took him to the top of the television tower on Alexanderplatz where they had a view of West Berlin: so close and yet out of reach. At 18 Matthes returned to East Berlin and secretly photographed the Wall – an act that would prove fateful.

On Whitsun 1987, Matthes photographed teenagers who had gathered at the Brandenburg Gate to hear a concert that their Western idols were playing on the other side of the Wall in front of the Reichstag. When the East German People's Police and State Security tried to stop this, the teenagers protested loudly, calling out "The Wall must go!" Detlef Matthes managed to get away, but he was shocked by the brutality of the state authority. He described what he saw in a report that he sent to Western broadcasting stations that was intercepted by the State Security. When the police searched his apartment, they found the illegal photographs he had taken. Matthes was arrested and charged with espionage and engaging in illegal contact with the enemy. He was sentenced to many years in prison.

The closing of the border on August 13, 1961 came as a shock to most residents of West and East Berlin. On both the political and individual level, the West side learned to deal with the Wall pragmatically, leading to a normalization of Berlin's division. The two half-cities developed separately from one another into independent centers and the people adjusted to the new situation. Inevitably they came to accept and become accustomed to the Wall. On the East side, the opposition movement and discontent within the population grew during the last years of the GDR. But it was not until opposition members and other discontented East Germans took to the streets to protest that a movement developed with a strong "dynamic, which unraveled the system, quickly bringing an end to the country and the fall of the Wall."[8]

1
Also see: Ole Giec/Frank Willmann (eds.), *Mauerkrieger. Aktionen gegen die Mauer in West-Berlin 1989*, Berlin 2014; Anne Hahn/Frank Willman (eds.), *Der weiße Strich. Vorgeschichte und Folgen einer Kunstaktion an der Berliner Mauer*, Berlin 2011.
2
See Hans Georg Lehmann, "Mit der Mauer leben? Die Einstellung zur Berliner Mauer im Wandel," in: *Aus Politik und Zeitgeschichte*, B 33 – 34/86, pp. 19 – 34, 1986.
3
See Stiftung Stadtmuseum Berlin, *West:Berlin. Eine Insel auf der Suche nach Festland*, Booklet, Berlin 2014; and the essays in: Stefanie Eisenhut/Hanno Hochmuth/Martin Sabrow (eds.): *West-Berlin, Zeithistorische Forschungen*, Jg. 11, H. 2, Göttingen 2014; Onlinedokumentation der Tagung des Stadtmuseums und des Zentrums für Zeithistorische Forschung: *Biotop Berlin. Neuere Forschungen zur Geschichte West-Berlins*, http://www.kongressradio.de/portal/tagung-biotop-berlin, Berlin, 4. – 5.12.2014.

4
Heinrich Dubel, *West-Berlin 1980 – 1989*, http://www.heinrichdubel.de/1_voe/11_westberlin.html (30.1.2015).
5
Patrick Süskind, "Deutschland – eine Midlife-crisis," in: *Der Spiegel*, 38/1990, pp. 118 – 125.
6
Lutz Rathenow, "Die Mauer und ihr Verdrängen aus dem Alltag der Ost-Berliner," in: *Deutschland Archiv Online, 50 Jahre Mauerfall*, Part 2, 7/2011, http://www.hsozkult.de/journal/id/zeitschriftenausgaben-6310.
7
See essays by Bruno Flierl and by Wolfgang Kil, in: Günter Schlusche/Verena Pfeiffer-Kloss/Gabi Dolff-Bonekämper/Axel Klausmeier (eds.), *Stadtentwicklung im doppelten Berlin. Zeitgenossenschaft und Erinnerungsorte*, Berlin 2014.
8
Jens Schöne, *Stabilität und Niedergang. Ost-Berlin im Jahr 1987*, Berlin 2011, pp. 73 – 75.

Opposition and Emigration Movement

Members of the peace movement
publicly demonstrate in Dresden,
September 18, 1987
unknown photographer, epd

Leading Up to the Fall of the Berlin Wall
Günter Jeschonnek

"And, of course, when the SED government learned that we had held discussions on this level, it wasn't pleased. We didn't make a moral case, we didn't even say: We don't like the GDR. But we let it be known of course. That was our strategy."

Interview, Stiftung Berliner Mauer, 2012

Günter Jeschonnek was born in 1950. His parents were members of the SED and were supportive of building the Berlin Wall. At age 15 he began an apprenticeship in farming and later decided to study agricultural engineering. When he refused to participate in the pre-military training, he was forced to serve as a tractor operator for a year "to prove himself practically." A plan to escape in 1973 failed, but could not be proven. He studied theatre directing and later worked as a theatre director. But after he submitted an application to emigrate in 1986, he was not offered any more jobs. Günter Jeschonnek co-founded the workgroup "Citizens' Rights in the GDR," which demanded the right of all GDR citizens to emigrate based on GDR law and international agreements. In 1987 the Ministry of State Security forced him and his family to emigrate and move to West Berlin.

Opposition

Despite surveillance and repression, voiced opposition was never completely silenced. In the 1980s, independent peace, environmental and human rights groups formed. Under the auspices of the Protestant Church, in whose rooms the groups held their meetings, they achieved a limited oppositional sphere.

Association of Total Conscientious Objectors

When the GDR introduced a compulsory military service in 1962, some young men refused to serve. Beginning in 1964, conscientious objectors were allowed to fulfill their military duty by serving as construction soldiers. But there were some men who refused to join any military service and they were willing to go to prison for their principles. As of 1986, these "total conscientious objectors" began organizing themselves throughout the country and establishing an international network. The "Association of Total Conscientious Objectors" was founded in East Berlin to support objectors and their families. By 1989 the association had established 17 regional chapters. It criticized the increased militarization of the GDR and protested against the international arms race.

Peace and Human Rights Initiative

The "Peace and Human Rights Initiative" (IFM) was founded in 1985. The group operated independently of the Protestant Church. In petitions to the state and party, it demanded basic democratic rights. It protested against human rights violations and the persecution of dissidents. The IFM used western media to spread its protest. Its members were under constant surveillance by the secret police, which used every means at its disposal, including smuggling informers (IM) into the group, to break it up.

Information poster from the "Friends of the Total Conscientious Objectors," 1980s
Robert-Havemann-Gesellschaft e.V.

Secret police photo of the IFM flyer campaign, 1987
BStU

First issue of the underground magazine "Grenzfall," 1986
In 1986, the IFM began publishing its own magazine. Seventeen issues, with 800 copies each, were printed between 1986 and 1989. Beginning with the third issue, the IFM intentionally refrained from including the protective note: "For internal church use only."
Robert-Havemann-Gesellschaft e.V.

Monika Haeger
IM "Karin Lenz"

Monika Haeger, 1980er Jahre
BStU

1945	Born in East Berlin
1982	Recruited as an informant (IM) for the secret police
1986	Founding member of the Peace and Human Rights Initiative
2006	Dies in Berlin

The East Berliner Monika Haeger had worked as an editor since 1971. The secret police recruited her as an informant and orchestrated her expulsion from the SED so that she could be more easily infiltrated into the opposition groups "Women for Peace" and "Peace and Human Rights Initiative." Under the alias "Karin Lenz," she reported to the secret police about the work of these groups. She was almost exposed in early 1989 when an IFM group photo surfaced on which Monika Haeger had identified the people by name. At first she denied her role as an informant and was able to dispel suspicion. A short time later she revealed herself. In 1990 she commented on her spying activities in a television interview.

Church from Below

In 1986, an agreement was made between the Berlin-Brandenburg church leadership and the GDR government. The state allowed the church to conduct a church congress in East Berlin. In return the church leadership agreed to curtail the autonomy of grassroots groups. It forbid the peace workshop planned in 1987, one of the most important information events organized by the East German opposition. Several groups reacted by organizing a very successful independent "church congress from below." After the church congress, the group continued to exist as the "Church from Below" (KvU). With its demands for "Glasnost in the State and Church," it expressed criticism of the authoritarian structures in East German society. The KvU primarily represented the concerns of the oppositional youth scene.

KvU event poster, September 11–12, 1987
Robert-Havemann-Gesellschaft e.V.

Members of the KvU at the closing ceremony of the Protestant Church congress demanding "Glasnost in the State and Church," August 26, 1987
Klaus Mehner,
Bild 87_0628_REL_EvKT_EndeC_02,
Bundesstiftung Aufarbeitung

Punks in the cellar of the Church of the Redeemer in Berlin-Lichtenberg, 1980s
SUBstitut

Opposition and the Wall
Most importantly, opposition groups in the GDR called for political and social changes in their country. The demands for an open border and German unity were at most marginal. Many members of the opposition felt that Germany's division was an historical consequence of its having started the Second World War. They criticized the closed East German border and demanded the legally protected right to travel to countries in the West. Very few in the opposition could imagine an end to the Wall regime and it was not their intention to bring an end to the GDR.

Samisdat magazine "Aufrisse," 1987
The initiative "Rejection of the Practice and Principle of Exclusion" criticized the Berlin Wall for creating enemy images and isolating the GDR from the rest of the world. It demanded complete travel freedom in western and socialist countries.
Robert-Havemann-Gesellschaft e. V.

Repression and Opposition

The SED and secret police tried to break up opposition groups in the late 1980s. But neither arrests nor expatriation succeeded in silencing the opposition. East German citizens usually gathered in the protected rooms of the Protestant Church to hold vigils in solidarity with the people who were persecuted. People throughout the GDR were informed of these events through western media reports. The state was no longer able to isolate the opposition from the larger population.

Rooms of the Environmental Library on the day of the raid, November 25, 1987
The Environmental Library in the Zion Church was a meeting place for East Berlin opposition members. It was raided by the secret police in 1987. They confiscated the printing press used for the magazine "Grenzfall" and arrested the staff that was there. But the secret police operation did not weaken the Environmental Library. Its prestige grew and acts of solidarity led to the release of its members from prison.
MfS photo, BStU

Appeal of solidarity with the arrested members of the Environmental Library, caricature by Dirk Moldt, 1987
Robert-Havemann-Gesellschaft e.V.

Dietrich Lusici

Emigration Movement
The policy of détente culminated in 1975 at the Conference on Security and Cooperation in Europe (CSCE). All the participating states, including the GDR, agreed to respect human rights and fundamental freedoms. They expressed their intention to support human contacts and consider favorably requests to reunify families. In response, almost 20,000 East Germans applied to resettle in the West. The number of requests to emigrate rose to more than 300,000 between 1977 and the summer of 1989.

The painter Dietrich Lusici grew up in the Spreewald. In 1974, he won first place at a poster biennale in Warsaw for a poster criticizing pollution. But in the following years, he experienced political constriction instead of artistic freedom. He was not allowed to accept invitations from Western countries. When he submitted an emigration application for himself and his family in 1984, the situation worsened. He received very few commissions and was only able to show his work in rooms of the church. The uncertain future and financial difficulties weighed heavily on the painter. This experience found expression in several of his art pieces. In 1986, Dietrich Lusici was permitted to leave the GDR with his family and his entire art collection, and resettle in West Berlin.

Dietrich Lusici, 1979
Dietrich Lusici

1942 Born in Ragow
1984 Applies to emigrate
1986 Resettles in West Berlin

Journal and sketchbook from the time of their emigration, 1985
While waiting for their application to be approved, Dietrich Lusici kept a journal with many drawings. The sketches show his deep preoccupation with German division and political repression in the GDR.
Dietrich Lusici, VG Bild-Kunst Bonn

273

Frank Sorge

Frank Sorge, mid-1980s
Frank Sorge

1969   Born in Straussberg
1985   Sister's escape through Hungary
1987   Immigration to Canada

Frank Sorge had close contact with relatives in West Germany who regularly visited his family in the GDR. The entire Sorge family maintained a distance to the SED state. Feeling constricted and patronized in the GDR, his sister fled to the West during a family holiday in Hungary in 1985. On returning home, Frank, who was 15 at the time, was interrogated by the secret police. His mother's marriage to a German-Canadian in 1987 made it possible for Frank to leave the GDR. Approval for emigration to Western countries other than West Germany was granted more quickly. Frank and his mother were allowed to leave that same year. In 1988, Frank Sorge, by then of full age, returned from Canada and moved to West Berlin.

Greetings from home on the back of a photo, 1987
Frank Sorge

Barbara Große

Barbara Große, 1970s
Barbara Große

1947 Born in Leipzig
1983 Arrested
1984 Ransom paid for release to West Germany

Barbara Grosse submitted the first emigration application for her and her family in 1976. The 29-year-old sound engineer yearned to travel freely and live a life without political paternalism. When her mother entered retirement in 1981 and was allowed to leave the GDR legally, Barbara Grosse requested that the family be reunited. She paid several visits to the Permanent Representation of West Germany in East Berlin and asked for support for her application. After visiting the West German embassy in Prague in 1983, she was arrested by the secret police. The Leipzig district court construed her contact to the embassy as "treasonous agent activity." Barbara Grosse spent 15 months in prison before West Germany paid ransom for her release in March 1984. Her husband and children were also permitted to leave the GDR a short time later.

Information from neighbors who spied on her, March 11, 1977
The secret police kept surveillance on Barbara Grosse and questioned neighbors about her. Some people provided information willingly, vilifying her and her family.
BStU

Repression and Protest

People had many different reasons for applying to leave the country. Leaving family and friends – probably forever – was not easy for anyone. Nevertheless the number of people wanting to emigrate continued to rise in the 1980s. Many had been denied the privilege to study, were harassed at work, or were banned from their profession. This put them in a difficult financial situation. Some of the applicants decided to form groups and make their demands public. The SED and secret police feared these groups and persecuted them severely.

A man who wanted to emigrate, after his arrest, 1980s
Public protest was often the last resort for people forced to wait many years for their emigration application to be approved. Most protestors were arrested, but usually, after a time, ransom was paid for their release to West Germany.
MfS photo, BStU

A banner confiscated by the secret police, November 8, 1988
A couple used a bed sheet to make a banner on which they wrote: "We want out of here!" The banner was attached to their balcony for all to see. The couple was arrested and sentenced to 16 months in prison.
MfS photo, BStU

Arrest of protestors wanting to leave the country, February 11, 1988
East Germans who wanted to emigrate protested in front of the Permanent Representation of West Germany in East Berlin. The East German police forcefully ended the demonstration and arrested the demonstrators. This did not, however, prevent the protest from becoming known.
Klaus Mehner, Bild 88_0211_POL-Ausreise_14, Bundesstiftung Aufarbeitung

People who applied to emigrate attend the church congress in Görlitz, 1988
Bernd Bohm, dpa Picture-Alliance

Katja Böhme

"You want to stay, we want to go"[1] – The Emigration Movement and the Political Opposition in the GDR

The people who took to the streets to protest and those who fled the GDR via Hungary, Czechoslovakia and Poland were pivotal in bringing about the collapse of the SED state. These movements destabilized the state, which led to the rapid downfall of SED rule. Each individual's action, however, reflected a crucial life decision: whether to stay or whether to go.

Before the mass exodus from the GDR began and the protests in the GDR evolved into a mass movement, most of the people who had decided to protest openly or to leave the country had organized into small groups of which the majority of the GDR population remained unaware. Many GDR citizens had either resigned themselves to the closed society in which they lived – and to the schizophrenic situation created by the state – or they had actively chosen to accept it. Before the democratic process and mass protests began in 1989, only a few openly questioned the situation in which they lived. Among them were to two distinct groups: people who had been opposed to the GDR from the very beginning and who had organized themselves into opposition groups, and people who, as of the mid-1970s, had submitted official applications to the state requesting permission to immigrate to the West. The first group tackled the prescribed silence of society in small groups and tried to create an alternative public sphere in which they could articulate and discuss their demands for change. Those in the second group chose to turn their backs on the GDR permanently, hoping for the chance to embark on a new, free life in the Federal Republic.

In addition to the changed political conditions at the end of the 1980s and the deteriorating economic situation in the East, these two groups, the emigration movement and the political opposition within the GDR, are generally cited as highly influential forces that contributed to the collapse of the SED. The interests of these two groups, however, could not have been more divergent. The one group wanted to change the GDR; the other group wanted to leave it. Thus, it is not surprising that tensions existed between them. In retrospect, and with the knowledge of the successful outcome, explaining the collapse of the GDR regime as the result of the combined impact of the mass exodus in 1989 and the demonstrations initiated mostly by opposition groups reflects a simplification of the relationship between these two movements. A more thorough examination reveals the conflicts and contradictions imbedded in the actions of the protagonists at that time and the synergetic effect that existed between them in spite of their differences.

"Stay home and defend yourself daily"[2]

As different as the GDR opposition groups were in their political aims and chosen methods of action, they tended to share a similar attitude towards emigration applicants. Their strong rejection of people who had applied to leave the GDR was based on a fear that emigration applicants would become politically involved in the opposition as a way to speed up their application process. Fearing exploitation by the applicants, the opposition systematically excluded them from their circles. The reforms taking place in the Soviet Union in the late 1980s spread the hope that change was possible, even in the GDR, and the opposition did not want to risk having its interests hindered by those applying to leave: Looking back, Klaus Wolfram describes the hope harbored by the movement: "The reform potential was revived and the dictatorship had been weakened … In this situation, linking the opposition to the emigration applicants would have meant isolating it from the atmosphere of reform and feeding arguments to the official party counter-forces."[3] This fear proved justified in January 1988: The State Security had already been planning to expatriate certain members of the opposition, but when a few of them joined emigration applicants and participated in the annual demonstration in memory of the murder of Rosa Luxemburg und Karl Liebknecht, the State Security used

Members of the opposition with homemade banners on the evening before the Luxemburg-Liebknecht demonstration, January 16, 1988
Bernd Freutel,
Robert-Havemann-Gesellschaft e.V.

Wolfgang Templin, Lotte Templin, Werner Fischer and Bärbel Bohley after their deportation to the West, February 6, 1988
unknown photographer, akg-images/AP

The group "Weisser Kreis" demonstrates on the "Platz der Kosmonauten" in Jena, 1983
BStU

the opportunity to carry out its plan, thus driving a wedge between the two opposition groups. In connection with the demonstration, the Stasi arrested more than 170 applicants and expelled them from the GDR with little warning. Those who wanted to leave the GDR had achieved their primary goal – emigration. But the Stasi had also arrested members of the opposition movement, including Wolfgang and Lotte Templin, Bärbel Bohley, Vera Wollenberger, Werner Fischer and Bert Schlegel. The State Security threatened them with long prison sentences if they did not agree to move to West Germany or Great Britain.

While in prison these individuals were unaware that their arrest had inspired expressions of widespread solidarity in the GDR. After their release to the West they learned that some members of their political circle interpreted their decision to leave the country as an act of betrayal. In an official statement in February 1988, the Environmental Library expressed its bitter disappointment over the emigration of its fellow member, Bert Schlegel: "We hope that he will someday be able to end his flight and find a new political and intellectual home. In any event, by leaving, Bert has damaged the reputation of the peace and environmental group of the Zion Church community. We plan to stay here and establish social and ecological conditions in our country that will make a more humane coexistence possible."[4] The circumstances led the group to make a harsh decision: "The peace and environmental circle of the Zion Church community has decided not to accept any more emigration applicants into its ranks in the future."[5]

The Environmental Library's bulletin "Umweltblätter" also contained angry attacks against emigration applicants. They were accused of "dreaming of West Germany, the land of milk and honey, Smarties, Onko coffee, Wienerwald chicken and a fairytale-like freedom." It described them as "incapable of solidarity and egocentric" and criticized their moral failure: "Self-help groups are started, but at the same time children are taken along as hostages to demonstrations. They leave their women and children, betray friends and supporters – any method is acceptable."[6]

In some places in the GDR, the events around the Luxemburg-Liebknecht demonstration helped mobilize the opposition, but in Berlin it was temporarily paralyzed. Having its members deported to the West weakened the opposition, both in numbers and morally. Moreover, the differences between the emigration applicants and the opposition in the GDR became permanently entrenched.

"Because we never had the chance to work with an opposition group…"[7]

Unlike the people in the political opposition, emigration applicants remained isolated. There are only a few examples of their forming groups such as the "Weisser Kreis" (white circle) in Jena and "Reisegruppe 88" (travel group 88) of the Denominational Church in Berlin-Treptow. Although the emigration movement was diffuse and unorganized, it was not necessarily non-political. The increased surveillance, discipline and punishment of applicants in the 1980s led many to become more politicized: they became more willing to take risks and go public with their concerns.[8]

Although most opposition groups showed little interest in the applicants' concerns, their need to support each other grew. In 1987, a group called "Citizens' Rights in the GDR" was founded in Berlin and became one of the few points where opposition and emigration applicants came together. It provided advice to people applying to leave and also demanded that the GDR government establish clear and legally-binding rules for legal emigration. It presented a statement on the United Nations' Day of Human Rights in 1987: "As long as the GDR continues to curtail human rights that are indispensable to a person's individual development, and as long as the real reasons for the emigration syndrome are not discussed publicly, the number of applicants applying to leave will continue to rise."[9] This plea to the GDR government could also be understood as an appeal to the opposition to recognize that the growing number of people applying to leave reflected their shared criticism of the social shortcomings in the GDR. Emigration applicants often felt misunderstood by the opposition and that their concerns and fears were not taken seriously. In the Environmental Library's "Umweltblätter," a reader who had applied to emigrate addressed the opposition's hostility: "You are lumping together everyone who has applied to emigrate. I think that is a big mistake." He was one of the applicants who had "searched for reasons to stay in this country." But as long as there is no mass pressure "from below, (…) I am unable to share your optimism regarding positive changes in the GDR. I am resigned, and out of concern for the future of my son, I will leave this country."[10]

Although the emigration applicants and the opposition members drew divergent conclusions from the political situation in the GDR, they shared an important similarity: At a time when the majority of the GDR population had accommodated itself to the ruling system in the GDR, they openly rejected their loyalty to the state, acted defiantly and became political, despite being well aware that this would lead to their social isolation and political persecution. Their actions were important in paving the way for the emancipation process that gripped the GDR population in the fall of 1989.

1
Günter Jeschonnek in the 68th meeting of the Enquete-Kommission, in: *Materialien der Enquete-Kommission "Aufarbeitung von Geschichte und Folgen der SED-Diktatur in Deutschland,"* Vol. VII,1, Baden-Baden 1995, p. 398.
2
Conspiratory text by Gerd Stadermann, founding member of the Pankow Peace Group, in which he votes for staying in the country in 1981.
3
Klaus Wolfram, *Geschichte des Guten Willens, Skizzen aus der Opposition*, Vol. 5, 1995.
4
Statement from the Environment Library on February 3, 1988, cited in: Thomas Klein: *Frieden und Gerechtigkeit. Die Politisierung der Unabhängigen Friedensbewegung in Ost-Berlin während der 80er Jahre*, Cologne 2007, p. 376.
5
Ibid.
6
Umweltblätter, February 12, 1988, 22/1988, p. 7.
7
See endnote 1.
8
Renate Hürtgen, *Ausreise per Antrag: Der lange Weg nach drüben. Eine Studie über Herrschaft und Alltag in der DDR-Provinz*, Göttingen 2014, p. 72.
9
Statement from "AG Staatsbürgerschaftsrecht der DDR" on the Day of Human Rights, December 10, 1987, printed in: Günter Jeschonnek: "Ausreise – Das Dilemma des Arbeiter- und-Bauern-Staates?," in: Ferdinand Kroh (eds.): *Freiheit ist immer Freiheit… Die Andersdenkenden in der DDR*, Berlin 1988, pp. 268 – 270, see also http://www.berliner-mauer-gedenkstaette.de/de/uploads/zeitzeugen_dokumente/jeschonnek-erklaerung-10-12-1987.pdf
10
Umweltblätter, March 3, 1988.

6

The Peaceful Revolution and Fall of the Wall

1989

East Berliners at the Bornholmer
Strasse border crossing,
November 9, 1989

Andreas Schoelzel

Erich Honecker on the VIP gallery during the military parade in East Berlin, October 7, 1989

Despite the mass exodus and increased protests throughout the country, the SED leadership chose to go forward with the traditional celebration of the 40th anniversary of the GDR.

unknown photographer, dpa Picture-Alliance

Occupation of the embassy in Prague, 1989

In the summer of 1989, tens of thousands of mostly young people fled to the West German embassies in Prague, Budapest and Warsaw. As many as 6,000 East Germans sought refuge in the Prague embassy. Tents and sanitary facilities were installed in the embassy courtyard for the refugees. Following negotiations with the GDR leadership, West German foreign minister Hans-Dietrich Genscher announced to the waiting refugees on September 30 that their long-awaited emigration had been approved. Over the next few days the refugees traveled by train to the West. But within a few days thousands of new refugees had arrived at the embassy, also hoping to emigrate.

Christian Seebode, Presse- und Informationsamt der Bundesregierung

Arrest of demonstrators, October 7, 1989

The official 40th anniversary celebration of the GDR did not pass without incident. Thousands of people throughout the country demonstrated for reforms. They demanded the recognition of the "New Forum," a new civil rights platform. The SED leadership reacted with severity. It had the police and secret police crack down on demonstrators with clubs and water cannons. Many people were injured and thousands were arrested. But the population did not allow itself to be intimidated. More and more people felt solidarity with those who had been arrested and joined the protests.

Nikolaus Becker,
Robert-Havemann-Gesellschaft e.V.

Monday demonstrations in Leipzig, October 9, 1989
After September 4, demonstrations were held every Monday following the peace prayers in the Nikolai Church. Despite the many arrests, the numbers of participants continued to grow. There was a strong fear after the harsh state action taken on October 7 that the protests might be put down by force. But more than 70,000 people gathered on October 9 to demonstrate for reforms. That was the turning point that caused the police forces to withdraw. The whole country learned from the western media that the demonstration had proceeded peacefully. The SED leadership's decision not to use violence led the protest to grow dramatically over the following weeks. On November 4, hundreds of thousands gathered at Alexanderplatz in Berlin.
unknown photographer, ullstein bild

Demonstration for the freedom of press, opinion and assembly on Karl-Liebknecht-Strasse in East Berlin, November 4, 1989.
unknown photographer, ullstein bild

285

East and West Berliners on top of the Wall at the Brandenburg Gate, November 9, 1989

There was no end to the exodus in the summer of 1989. The situation continued to worsen for the GDR leadership. At an international press conference broadcast live on East German television on the evening of November 9, Günter Schabowski, a member of the SED politburo, announced a new travel regulation. An hour later it was declared on western television: "The GDR is opening its borders." Thousands of East Berliners rushed to the border crossing to take advantage of the promised travel freedom. So many people had gathered at the Bornholmer Strasse border crossing in such a short period of time that the guard in charge at the checkpoint felt compelled to open the barrier shortly before midnight. Soon all the border crossings in Berlin were opened and tens of thousands of East Germans flocked to West Berlin.

Schraps, ullstein bild

Embracing at the Invalidenstrasse border crossing, November 9, 1989
Klaus Lehnartz, Photonet

An East Berlin family leaves the GDR from the Bornholmer Strasse border crossing, November 9, 1989
On the night of November 9, no one knew whether the border would stay open. This led many East Berliners to take advantage of what might be their only chance to leave the GDR.
Werner Mahler,
OSTKREUZ – Agentur der Fotografen

Regina Webert

Regina Webert moved to Berlin-Friedrichshain in 1988. She squatted a rundown apartment and worked for a taxi company. This is where she met her future husband. He had been planning to leave the GDR for a long time. Regina Webert decided to go with him, but didn't tell anyone about her plans. The young couple drove to Hungary during the summer holidays in 1989. They met friends from West Germany there, who helped them escape. On August 25, they set off together towards Austria. From Austria, they continued on to West Berlin. Regina Webert once again lives in her childhood home in Berlin-Rahnsdorf.

Regina Webert, 1989
Regina Webert

1967 Born in Bad Saarow
1985 Inherits a Trabi
1989 Flees via Hungary to Austria and West Berlin

Regina Webert's car key and waist bag, 1970s and 1980s
Regina Webert took only her waist pack with her when she fled. It contained her ID, car key and diary.
Donated by Regina Webert,
Stiftung Berliner Mauer

Marianne Birthler

The Year 1989 – Citizens' Movement and Revolution

This essay is based on: Marianne Birthler: Halbes Land. Ganzes Land. Ganzes Leben, 2nd edition, Berlin 2014.

The photos from the evening of November 9, 1989 of people hugging, cheering and shedding tears of joy are by now iconic images. Throughout the world this moment has become a symbol of liberation. But it is not the fall of the Wall that brought the people freedom, but the opposite: the fall of the Berlin Wall was only possible after the citizens of the GDR began their struggle for freedom. Yet their struggle could not have succeeded without the previous citizens' movements in Poland, Hungary and Czechoslovakia.

There had always been political opposition and protest in the GDR, but this always ran up against the tight boundaries set by the political system. People often paid for their actions with long prison sentences, and sometimes even with their lives. In the seventies and eighties, those who opposed the system no longer had to fear loss of life, but the state continued to react severely and brutally to acts of self-assertion or willfulness, even when they were initially non-political, i.e. expressed in music, dress or lifestyle. Those who aligned themselves with the independent peace movement, who addressed concerns about environmental pollution, or who organized themselves in gay and lesbian groups quickly drew the attention of the state. Dissidents often became political only after they encountered the brutality of the state. After experiencing such brutality first hand, people sought out others with similar experiences and shared concerns. Friendships formed and solidarity networks and political groups were created. Mutual trust and common values were often stronger than fear of persecution and repression.

But those who organized themselves outside of state structures risked being accused of and charged with "seditious formation of groups" or "unconstitutional association." Many groups therefore met in the rooms of the Protestant Church: if a group was accepted into the church community, it was regarded as part of the church's working groups and therefore legal. The numbers of groups seeking and acting under the protection of the church rose dramatically in the late eighties. Together with parish discussion groups and peace circles, they formed an interesting and diverse milieu that drew more and more people, attracting attention through various activities. At the behest of the SED, the State Security responded to this phenomenon with increased surveillance, harassment, and open repression.

But by then opposition groups were no longer willing to silently tolerate the SED's intimidation efforts. In the fall of 1987, when the State Security raided the Environmental Library in the Zion Church parish in Berlin and arrested several activists, a vocal protest was formed through vigils and intercession prayers. As expected, the GDR media kept quiet about this protest, but reports from accredited Western journalists stationed in East Berlin reached people in the GDR through the circuitous route of Western radio and television. After this, more and more people were prepared to speak out publicly on important political issues and protest against repressive measures and arrests. Compared with the silent majority, few people dared to organize themselves against the SED and lend public expression to their dissatisfaction. Although the movement continued to grow, far more people opted to escape the oppressive conditions by officially applying for permission from the state to leave the GDR.

Vigil in the Zion Church for the members of the Environmental Library who were arrested, November 27, 1987
Andreas Schoelzel

Those who recognized the sign of the times in early 1989 expected things to change. But which direction would the SED take? Would it follow the example of the Soviet Union and other Eastern bloc countries and risk cautious reform? Or would it use increased pressure and brutality against anyone who rebelled against the SED? After tanks crushed peaceful demonstrators on Tiananmen Square in Peking in June 1989, the SED offered its congratulations to the Chinese leaders. Thereafter, the term "Chinese solution" began to make the rounds: if the SED and GDR government welcomed the action taken by the military in Peking, then the GDR opposition had reason to fear this response from its leaders as well.

Several new groups were founded in September 1989: "New Forum," "Democracy Now," "Democratic Awakening" and the "United Left" all announced their establishment in the same week. Since early summer there had been talk of establishing a social democratic party. Environmental groups that had enjoyed growing popularity were also merging to establish a joint organization. In the following weeks, these associations, along with the three-year-old "Initiative for Peace and Human Rights," gave a form and voice to the growing and diverse citizens' movement. "New Forum," which acquired thousands of new members within a very short time, had the broadest public impact.

October 7, 1989 was the 40th anniversary of the founding of the GDR. The SED wanted to celebrate this day throughout the country with great fanfare, a large military parade and local fairs. While the leaders were celebrating themselves and the GDR, in many cities the opposition used the anniversary as an opportunity to speak out. Thousands came to the "Erlöserkirche," a large Protestant church in Berlin-Lichtenberg, where they demanded free elections under the auspices of the UN. Opposition groups also announced the formation of an electoral alliance – a seemingly utopian idea at the time.

In East Berlin the Gethsemane Church in the Prenzlauer Berg district became the main site of the revolution. Its doors stood open around the clock in early October 1989 and candles burned day and night in front of the entrance. A highly visible banner had been hung over the door with the words: "Keep watch and pray. Vigil for those who have been wrongly arrested." There was a continual coming and going at the church, which was both a place of refuge and an information center, a trouble spot and a place of rest. The Environmental Library organized a solemn vigil in the church. An increasing number of young people joined the group, which had begun a fast in the sanctuary, demanding freedom and democracy. The opposition groups' contact telephone also found a place in the Gethsemane parish, which became the delivery point for information.

On the afternoon of October 7, a spontaneous demonstration formed at the World Clock, a popular meeting place at Alexanderplatz, and it quickly grew. The crowd moved on to the Palace of the Republic, where the official state ceremony was taking place. The demonstrators remained peaceful, calling out slogans such as "Democracy – now or never" and "We are the people." The police and armed security units pushed the demonstrators back and the procession moved north towards the Gethsemane Church. The peaceful demonstrators were assaulted by police. In different areas dozens of people were violently loaded onto waiting trucks and taken away. The next day and night, armed police and "Stasi civilians" continued to brutally assault the peaceful demonstrators and make arrests. As many as 1,200 people had already been arrested.

October 9 was a Monday and demonstrations had been taking place every Monday in Leipzig for weeks. With each new week, the demonstrations grew larger. On that particular Monday, the leadership of the party and the security units were more nervous than ever before. There had been rumors that schools and day-care centers in the city had been closed, that hospitals had been put on alert, and that heavy vehicles were parked around the Leipzig city center, ready to take action against demonstrators. As the Leipzig residents swarmed to their churches, the Berliners prepared for another night of violence and arrests. But the fear was greatest in Leipzig. What no one could imagine until then seemed possible that day: the SED might use armed force against its own citizens. More than two thousand people had gathered in the Gethsemane Church, sensing that the situation was going to come to a head and that a decision was soon to be made.

The New Forum of Prenzlauer Berg introduces itself in the Gethsemane Church, November 10, 1989
Andreas Kämper
Robert-Havemann-Gesellschaft e.V.

Demonstrators on Alexanderplatz demand the end of SED rule, October 7, 1989
Harald Hauswald,
OSTKREUZ Agentur der Fotografen

Vigil in the Gethsemane Church in East Berlin for the people who were arrested, October 9, 1989
Bernd Bohm, epd

Banner at the demonstration on Alexanderplatz in East Berlin, November 4, 1989
Klaus Lehnartz, Photonet

Finally, the news that they had been waiting and hoping for arrived from Leipzig. Till Böttcher from the Environmental Library had used his dictation machine to record the phone conversation and he played it back in the Gethsemane Church: the people in Leipzig had demonstrated without interference. Totally unsure of what awaited them, they held hands or linked arms before leaving the church.

The church was completely silent when Till Böttcher held the recorder up to the microphone. Then came a burst of applause and people embraced each other in joy. We felt an immense sense of relief. the situation around the Gethsemane Church had also changed. Police and security had withdrawn. Instead, countless candles were burning in windows and in the middle of the Stargarder and Greifenhagener streets – probably put there by the neighborhood residents. Someone let the church bells ring. It was unbelievable: The leaders were in retreat. We didn't know if anything had been decided yet, but many were enjoying a taste of freedom for the first time.

On Saturday, November 4, Berliners demonstrated for freedom of the press and assembly on Alexanderplatz. The demonstration, initiated by "New Forum" and Berlin theatre people, drew hundreds of thousands. They arrived carrying banners and signs to express their protest and make public demands. Berlin was not the only city to demonstrate that day. Never before or again during that autumn would so many people take to the streets of the GDR as they did that Saturday. With each day the certainty grew that the way things had been previously was gone once and for all. More people stopped being afraid and joined the public demonstration.

The slogans and chants became more decisive and radical, focusing on citizens' rights, a change of leadership, demands for freedom and democracy. The wonderfully simple and confident declaration "we are the people" became the queen of all slogans. An overwhelming amount of information and news reached us each day.

Reports came in one after another, most importantly: leading functionaries were resigning in scores. The entire government stepped down on November 7, and the Politburo followed the following day. Even though several functionaries and ministers were quickly reinstated into their previous positions, these events were seen as a clear sign of political erosion. In the wake of these major political changes, urgent topics, free of taboos, were finally put on the agenda. A society had begun to take its fate into its own hands.

Peaceful Revolution and the Fall of the Wall
Konrad Weiß

"The atmosphere was truly unbelievable, an unbelievable life, such a feeling of happiness […] We passed by a disco there and this whole throng of GDR citizens […] went into this disco. I will never forget it […] and they danced there. They were dancing to celebrate the fall of the Wall and then moved on to Ku'damm. […]

Interview, Stiftung Berliner Mauer, 2012

Konrad Weiß was born in Lauban (Silesia) in 1942. He began studying at the German film school in Potsdam-Babelsberg in 1966 and graduated in 1969. Afterwards he worked as a director in the DEFA studios for documentaries in East Berlin. He was prevented from publishing a text on neo-fascist tendencies in the GDR in 1988. Some of his other texts circulated illegally. In 1989 Konrad Weiß co-founded the citizens' group "Democracy Now." He served as its spokesmen and, in 1989/90, became a member of the Volkskammer, the East German parliament. He served as a representative in the German Bundestag from 1990 to 1994.

7
The Path to Unity

Storming the headquarters of the secret police on Normannenstrasse in East Berlin, January 15, 1990
After January 15, citizens committees oversaw the dissolution of the secret police.
Rolf Zöllner, imago stock & people

The Path to Unity

During the eleven months between the opening of the border and German unification, events moved quickly in the GDR: every week new reports emerged about the SED's abuse of power. The people in charge resigned or were arrested. The magnitude of the economic misery came to light.

The government established under Lothar de Maiziere following the East German parliament elections in March 1989 oversaw the process of unification with West Germany. On August 23, the East German parliament passed a resolution based on Article 23 of the West German Basic Law to have the GDR join the Federal Republic of Germany. For many within the citizens' movement, this did not represent a union based on equality. One of the few issues on which activists were able to assert their interest was the establishment of a special agency to administrate the records of the secret police.

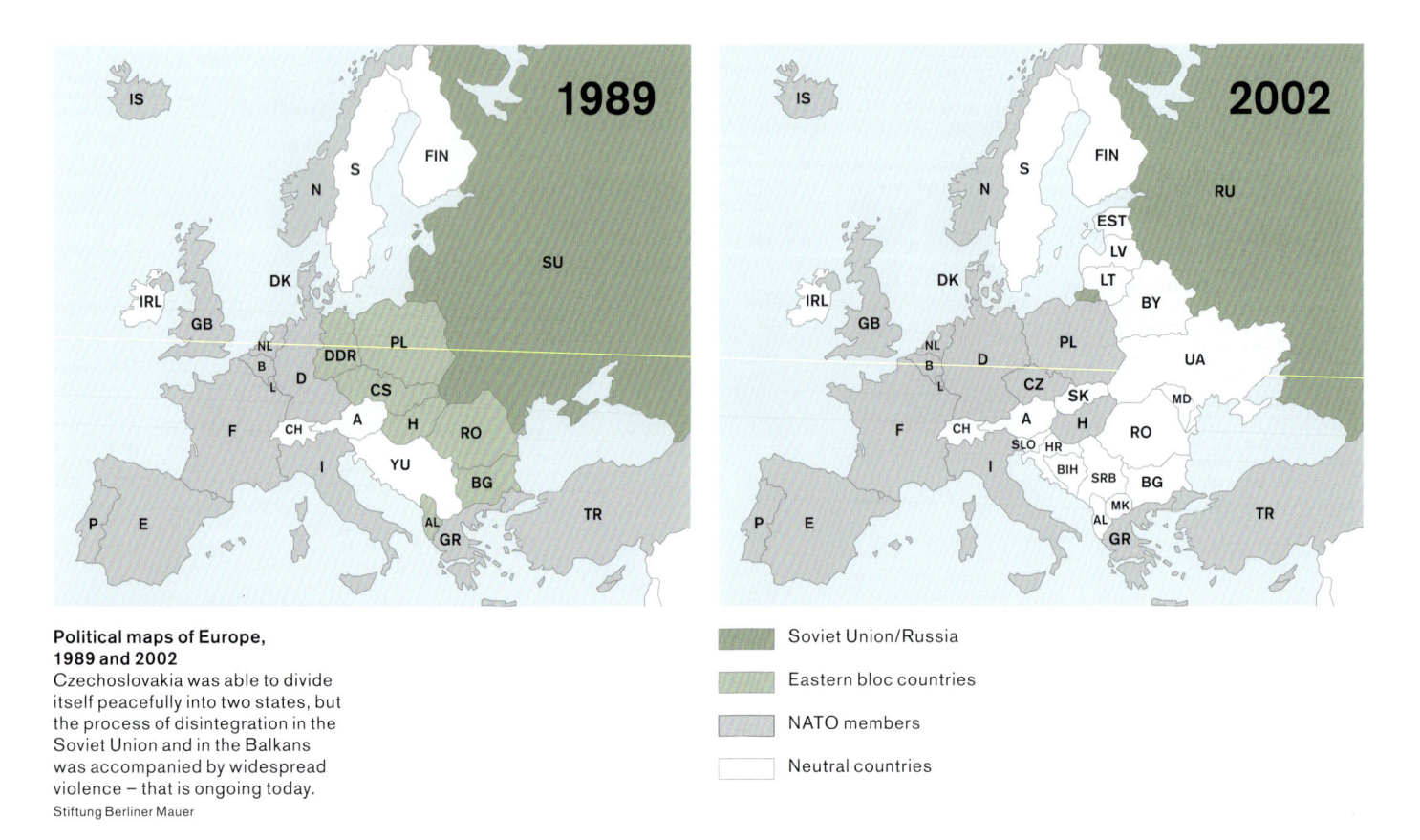

Political maps of Europe, 1989 and 2002
Czechoslovakia was able to divide itself peacefully into two states, but the process of disintegration in the Soviet Union and in the Balkans was accompanied by widespread violence – that is ongoing today.
Stiftung Berliner Mauer

- Soviet Union/Russia
- Eastern bloc countries
- NATO members
- Neutral countries

An End to the Confrontation?

Even before the Wall fell, Moscow's paternalistic role in the Eastern bloc had caused widespread dissatisfaction. In late 1989, the communist governments in Czechoslovakia, Bulgaria and Rumania had to step down, making way for democratic forces. Within the Soviet Union, the Baltic states, Ukraine and White Russia also achieved their independence. In Yugoslavia, national differences that had been subdued under Tito's regime erupted, leading to a war in the Balkans. Here in 1999, German soldiers were involved in a military conflict for the first time since World War II.

> *"We, the Foreign Ministers of the Alliance, express our determination to seize the historic opportunities resulting from the profound changes in Europe to help build a new peaceful order in Europe, based on freedom, justice and democracy. In this spirit, we extend to the Soviet Union and to all other European countries the hand of friendship."*

Message from the NATO Foreign Ministers, June 7, 1990

The statue of Lenin in Vilnius is taken away, August 23, 1991
As a sign of their new found independence, new governments removed symbols of communist rule. In Berlin, the Lenin statue on what is today "Platz der Vereinten Nationen" was taken down.
Juraitis, ullstein bild

Draft from the "Peace and Human Rights Initiative" for the "Round Table," February 19, 1990
This document illustrates just how controversial and uncertain the status of a future Germany was: Even the conservative participants did not vote for a unified Germany to remain in the NATO.
Robert Havemann Gesellschaft e.V.

Coming to Terms with the Past

The judicial investigation of SED injustices began even before unification. In early December 1989, the GDR public prosecutor initiated criminal investigations against the 30 former top functionaries in the GDR, including ten members of the Politburo. But due to their old age and poor health, most of them were spared prison. For the dictatorship's victims, a painful lesson was learned: criminal proceedings cannot always sufficiently redress injustices suffered.

Erich Honecker on trial before the Berlin district court, November 30, 1992

The judiciary instituted several proceedings against Erich Honecker. He had to stand trial for the deaths at the Wall as well as for other charges. In January 1993, he was released from pre-trial confinement because of his poor health and all proceedings against him were closed.

unknown photographer, dpa, ullstein bild

Heinz Keßler

Heinz Keßler, 1988
unknown photographer, Bundesarchiv

Heinz Kessler was born in today's Poland and grew up in Chemnitz. Like his parents, he was a committed communist. He was drafted into the Wehrmacht in 1940, but defected to the Red Army. He returned to Germany in 1945 and began his rise in the GDR armed forces in 1950. In 1985, he took charge of the office of defense minister and became a member of the SED Politburo in 1986. Kessler was forced to resign in November 1989 and was arrested two months later. He was held in the Hohenschönhausen remand prison until April 1990. In 1993, the Berlin district court sentenced him to seven-and-a-half years in prison for "incitement to manslaughter." Kessler continues to deny that there had ever been an order to shoot.

The Changing Significance of the Wall

When the Wall fell on November 9, 1989, it was not foreseeable that it would almost completely disappear from view within a year. "Wallpeckers" were everywhere, hammering out pieces of concrete from the Wall. The "East Side Gallery," a section of the inner wall painted by artists from all over the world, was created on Mühlenstrasse in East Berlin. The Berlin Wall soon became a worldwide symbol of liberation from dictatorship. Today, segments of the Berlin Wall can be found on every continent. Some stand in museums and on public squares, others on private property. Some have been altered, others preserved in their original form. Wherever they are, they serve as a symbol for the universal importance of freedom and human rights. Researchers named a piece of rock on Mars "Broken Wall" in commemoration of the fall of the Berlin Wall.

Wall demolition on Bernauer Strasse, 1990
In June 1990, members of the GDR border troops began the organized demolition of the Wall. By the end of the year, the job was almost complete. Some of the Wall remnants were used for street construction.
Rolf Zöllner

East Side Gallery, 1990
In February 1990, artists began painting a section of the inner wall facing East Berlin. It became the "East Side Gallery" and has been protected as a monument since 1991. It is the longest preserved piece of the Berlin Wall.
Urs Schweitzer, akg-images

Two City Halves Grow Together

East and West Berlin had grown apart during the period of division. After the Wall fell, new border crossings opened almost every day. Over time the city's infrastructure was connected and the two halves of the city grew back together. Berlin shifted from the fringe to the center of political events. Established as the German capital in 1991, the new metropolis became the seat of the German federal government and the German Bundestag in 1999.

The Jannowitzbrücke underground station reopens, November 11, 1989
From 1961 to 1989, the station, which was situated in East Berlin, was a so-called Ghost Station. Only West Berliners could use the subway line and travel through the dark station on slow-moving trains.
Robert Roeske, Bundesarchiv

East German police officer with a repainted police car, 1990
Even before the police forces were merged together, 200 patrol cars from the East German police were painted over in the colors of the West Berlin police.
Norbert Michalke, ullstein bild, imagebroker.net

The two mayors, Walter Momper (West Berlin) and Tino Schwierzina (East Berlin) in the Berlin Town Hall, June 12, 1990
A half year after this first joint meeting, Berliners from East and West elected their representatives for the Berlin city parliament together.
unknown photographer, dpa, ullstein bild

Hermann Wentker

The Fall of the Wall and German Unity

Following the press conference held by Günter Schabowski on the evening of November 9, 1989, the East Berlin masses forced the Berlin Wall to be opened. In the German Bundestag in Bonn, Chancellery Minister Rudolf Seiters read a brief government statement. A short debate was conducted after which the West German delegates rose and sang the national anthem.[1] The mood among the heads of the security forces in East Berlin was a very different one. Karl-Heinz Wagner, Chief of Staff of the People's Police, and Colonel Hans-Joachim Krüger from the Ministry of State Security met for midnight talks during which they abandoned their commitment to socialism.[2] Willy Brandt, meanwhile, flew to Berlin on November 10, optimistic about the future. He told a reporter from the radio station "Freies Berlin": "We find ourselves in a situation in which what belongs together can now grow together."[3] Marianne Birthler recalls that acquaintances of hers at the time were quick to realize that the end of the border regime also signalled the end of the GDR.[4] These statements suggest that many people understood that, with the fall of the Wall, the future of the GDR's existence was being called into question. Over the next few days "what at first had seemed unfathomable, became possible and then increasingly likely,"[5] i.e. the reunification of the two German states. Looking back, it is clear that the ninth of November represented a "change within a change"; this date came to mark the beginning of the "national phase" of the Peaceful Revolution.[6]

The division of Germany after 1945 was not the final word on the German question. The East-West conflict that divided the European continent was the basic condition on which division rested. A change in this situation demanded that the German question be readdressed. During the forty years of its existence, the GDR had failed to achieve the internal legitimacy it needed to sustain itself: its citizens did not identify with their country, but, rather, measured its "achievements" against the conditions in the Federal Republic. Hence, to secure its rule, the SED leadership was dependent on two constants – both of which demonstrated its weakness, not its strength: the Soviet "guarantee of existence" and the Berlin Wall. But given Moscow's weakening commitment to the Brezhnev Doctrine and the evident restraint Soviet troops had exhibited during protests that autumn, it could be assumed that the Soviet Union would not intervene militarily on behalf of the GDR. And, unlike Hungary and Poland, the GDR did not consider introducing domestic reforms as a way out of the crisis because the GDR's "socialist identity" lay at the very "core of the issue." According to the SED social scientist Otto Reinhold, a "capitalist GDR" could not justify its existence alongside a "capitalist Federal Republic."[7]

"For our country," an appeal from 31 East Germans calling for the GDR to be preserved, November 29, 1989
At first the idea of preserving the GDR as a democratic, sovereign state found broad support. This changed when the extent of the economic misery in the GDR came to light.
Neues Deutschland/Staatsbibliothek zu Berlin – Preußischer Kulturbesitz

The Brandenburg Gate is opened in the presence of Chancellor Helmut Kohl, GDR leader Hans Modrow and West Berlin's Mayor Walter Momper, December 22, 1989
unknown photographer, dpa Picture-Alliance

The Checkpoint Charlie border crossing is torn down at the start of the Two-Plus-Four talks, June 22, 1990
The Two-Plus-Four talks were attended by representatives of both German governments and the four Allies – the Soviet Union, United States, Great Britain and France.
Christian Stutterheim, Bundesregierung

Admittedly, at demonstrations that took place in the GDR before the Wall fell, one heard only a few isolated calls for getting rid of the Wall or for reunification. During the first phase of the Peaceful Revolution between early September and October 9, slogans such as "We're staying here!" and "We are the people!" served to establish a mass movement, demonstrate courage and emphasize peace. It was only after the successful Monday demonstration in Leipzig on October 9, after which the people's fear had dispelled, that calls for the government to step down, for political reforms and for free elections became louder.

When the Wall opened during the night of November 9, the door to German unity was also pushed open. The international and national situation was initially confusing, making it difficult for demonstrators and the West German government – which had shown considerable restraint until then – to take steps towards unity. Following a telephone call with Mikhail Gorbachev on November 11, German Chancellor Helmut Kohl understood that the Soviet troops were going to stay in their barracks.[8] Thus, the fate of the GDR in its current form was sealed. At that time, however, it still remained unclear whether the two German states would reunify. Changes began to take place in the GDR that clarified the situation. In the twelve days following the Wall's opening, eleven million people visited West Berlin and West Germany, witnessing with their own eyes how their countrymen in the West lived. After this, calls for reunification became louder on the streets of the GDR, but other demands were also heard.

As unification advocates and unification opponents became increasingly polarised on the streets, various civil rights groups, which had come to the fore at demonstrations in October, were pushed out by the growing masses. This was because most opposition groups supported either a reform-socialist future for the GDR or were committed to a vision of civil society in which the state would be replaced by a body of responsible citizens willing and able to participate in the political decision-making process. Both ideas implied preserving the GDR as an independent political unit, which set them apart from the majority. Given the advanced signs of crisis in the GDR, most people did not want any more experiments with socialism. They wanted to rely on the functional, political and economic model that already existed in the Federal Republic. In the second half of November, when unification advocates appeared to be gaining support on the streets, opinion polls – to be treated with caution – indicated that a majority of the population still supported the idea of developing an independent GDR, at least for the time being.

Two initiatives emerged simultaneously that caused the debate to escalate. On November 26, Christa Wolf read on East German television "For Our Country," an appeal which argued for a reformed GDR that would develop as "a socialist alternative to the Federal Republic."[9] The appeal was signed by important members of the opposition, intellectuals and actors; but it was also supported by members from the party and state apparatus whose political thinking had evidently changed. Egon Krenz and Hans Modrow, for example, saw it as something to latch onto as the GDR was sucked into the maelstrom. Just two days later, on November 28, Helmut Kohl announced his "ten-point plan" in the German Bundestag, in which he proposed "developing confederative structures between both states in Germany, with the objective of creating a federation, that is, a federal system, in Germany."[10] He did not provide a time schedule for his plan, but he followed the recommendation of his advisor Horst Teltschik and adopted the role of leading opinion maker in the political debate over Germany. This earned Kohl criticism from both the opposition in Bonn and abroad, but in the GDR, especially in the country's southern districts, his ideas were met with enthusiasm. Although the appeal "For Our Country" received some support, it was generally agreed that it was counterproductive: most people were put off by the socialist experiment that it promoted and even civil rights activists recognized that the inclusion of signatures of leading SED cadre members pushed it to the point of absurdity.

Economic, currency and social union: people queue in front of a bank to exchange East German marks for the West German D-Mark, July 1, 1990
ADN-Bildarchiv, ullstein bild

In the next phase, two decisive factors emerged in addition to the stronger calls for reunification at demonstrations: the failure of the GDR leadership under Premier Modrow to get the domestic situation under control and Chancellor Kohl's decision to exploit the power vacuum in the GDR and speed up the reunification process. His decision went back to December 19, when Kohl met Modrow in Dresden to discuss their respective ideas of a German-German "treaty partnership" (Modrow) and the "ten-point plan" (Kohl). Before the two heads of state met for evening talks, Kohl received an overwhelming welcome from the East German people. Kohl instinctively sensed that reunification was not going to be a medium-term project, which would be developed over a period of ten years. The mood of the people told him that it was both necessary and possible to act much more quickly.

Discussions in the GDR and the Federal Republic soon came to focus on German reunification because of the important role the Berlin Wall played in maintaining the GDR's existence. That the subsequent events would lead to German reunification on October 3, 1990 were, however, anything but inevitable. The path to German unity was paved by the fall of the Wall, but not decided by it.

The German question… reopened!
Jupp Wolter (artist),
Haus der Geschichte, Bonn

1
Deutscher Bundestag, *Stenographischer Bericht, 11. Wahlperiode*, 9. 11. 1989, pp. 13221 – 13223.
2
See Hans-Hermann Hertle, *Der Fall der Mauer. Die unbeabsichtigte Selbstauflösung des SED-Staates*, Opladen 1999, p. 230.
3
Cited in Günter Bannas, "In der Erinnerung zusammengewachsen," in: *Frankfurter Allgemeine Zeitung* on October 14, 2014.
4
Marianne Birthler, *Halbes Land, ganzes Leben. Erinnerungen*, Berlin 2014, p. 192.
5
Ibid.
6
See Konrad Jarausch, *Die unverhoffte Einheit 1989 – 1990*, Frankfurt a. M. 1995, p. 106.
7
Otto Reinhold on August 19, 1989, cited in Volker Gransow/Konrad H. Jarausch (eds.), *Die deutsche Vereinigung. Dokumente zu Bürgerbewegung, Annäherung und Beitritt*, Cologne 1991, p. 57.
8
Kohl's telephone call with Gorbachev, Nov. 11, 1989, in: *Dokumente zur Deutschlandpolitik. Deutsche Einheit. Sonderedition aus den Akten des Bundeskanzleramtes*, edited by Hanns Jürgen Küsters and Daniel Hofmann, Munich 1998, pp. 515 – 517.
9
The appeal in: Gransow/Jarausch (ed.), *Die deutsche Vereinigung*, pp. 100 f.
10
The ten-point plan, in: Gransow/Jarausch (ed.), *Die deutsche Vereinigung*, pp. 101 – 104.

"Peaceful Revolution and the Fall of the Berlin Wall" in the exhibition in the Documentation Center, 2015
Berthold Weidner

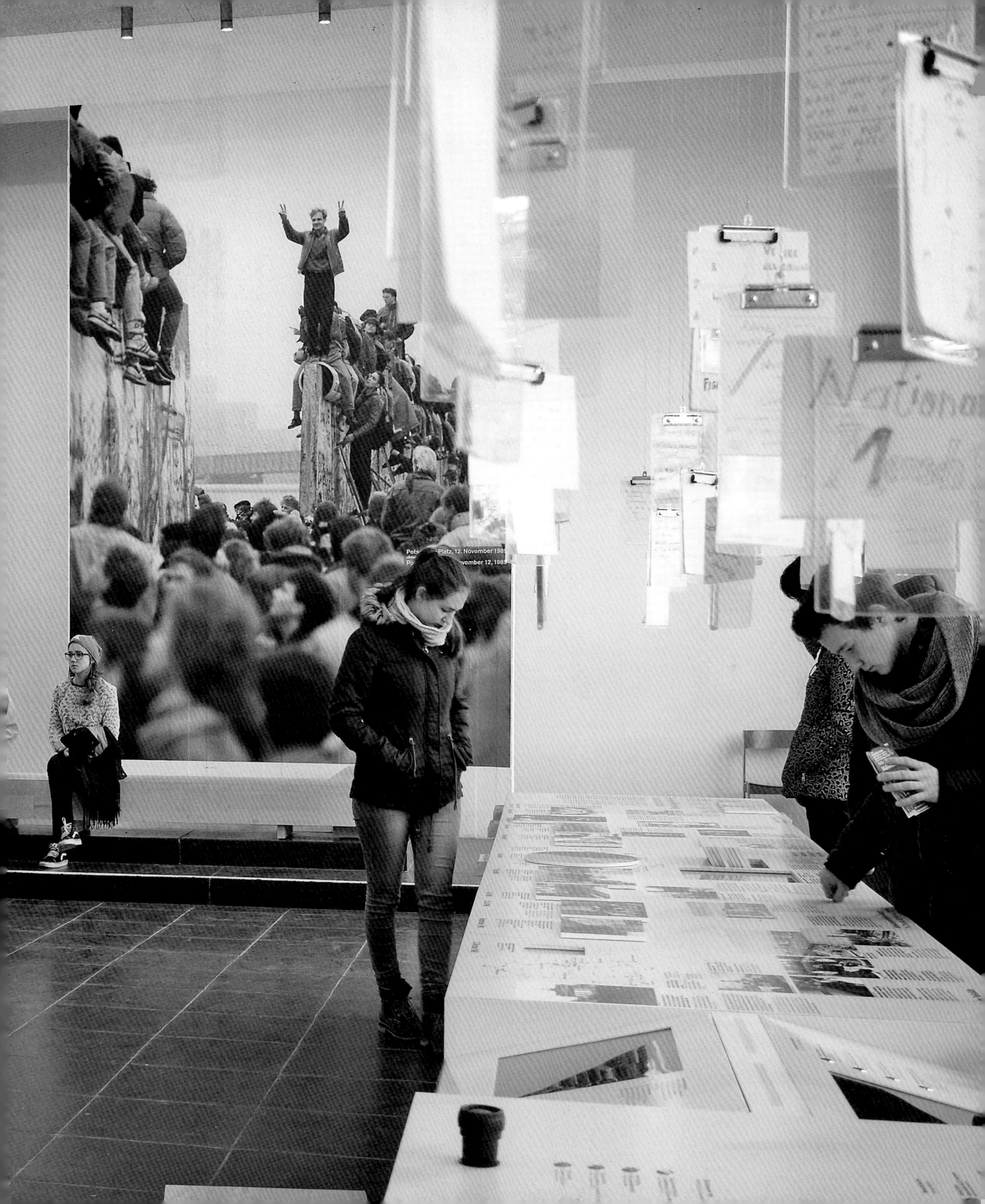
Platz, 12. November 1989
vember 12, 1989

Axel Klausmeier

"In order to grasp something, there must be something to grasp." Or: The Remnants of the Berlin Wall as Objects of Monument Preservation[1]

When Pastor Manfred Fischer (1948 – 2013) began his laborious years-long struggle to create the Berlin Wall Memorial in January 1990, he already understood that the barrier that had divided Berlin would be very important in the future. He realized that its physical presence, even in the form of fragmented remnants, had the power to vividly convey the city's history of division. During this time, the former pastor of the Protestant Reconciliation Church in Wedding would often rush over to Bernauer Strasse when he heard bulldozers or "wall peckers" (people chiseling away pieces of the wall for souvenirs) destroying the Wall, and he would chase them away before they could do further damage to the structure.[2] For Fischer, who had begun working at the parish in 1975 and who saw the Wall everyday from his office window, and for the others who joined him in his struggle, there was no question that this world-famous barrier was a historical testimony that had to be preserved. A vivid historical site – he had often maintained – has a strong emotional component and contains unknown possibilities for teaching history. Fischer was promoting this view when the demolition of the border fortifications was already well underway; yet it remained unclear where the political journey would end. Would the GDR be able to assert itself as an independent state? And if so, what would happen to the border fortifications in Berlin? The GDR did not stop its practice of stamping passports until July 31, 1990, nearly nine months after the Wall fell. The last units of the border troops officially ended their operations on September 30, 1990, just days before the two German states were reunified on October 3, 1990.

The assault on the physical border fortifications, and thus its material integrity, began on Bernauer Strasse on November 10, 1989, and was carried out simultaneously on two very different levels: the official level based on orders and military implementation and the spontaneous anarchical level, during which the Wall was appropriated by "fun-seeking" Berlin residents and visitors. Following their commanders' orders, pioneer units of the border troops opened the border grounds to create new border crossings. At the same time, thousands of people flocked to the Wall with hammers and chisels, breaking off pieces of the Wall to take home with them as a trophy or souvenir. Because of the border troops' heavy machinery and the wall peckers' chaotic picking, the Wall had almost completely disappeared within a matter of months. When reunification came into effect on October 3, 1990, responsibility for the demolition fell to the Bundeswehr.[3]

The predominant mood at the time, which ultimately led to the almost total destruction of the Wall, is, in retrospect, not completely understandable.[4] Political groups seemed to share an almost unquestioned consensus that the border fortifications, including the 112-kilometer-long "outer ring" that ran around the state of Brandenburg, which had been transformed overnight from a barrier to a monument, should disappear from the cityscape as soon as possible.

Remnants of Border Wall 75 with marks left by "wall peckers," 2010
Jürgen Hohmuth, Stiftung Berliner Mauer

Repaired "perimeter-fence fence," 2011
Axel Klausmeier, Stiftung Berliner Mauer

Translocated segments of the Berlin Wall, 2010
Axel Klausmeier, Stiftung Berliner Mauer

Remnants of the inner wall, 2011
Axel Klausmeier, Stiftung Berliner Mauer

Protective cover over an archeological site, 2011
Axel Klausmeier, Stiftung Berliner Mauer

Of course the Wall had to "fall." Its physical demise was a factual and symbolic necessity. It was the tangible evidence of the triumph of freedom. But conquering the Wall is not the same as extinguishing it. The relentless demolition of the Wall was carried out, it was often said, so that Berlin could become "a metropolitan city like others." Evidently, official Berlin had no understanding of the Wall's worldwide historical significance. It did not recognize that a "unique selling point" could be achieved by preserving the Wall. This view stood in contradiction to the widespread international interest in the Wall that was soon evident in the commercial success of selling wall segments.[5] This lack of reflection was understandable, if unfortunate. It is natural to want to erase places and objects that remind us of painful events, but destroying physical evidence cannot undo history. The dedicated historical preservationists who advocated protecting this unwieldy structure were often fighting a losing battle, although they did succeed in having twelve sections of the Wall added to the state of Berlin's register of monuments before Germany's reunification in October 1990.

The "Berlin Wall" has since become a monument of international standing. No structure better and more enduringly characterizes the communist dictatorship than these border fortifications. Consequently, the few remaining border fortifications have since become the most famous structure of East Germany. Both the process of overcoming the Wall and the process of tearing it down have become an integral part of the Berlin Wall as a monument. The peaceful victory over the Wall is inseparable from the iconic media images of November 9, 1989, which allowed the world to share in this joyous and historic event. Many of the preserved remnants of the Berlin Wall fortifications are now kept and displayed as collector items, relics and monuments, a fact that lends a special significance to the "Berlin Wall" as a whole.[6]

From the Cultural significance to the practice of Preservation

For many years the idea that conservation methods might be applied to preserve and even "care for" the despised border grounds was unthinkable. A general concept to preserve and maintain the individual existing pieces dispersed throughout the city has never existed. At Bernauer Strasse, the first 15 years after the Wall fell were focused mainly on preventing the further loss of Wall remains and establishing the initial foundations of a memorial site. The question of how to sustainably maintain this unusual testament to history did not become relevant until 2009. That year engineers determined that it was impossible to assess or verify the stability of various elements of the Berlin Wall and inner wall. In previous years, very different, strongly debated efforts had been made to implement the practical conservation of individual parts and sections of the structure.[7] Various conservation methods were even applied to similar structural elements that stood at different places. The evaluation of each individual remnant served as the basis for future decisions and became the most significant criteria for determining what historic preservation methods should be applied. Take the example of the East Side Gallery in Berlin: the "longest gallery in the world," it was created spontaneously in 1990 by 118 artists from 21 different countries, and has been completely restored at least twice. The paintings were redone and the underlying surface, the actual Wall, was stripped down to the concrete reinforcement and replaced.

A preserved segment of the original Berlin Wall on Bernauer Strasse underwent restoration between 1996 and 1998 during construction of the official Wall Monument designed by the Stuttgart architects Kohlhoff + Kohlhoff. Here, too, little care was given to the original building material, but the inner supporting structure of the L-shaped Border Wall 75 was at least retained, along with a few segments of the inner wall. When the inner wall on the Invaliden Cemetery in Berlin-Mitte was restored in 2002, yet another restoration approach was pursued. In this case, they overshot the restoration aim by adding a coat of white paint to the former inner wall. But, unlike the white paint that had once served to enhance border security at night, the restoration measure was applied with historical inaccuracy to the wrong side of the wall. Another preserved piece of Berlin Wall stands on the grounds of the "Topography of Terror" exhibition in

Archeological excavation of a destroyed border building, 2011
Axel Klausmeier, Stiftung Berliner Mauer

Outline of the destroyed Reconciliation Church on the plaza in front of the Chapel of Reconciliation, 2011
Axel Klausmeier, Stiftung Berliner Mauer

Archeological excavation of a destroyed border building with protective roof
Axel Klausmeier, Stiftung Berliner Mauer

Berlin-Mitte. This segment was heavily damaged by "wall peckers." Its historic structure has been carefully monitored at regular intervals for years, but no extensive conservation measures have been taken. Instead, the fragile structure is kept under observation following the concept of minimal intervention, which means that only supporting measures are taken. A protective fence was added to the Wall to make it more difficult to access (in particular to ward off the never-tiring "wall peckers"). These few examples demonstrate that each site has followed its own directives and that there are no patent remedies to preserve structures listed as historical monuments.

Hence we had no authoritative, fully-accepted conservation method to employ when repairing the assessed damage, which included "exposed reinforcement without contact to concrete," or "a strongly reduced concrete profile," on the remains of the Wall along Bernauer Strasse.

Based on the findings of a scholarly conference[8] and of a later established expert commission, it was agreed that the special historical significance of the existing structural remnants of the border fortifications lay not only in their sheer existence, but also in their fragmentation. A constitutive part of this "story" is how the Wall was brought down peacefully by courageous East Germans who risked the consequences of standing up to a dictatorial regime. They actually made it possible for the "wall peckers" to leave their mark on the Wall. The widespread demolition and vacant space left in the city also tell a story of civilian appropriation. Hence, it was agreed that the Wall remains along Bernauer Strasse should be cautiously repaired using a method of minimal intervention in order to allow the fragile condition of the Wall at the moment of its defeat to also be preserved. The temptation to give in to the alluring appeal of technical advancements was intentionally resisted. The main concerns were conserving the original substance, structural reinforcement and reversibility so that various options would remain open to future generations when they become responsible for the monument. We are, after all, merely momentary trustees of the monument's preservation. Another issue for memorial sites is that the key to their acceptance is often linked to the credibility of the material substance that has been handed down and the persuasiveness of the historical site. The physical remnants that still exist possess a document-like character, not unlike the written sources that are so indispensible to a historian's work. But, like a palimpsest, they are often ambiguous and difficult to comprehend. They show how important physical sites are to humans as commemorative and visual aids, creating points of reference and illustrating a site's history.

In the end, a Conservation and Management Plan was developed that recommended the implementation of essential, continual maintenance and preservation measures, and which suggested monitoring the structure at regular intervals. In 2011, a scientifically-based maintenance concept was presented that defined short, middle and long-term measures.

Summary

Today, historical preservation methods are used to conserve the remnants of the Berlin Wall at many different sites. The site of the Berlin Wall on Bernauer Strasse was established as a place of historic and civic education and to commemorate the Wall's victims. It is fitting that the site is visited by so many young people from around the globe who have no personal recollection of the era of division and the suffering it caused. Soon, the length of time during which the Wall spread fear and terror will be equal to that which has passed since its demise. As these historical events slip further into the past, the importance of physical remnants, which function as structural testimony, increases: they were there when freedom became possible and the people in the GDR fought for their rights through a peaceful revolution, and thus constitute evidence of these events as well. Through their fragmentation, they are able to spread a message of hope to a crisis-ridden world in which many still are not free.

Representation of the border wall, 2011
Jürgen Hohmuth, Stiftung Berliner Mauer

Tourists in front of the Monument; the Wall as a tourist attraction, 2010
Axel Klausmeier, Stiftung Berliner Mauer

Archeological excavations of a border building with information panels and protective roof, 2011
Christian Fuchs

1
The quote in the title is from Pastor Manfred Fischer, the intellectual "constant" in the struggle to establish the Berlin Wall Memorial. The basic ideas of this essay are based on other publications by the author, including: Axel Klausmeier/Günter Schlusche (eds.), Denkmalpflege für die Berliner Mauer. Die Konservierung eines unbequemen Denkmals, Berlin 2011; Axel Klausmeier, "Die Bedeutung der Denkmalpflege für die Erhaltung und die Erweiterung der Gedenkstätte Berliner Mauer", in: Thomas Drachenberg/Axel Klausmeier/Ralph Paschke/Michael Rohde (eds.), *Denkmalpflege und Gesellschaft. Detlef Karg zum 65. Geburtstag*, Rostock 2012, pp. 146–149. Additional bibliographical references are provided here.
2
See Gabriele Camphausen/Manfred Fischer, "Die bürgerschaftliche Durchsetzung der Gedenkstätte an der Bernauer Straße," in: Klaus-Dietmar Henke (ed.), *Die Mauer*, Berlin 2011, pp. 355–377.
3
Gerhard Sälter, "Das Verschwinden der Berliner Mauer," in Klaus-Dietmar Henke (ed.), *Revolution und Vereinigung 1989/90*, Munich 2009, p. 353–355; See also Gabi Dolff-Bonekämper, "Denkmalschutz für die Mauer," in: *Die Denkmalpflege 58 (2000) 1*, 2000, pp. 33–40.

4
On the following ideas see also: Axel Klausmeier/Leo Schmidt, "Mauerrelikte," in: Henke (ed.), *Die Mauer*, pp. 342–355.
5
Ronny Heidenreich, "Beton zu Geld. Das Geschäft mit der Berliner Mauer," in: Anna Kaminsky (ed.), *Die Berliner Mauer in der Welt*, Berlin 2009, pp. 236–238.
6
For more detail, see Leo Schmidt, "Die Botschaft der Mauersegmente," in: Kaminsky (ed.): *Die Berliner Mauer*, pp. 228–236.
7
See here Klausmeier/Schlusche (eds.), *Denkmalpflege*.
8
Jörg Haspel, Ergebnisse der Tagung „Erhaltungsstrategien für die Berliner Mauer – Status – Beispiele – Konzepte" am 25./26. Februar 2010, in: Klausmeier/Schlusche, *Denkmalpflege*, pp. 176–177.

Remnants of the Berlin Wall on Bernauer Strasse, 2010
Jürgen Hohmuth, Stiftung Berliner Mauer

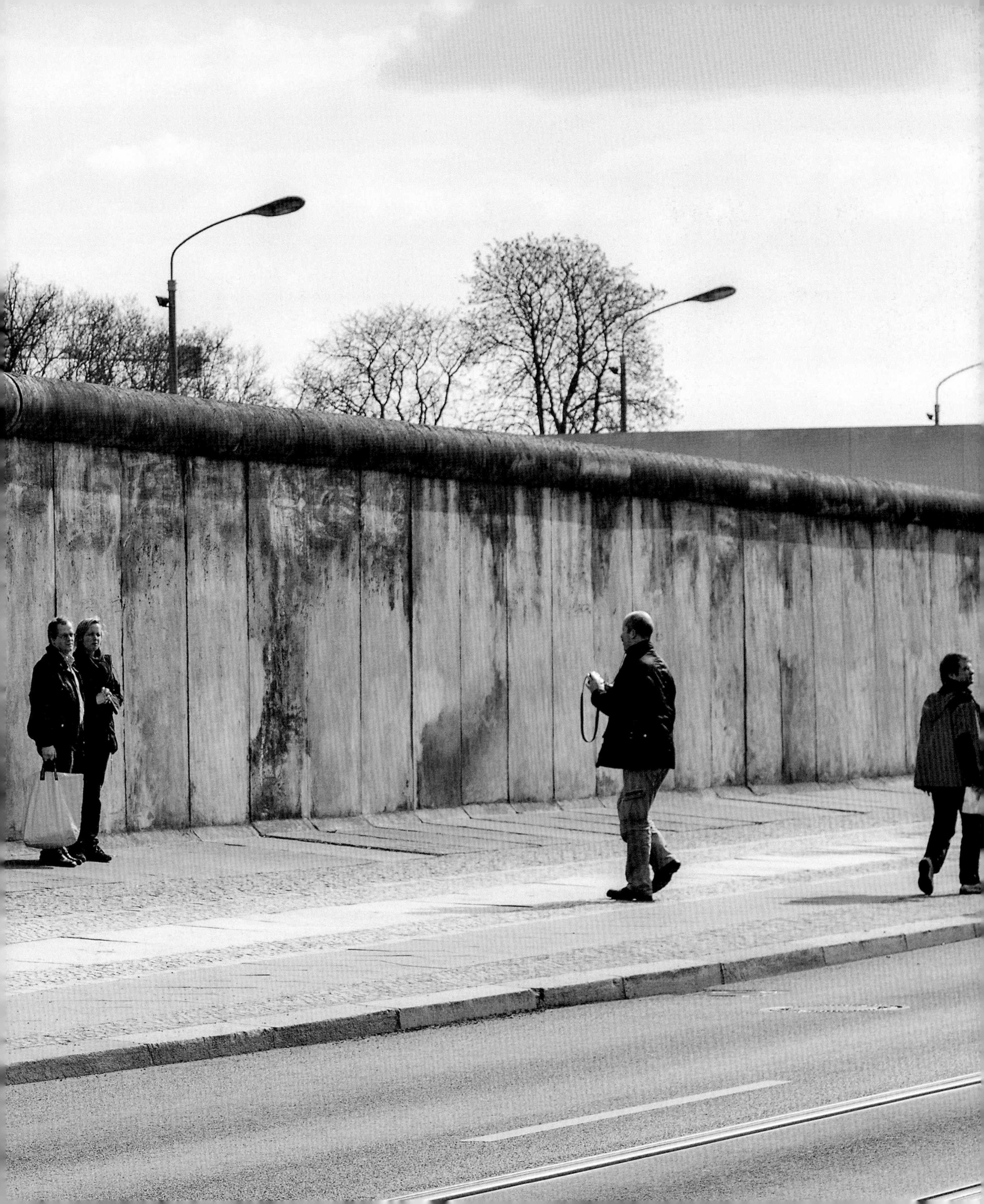

Klaus-Dietmar Henke

The Dimensions of the Berlin Wall

"And it came to pass, when the people heard the sound of the trumpet, and the people shouted with a great shout, that the wall fell down flat, so that the people went up into the city, every man straight before him, and they took the city." According to Joshua's account in the Bible, this is how the wall of Jericho fell. The fall of the Berlin Wall, too, has acquired an almost mythical quality, despite the thousands of iconic images of people standing on the Wall at the Brandenburg Gate, wearing jeans and revealing themselves to be very much of this world. The Berlin Wall has become a myth of humanity and a world icon – but why is this?

The word "wall" itself triggers everyone's imagination. Walls are universal cultural testimonies; they are protective fences, imprisoning barriers, guarantors both of freedom and of freedom's denial. Over the course of thousands of years, walls have been built and defended in the name of various causes; they have been attacked from within and from without, and they have been torn down, both literally and metaphorically. This is why so many great narratives revolve around them.

The city walls of Babylon were originally one of the seven world wonders. The Great Wall of China formed the border between barbarism and civilization. The walls of the Bastille seemed to have been built for eternity. Wall narratives are most prevalent when people, with God's help, succeed in overcoming seemingly insurmountable walls, through trickery, perseverance or cunning. The walls of Jericho acquired mythical status only after their wondrous collapse.

In the moment of its fall, the Berlin Wall, a symbol of the Cold War for 28 years, transformed from a political scandalon into a monument, and more importantly, into a timeless sign of hope. Its message: it is possible to change the unalterable; injustice cannot endure; freedom will prevail.

"A mury runś, runś, runś/I pogrzebia stary świat." The walls will fall and bury the old world beneath them. These are the lyrics of a battle song from the Solidarity trade union movement in Poland that brought about the collapse of Communist dictatorships throughout Europe. A quarter of a century later, at a memorial ceremony along the former border strip, during which the tradition of sounding trumpets was also maintained, the theologian and civil rights activist Ehrhart Neubert, noted that the "the tears of joy on November 9, 1989 do not wash away the blood that was shed here." But these tears of joy, he added, "remind us that the commitment to freedom and human rights is always rewarded."

The Berlin Wall's construction in 1961 was as improbable as its fall in 1989. That a major city like Berlin could be cut down the middle with one half enclosed by a 150-kilometer-long-wall was about as likely as Buckingham Palace and Westminster Abbey being moved to different continents in a single day. "This building used to stand in a different country" reads the inscription on a wall not far from the former death strip, in an area that was previously part of East Berlin. Much of the world's population living in metropolises and megacities can relate to this kind of dramatic anomaly. In retrospect, feeling sympathy with Berlin's fate becomes easier because the sudden separation of neighborhoods, communities, families and friends has been broadly documented and the moving stories of personal tragedy and misfortune told. Mythical narratives, political hope and personal experience have made the dramatic history of the Berlin Wall accessible to all.

The world-historical events that took place in Berlin are certainly far better documented than those of Jericho. Long after the Wall was deconstructed into colorful fragments with only a few hundred meters of it preserved for posterity, what remains are the pictures of the Wall's brutal construction and the people's ecstatic enthusiasm following its collapse, the overwhelming relief that was felt when the political isolation and personal restrictions came to an end. It is difficult to remain unaffected by the contrast of these images.

After it fell, the Berlin Wall almost completely disappeared from the city. Yet, as a great political icon of humanity, it is more present than ever, a fact demonstrated by its "universal iconization" (Leo Schmidt). Approximately 240 wall monuments consisting of original segments of the Berlin Wall are dispersed throughout the world. They exist on every continent – with the exception of the Antarctic – underscoring the international dimensions of the demolished barrier. These painted pieces of concrete, removed from the historical context of the original Wall, were placed in new locations and imbued with new meaning. The remnant of the Wall in Seoul transmits a message that is different from the one in Danzig, Buenos Aires and Los Angeles. At one place it recalls a nation's ongoing division, at another the struggle against communism, an overthrown dictatorship or the superiority of the Western way of life and government.

The Berlin Wall is also one of the most frequently used political metaphors. Few politicians have refrained from making reference to the Berlin Wall when drawing attention to pleasing or unpleasing issues, to desires or fears. It was evoked, for example when, after decades of separation, a new bus line opened across the Indian-Pakistani border. Vladimir Putin used the Wall to make a comparison that conveyed the risks of a confrontation with the West over Ukraine. The "Wall" is often cited when a great firewall is denounced on the Internet, when a Nobel Laureate attests to the fragility of market fundamentalism or when Barack Obama and Angela Merkel meet to address the "walls of today."

Like the demolished Bastille of the French Revolution, the Wall is a changeling that can imbue both the positive and the negative. All over the world, Berliners use it to win appreciation. When a Berliner, upon entering a taxi in Ushuaia in Tierra del Fuego, tells the driver where he is from, the driver will inevitably beam: "Aah! Berlino! Muro!" And in the world of advertising and product placement, the Wall is spared nothing. Just shortly after its fall, the advertising giant Saatchi & Saatchi posted a slogan on the East Berlin side of the city proclaiming "First over the Wall". The "Wall" is everywhere. Having freed itself from the physical structure, it now embarks on its own journey. The Wall has joined the likes of "Stalingrad" and "Dachau" in becoming a catchword.

These circumstances make it all the more important that the Wall's connection to the actual site of the events be restored. The aura embodied in the preserved remnants that stand in Berlin make it a secure collection point for the thousands of different ideas that people from all over the world bring with them when they come to the German capital in search of the Wall.

Today, the Berlin Wall Memorial on the famous Bernauer Strasse has established itself as the central site of the Wall in the city. It owes its existence to a few determined citizens led by Manfred Fischer, a man whose lively creative spirit remains unforgotten. He was the pastor of the Reconciliation parish, whose church, deserted in the death strip, was blown up by the East German border troops in 1985. He and his fellow campaigners strongly opposed the final demolition of the Wall here and built the Chapel of Reconciliation upon the foundations of their old church.

Thanks to the carefully curated exhibition by Gerhard Sälter and the excellent design along 1.4 kilometers and 4.4 hectares of grounds, the memorial, which was completed in 2014, provides ideal conditions for restoring the connection between the multitude of Wall images and the actual remains. At this important site of history and place of commemoration dedicated to the victims of the GDR regime, visitors can be sure that what they are seeing is not a replica or a reconstruction. Its restrained presentation allows the full power of authenticity to prevail.

Every visitor, regardless of where he comes from, witnesses the tension created by the designed presentation and original remnants. The images he brings with him collide when he enters the site, helping him to reconsider what he sees and to establish his own historical authenticity. In the words of the memorial's director Axel Klausmeier, this experience "allows an emotional response and thoughtful reflection to take place that unlocks history."

The memorial on Bernauer Strasse helps visitors give substance to their imagination. The after-life of the Berlin Wall and the boundless imagination of its incredulous story will endure for far longer than the physical structure ever did.

Five segments of the Wall with information panels on the history of German division and a replica of the Brandenburg Gate in the Peace Park in Uijeongbu, South Korea, 2014
Tobias Dollase

Appendix

The Marienfelde Refugee Center Museum – the Berlin Wall Foundation's Second Location

Large crowds at the emergency refugee center on the day after the Wall was erected, August 14, 1961
unknown photographer, Deutsches Historisches Museum

The Berlin Wall Foundation includes both the Berlin Wall Memorial on Bernauer Strasse and the Marienfelde Refugee Center Museum. The Refugee Center Museum is the central site dedicated to escape and emigration from the GDR. Located on historic grounds, it presents a permanent exhibition on the history of the camp, which was established in 1953 as the main reception facility for GDR emigrants and refugees. In 1964 it also began taking in ethnic Germans from Eastern Europe and the Soviet Union. By 1990, the center had served as the arrival point in West Berlin for 1.35 million people from the GDR.

The building complex contained all the Allied and German offices, organizations and associations involved in the emergency reception procedure that new arrivals had to undergo to receive a residence permit for the Federal Republic and West Berlin. The mass exodus of refugees ended with the construction of the Berlin Wall in 1961. The center did not experience a sharp rise in refugees again until 1989. When the economic, social and currency union between the Federal Republic of Germany and the GDR came into effect on July 1, 1990, the site's function as a reception camp for GDR refugees and emigrants became obsolete.

The permanent exhibition "Flight in Divided Germany" is located in the former refugee center's main building. The exhibit uses artefacts and eyewitness accounts to describe the different reasons people left, as well as the opportunities and problems they experienced when starting a new life in West Germany. The various facets and functions of the refugee center are also presented, from the reception procedure and everyday life of the residents to the surveillance carried out by the Stasi. A replica of a refugee apartment conveys an impression of the living conditions in the reception center. Today refugees and political asylum-seekers from current areas of conflict are housed on the grounds.

www.notaufnahmelager-berlin.de

Memorial at an historic site
Andreas Tauber, Stiftung Berliner Mauer

Visitors in the permanent exhibition "Flight in Divided Germany"
Gesa Simons, Stiftung Berliner Mauer

Replica of a refugee apartment in the permanent exhibition
Andreas Tauber, Stiftung Berliner Mauer

Imprint
The Berlin Wall
Permanent Exhibition on the Memorial Grounds at Bernauer Strasse 111

General Management
Pastor Manfred Fischer †
(until January 2009)
Prof. Dr. Axel Klausmeier

Curator
Dr. Gerhard Sälter

Scholarly Research
Dr. Sarah Bornhorst
Ronny Heidenreich
Dr. Susanne Muhle
Tina Schaller

Scholarly Advisory Board
Prof. Dr. Klaus Dietmar Henke (Chairman)
Prof. Dr. Karl F. Schumann (Deputy Chairman)
Marianne Birthler
Prof. Dr. Monika Flacke
Dr. Hans-Hermann Hertle
Prof. Dr. Hans Walter Hütter
Dr. Anna Kaminsky
Holger Kulick
Dr. Ehrhart Neubert
Petra Morawe
Prof. Dr. Leo Schmidt
Prof. Dr. Waltraud Schreiber
Rainer Wagner
Prof. Dr. Hermann Wentker
Prof. Dr. Manfred Wilke

until October 2010:
Prof. Dr. Rainer Eckert
Dr. Joachim Gauck
Roland Jahn
Prof. Dr. Alfons Kenkmann
Prof. Dr. Günter Morsch
Dr. Manfred Rexin
Dr. Rüdiger Sielaff
Prof. Ingrid Stahmer
Prof. Dr. Peter Steinbach
Dr. Clemens Vollnhals
Dr. Dieter Vorsteher

Texts
Dr. Sarah Bornhorst
Ronny Heidenreich
Dr. Susanne Muhle
Dr. Gerhard Sälter
Tina Schaller

Editing
Dr. Sarah Bornhorst
Dr. Gabriele Camphausen
Manfred Fischer
Ronny Heidenreich
Prof. Dr. Axel Klausmeier
Hartlef Knoch
Dr. Susanne Muhle
Dr. Maria Nooke
Tina Schaller
Eva Wiebel

Final Editing
Dr. Gerhard Sälter

English Translation
Miriamne Fields, Berlin

Planning and Construction Coordination
Dr. Günter Schlusche

Project Organization
Dörte Fritzsche (until July 2013)
Hans Göhler
Grün Berlin GmbH

Landscape Planning
sinai, Freiraumplanung und Projektsteuerung, Berlin

Architecture of Visitor Center and Border House Roof Shelter
Mola/Winkelmüller, Berlin

Exhibition Architecture
Christian Fuchs,
ON architektur, Berlin

Exhibition Graphics
Weidner Händle Atelier, Stuttgart

Archaeology
ADB Dressler, Glienicke/Nordbahn

Project Staff of the Administration and Planning Offices
Christian Freiesleben
Roland Eggers
Harald Krüger
Peter Hausdorf
Rainer E. Klemke
Ole Saß

This project was funded by
the Federal Commissioner for Culture and Media,
the State of Berlin,
the joint scheme for the "improvement of regional economic structure,"
the German Lottery Foundation of Berlin,
and the European Fund for Regional Development – "Investment in Your Future".

Imprint
1961 | 1989 The Berlin Wall
Permanent Exhibition in the Documentation Center at Bernauer Strasse 111

General Management
Prof. Dr. Axel Klausmeier

Curator
Dr. Kay Kufeke

Scientific and Conceptual Advice
Dr. Gerhard Sälter

Scholarly Research
Katja Böhme
Dr. Elke Kimmel
Dr. Susanne Muhle
Cornelia Thiele

Scholarly Advisory Board
Prof. Dr. Klaus Dietmar Henke (Vorsitzender)
Prof. Dr. Karl F. Schumann (Stellvertretender Vorsitzender)
Marianne Birthler
Prof. Dr. Monika Flacke
Dr. Hans-Hermann Hertle
Prof. Dr. Hans Walter Hütter
Dr. Anna Kaminsky
Holger Kulick
Petra Morawe
Dr. Ehrhart Neubert
Prof. Dr. Leo Schmidt
Prof. Dr. Waltraud Schreiber
Rainer Wagner
Prof. Dr. Hermann Wentker
Prof. Dr. Manfred Wilke

As guests of the Foundation Association
Pfarrer Manfred Fischer †
Dr. Helge Heidemeyer
und für die Zuwendungsgeber
Christian Freiesleben (BKM)
Rainer E. Klemke
(until September 2012)
Dr. Christine Regus
(Senatskanzlei für Kulturelle Angelegenheiten des Landes Berlin)

Texts
Katja Böhme
Prof. Dr. Klaus Dietmar Henke
Dr. Elke Kimmel
Prof. Dr. Axel Klausmeier
Dr. Kay Kufeke
Dr. Susanne Muhle
Dr. Gerhard Sälter
Cornelia Thiele
Prof. Dr. Hermann Wentker
Prof. Dr. Manfred Wilke

Final Editing
Dr. Elke Kimmel
Dr. Kay Kufeke
Dr. Susanne Muhle

Additional Research
Dr. Nina Burkhardt
Angelika Heider
Dr. Manfred Wichmann

Contempory Witness Interview Concept
Dr. Kay Kufeke
Alexandra Pohlmeier

Interviews conducted by
Anna von Arnim-Rosenthal
Lydia Dollmann
Dr. Elke Kimmel
Dr. Kay Kufeke
Dr. Susanne Muhle
Dr. Maria Nooke

Filming and Editing of Interviews
Alexandra Pohlmeier

Research and Film Concepts
Qlick Media
Holger Kulick, Berlin

Film Editing
René Perraudin Filmproduktion, Berlin

Concept and Texts of Children Trace
Zera Berlin, Johanna Muschelknautz

Consulting for Children Trace
Dr. Katrin Passens

English Translation
Miriamne Fields, Berlin

Exhibition Office
Annika Estner
Margarethe Wengler

Planning and Construction Coordination
Dr. Günter Schlusche

Remodeling Architecture
ZHN Architekten, Berlin

Exhibition Architecture
Christian Fuchs,
ON architektur, Berlin
Martin Bennis Architekt, Berlin

Lighting Design
Anne Boissel,
Licht- und Raumgestaltung, Berlin

Exhibition Graphics
Weidner Händle Atelier, Stuttgart

Exhibition Construction
Schelm & Sohn, Hannover
Weisse GmbH & Co. KG, Eberswalde

Exhibition Prints
Eicher Werkstätten GmbH & Co. KG, Kernen im Remstal

Exhibition Technology
CPB Computer-Präsentationsund Bildtechnik GmbH, Berlin

Post-Production
Framegrabber Medien GmbH, Hamburg

Press and Public Relations
Hannah Berger

Finances
Maren Hüttig
Rainer Waldow-Buchmeier
Barbara Merkel
Steffen Richter

The exhibition was funded by
Die Beauftragte
der Bundesregierung für Kultur
und Medien.

The building renovations and remodeling were funded by
Landes Berlin,
„Gemeinschaftsaufgabe
Verbesserung der regionalen
Wirtschaftsstruktur" and the
Stiftung Deutsche Klassenlotterie
Berlin.

We especially thank the following for their non-paid assistance
Alliiertenmuseum Berlin,
Bundesarchiv,
Bundesbeauftragten
für die Unterlagen des Staatssicher-
heitsdienstes der ehemaligen DDR,
Bundesstiftung zur Aufarbeitung
SED-Diktatur,
Deutsches Rundfunkarchiv,
Deutsche Bahn AG,
Deutschlandradio,
Deutsches Zollmuseum,
Landesarchiv Berlin,
Militärhistorisches Museum
Dresden,
Museum Haus
am Checkpoint Charlie,
Polizeihistorischen
Sammlung Berlin,
Archiv der Robert-Havemann-
Gesellschaft e.V.,
Senatsverwaltung für
Stadtentwicklung Berlin,
SPIEGEL TV,
Stiftung Stadtmuseum Berlin,
Archiv der Versöhnungsgemeinde
Berlin-Wedding.

A very special thanks to all the contemporary witnesses who agreed to be interviewed and/or provided documents and objects.

Despite major efforts, we were not always able to identify the holders of publication rights. We ask anyone wishing to lay claim to the publication rights of photos shown here to please contact the Berlin Wall Foundation.

Contributors

Anna von Arnim-Rosenthal
studied political science and cultural studies in Oldenburg, Bremen und Leipzig. She worked from 2007 to 2010 on various contemporary and cultural history exhibitions and book projects, for example for the Foundation Memorial to the Murdered Jews of Europe, the Ravensbrück Concentration Camp Memorial and the Spandau Citadel. She served as a research trainee with the Berlin Wall Foundation until 2012. After this she became an education consultant for the Berlin Wall Memorial and was an editor for the German Federal Agency for Civic Education until 2014. Anna v. Arnim-Rosenthal is currently employed in the school education department of the Federal Foundation for the Reappraisal of the SED Dictatorship.

Marianne Birthler
Marianne Birthler initially worked in GDR international trade and completed a correspondence degree in foreign trade studies. She later became a parish assistant and youth consultant for the Protestant Church's children and youth services. In the mid-1980s, she was active in the Solidarity Church Workgroup and the Initiative for Peace and Human Rights. She was spokeswoman of the Alliance '90 parliamentary group in the last People's Chamber, the GDR parliament. Until 1992, Marianne Birthler served as the Brandenburg Minister of Education, Youth and Sport. She later served as a federal spokesperson of the board of Alliance '90/The Greens and, in 1995, became the director of the Berlin office of the Green Party parliamentary group in the Bundestag. Later she was the parliamentary group's consultant for personnel development and continuing education. Marianne Birthler served as Federal Commissioner for the Stasi Records from 2000 to 2011. She is on the Berlin Wall Foundation's advisory board.

Katja Böhme
studied history, sociology and general and comparative literature at the FU Berlin. After completing her studies, she worked as a research assistant at the Center for Contemporary History in Potsdam (ZZF) and, from 2009 to 2012 as research associate at the Documentation Center on Everyday Life in the GDR in Eisenhüttenstadt. She later served as a research trainee at the Berlin Wall Foundation. Katja Böhme became a doctoral candidate at ZZF in December 2014.

Miriamne Fields
has worked as a professional translator of German texts into English since 2001. Specializing in German history, she has translated several books, articles and museum exhibitions addressing topics of Jewish life, the Nazi era and GDR history. She has a bachelor's degree in history from Barnard College in New York City and a master's degree in history and English literature from the TU Berlin.

Klaus-Dietmar Henke
studied modern history and political science in Munich. After completing his PhD there in 1977, he worked until 1992 as a research associate for the Institute for Contemporary History in Munich. Later he served there as deputy editor-in-chief of the Vierteljahreshefte für Zeitgeschichte and as acting director. He subsequently headed the education and research department of the Stasi Records Agency. From 1997 to 2012 he was a professor of contemporary history at the TU Dresden and from 1997 to 2002, director of its Hannah Arendt Institute for Totalitarianism Research. He is spokesman of the Independent Commission of Historians Researching the History of the German Intelligence Service and chairman of the Berlin Wall Foundation's advisory board.

Elke Kimmel
studied modern history and film studies in Berlin. She completed her doctorate at the TU Berlin in 1999. Afterwards she worked as a research associate on various exhibition and publication projects, for example for the German Technology Museum, the Marienfelde Refugee Center Museum, the Federal Agency for Civic Education, the Documentation Center on Everyday Life in the GDR, the Neuruppin Museum, the German Historical Museum in Berlin and the Center for Contemporary History in Potsdam. Since 2006 she has created a number of radio features on contemporary history topics. She worked as a research associate at the Berlin Wall Memorial from 2013 to 2014. She was also involved in creating the permanent exhibition of the Stasi Records Agency from 2013 to 2015. The freelance curator and author lives in Berlin.

Axel Klausmeier
studied art history, modern and medieval history in Bochum, Munich and Berlin. From 1999 to 2001 he completed a traineeship with the Foundation of Prussian Castles and Gardens in Berlin-Brandenburg. Afterwards he became an academic assistant in the department of architectural conservation at the BTU Cottbus. After working at the Institute for Historical Preservation at the ETH Zurich, he joined the DFG research project conducted at the BTU Cottbus in 2007/2008 on the Berlin Wall's transformation from a mechanism of SED domestic policies to an international monument. In January 2009 he became director of the Berlin Wall Foundation. In 2012, Axel Klausmeier was awarded an honorary professorship from the BTU Cottbus-Senftenberg.

Margret Kowalke-Paz
completed an apprenticeship as a photo retoucher. She worked from 1984 to 1989 as an editor of the Neue Zeit. Afterwards she studied printing technology (FH) in Leipzig. She was employed for many years with the Galrev Print and Publishing Company. She has worked since 2008 as a freelance editor, mostly for Ch. Links Publishers, and has edited several book projects, including publications of the Berlin Wall Foundation.

Kay Kufeke
completed an apprenticeship in reproduction photography and studied history and philosophy in Hamburg and Perugia (Italy). He was a research associate at the Sachsenhausen Concentration Camp Memorial from 1996 to 2000. He subsequently worked on several exhibitions on contemporary history and art history, for example at the House of History of the Federal Republic of Germany, the German Historical Museum in Berlin, the Topography of Terror Foundation and Dachau Concentration Camp Memorial. From 2012 to 2014 he was a research associate at the Berlin Wall Memorial in the research and documentation department. In late 2014 Kay Kufeke became a research associate at the Nazi Forced Labor Documentation Center in Berlin-Schöneweide.

Susanne Muhle
studied modern and contemporary history, European ethnology and sociology at the WWU Münster. She worked from 2003 to 2005 at the Villa ten Hompel in Münster. She subsequently became a scholarship holder from the Federal Foundation for Reappaissal of the SED Dictatorship and the Stasi Records Agency. She later served as a research trainee at the Berlin Wall Foundation in the research and documentation department. Susanne Muhle wrote her PhD dissertation at the WWU Münster and has been employed at the Berlin Wall Foundation as a research associate in the areas of civic education and historical research since 2013.

Maria Nooke
completed a religious education apprenticeship and worked with children and teenagers in the church. In 1985 she became active in peace and environmental groups within the church in the GDR and was co-editor of the opposition paper "Aufbruch." She studied sociology, psychology and pedagogy at the TU Berlin from 1992 to 1997 and has worked on several contemporary history projects on National Socialism and GDR history. She has been employed at the Berlin Wall Memorial since 1999. She completed her PhD at the FU Berlin in 2007. Maria Nooke is deputy director of the Berlin Wall Foundation and head of the Marienfelde Refugee Center Museum.

Gerhard Sälter
studied history, philosophy and political science at the FU Berlin. After completing his PhD in 2000, he worked as a freelance scholar with the Bautzen Memorial and with the State Commissioner for Stasi Records in Saxon. He began working for the Berlin Wall Association in 2001 and has been employed as a research associate for the Berlin Wall Memorial in the research and documentation department since 2002. Gerhard Sälter has been on leave since 2012, currently working for the Independent Commission of Historians Researching the History of the German Intelligence Agency.

Günter Schlusche
studied architecture at the TU Berlin and urban and regional planning at the London School of Economics. From 1982 to 1987 he was project coordinator of the International Building Exhibition in Berlin. He received his doctorate degree in engineering in 1996 from the TU Berlin. He worked as planning and building coordinator for the Memorial for the Murdered Jews of Europe until 2005. Günter Schlusche was responsible for overseeing the project to extend the Berlin Wall Memorial from 2005 to 2014.

Cornelia Thiele
studied modern and contemporary history at the Friedrich Schiller University in Jena and at the Humboldt University. She specialized in the areas of GDR history, sociology and gender studies and wrote her dissertation on German intellectual history and the German question in the unification process of 1989/90. She worked as a research trainee at the Berlin Wall Foundation from 2012 to 2014. Cornelia Thiele is currently developing a plan to redesign the German-German Museum in Mödlareuth.

Berthold Weidner
studied design in Schwäbisch-Gmünd and was employed by Otl Aicher. He became self-employed in 1989 and established an office partnership with Luisa Händle in 2003. The focus is on the design of exhibitions, guidance systems, images and books. Projects have been done with Norman Foster in London, Valencia, Bilbao. Other clients include the Berlin Wall Memorial and the Brandenburg Memorials Foundation. Berthold Weidner taught at the Merz Academy in Stuttgart, the Academy of Design in Bozen and the Darmstadt University.

Hermann Wentker
studied history and German studies in Erlangen and Bonn. After receiving his doctorate degree in 1990, he became an academic assistant in the department of modern and contemporary history at the University of Bayreuth. In 1998 he was appointed head of the Berlin office of the Institute for Contemporary History Munich-Berlin. Hermann Wentker was promoted to professor at the University of Leipzig in 2001 and is now a professor of modern and contemporary history there. He is on the advisory board of the Berlin Wall Foundation.

Other publications of the Berlin Wall Foundation

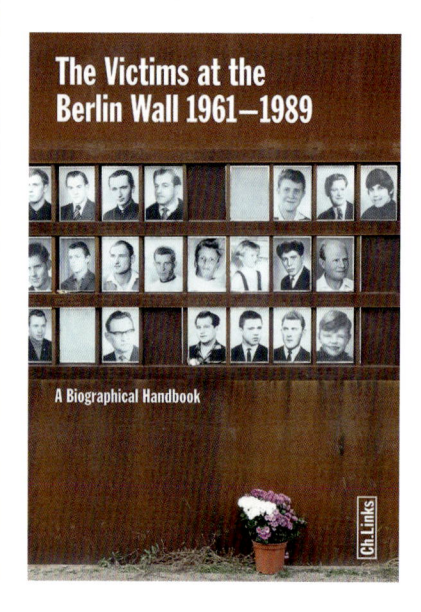

Hans-Hermann Hertle/Maria Nooke (Ed.):
The Victims at the Berlin Wall 1961–1989
512 p., 117 figs., hardcover with jacket, 19,5 x 21 cm
ISBN 978-3-86153-632-1, 25,00 €

Although many deaths at the Berlin Wall have been publicized over the years in the media, the number, identity and fate of the victims still remain largely unknown. This handbook changes this by answering the following questions: How many people actually died at the Berlin Wall between 1961 and 1989? Who were these people? How did they die? How were their relatives and their friends treated after their deaths? What public and political reactions were triggered in the East and the West by these fatalities? How have the victims been commemorated since their deaths?

By documenting the lives and circumstances under which these men and women died at the Wall, these deaths are placed in a contemporary historical context.

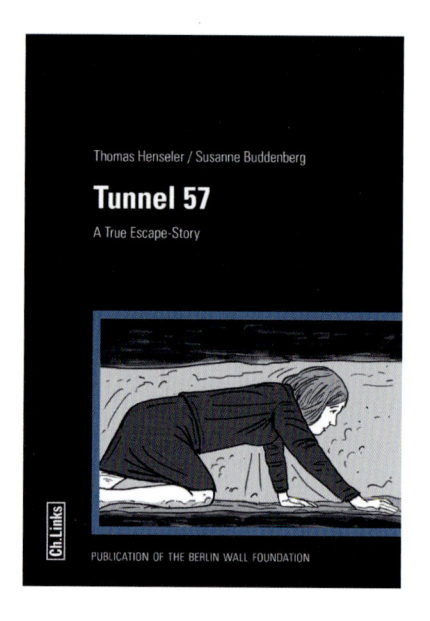

Thomas Henseler/Susanne Buddenberg
Tunnel 57. A True Escape-Story
32 p., softcover, 21 x 25 cm
ISBN 978-3-86153-729-8, 5,00 €

This historical comic book is an escape helper's first person account of the construction of a tunnel beneath the divided city of Berlin in 1964: From the preparations on the West Berlin side, the digging of the 145 metre long tunnel into East Berlin, the tunnel opening and the successful escape on the first day, and the dramatic events of the second day which were to have grave consequences.

Drawing on authentic interviews with the tunnel builders and refugees and original photographs and documents, writers and illustrators Thomas Henseler and Susanne Buddenberg recreate down to the last detail the dramatic events surrounding Tunnel 57.

Ch. Links Verlag, Schönhauser Allee 36, 10435 Berlin, www.christoph-links-verlag.de